DANCING THE EDGE TO SURRENDER

An Erotic Memoir of Trauma and Survival

Dear Jo

I wish you joy
on your Journey

much love,

Jm. Beth Bidbey

DANCING THE EDGE TO SURRENDER

An Erotic Memoir of Trauma and Survival

Lori Beth Bisbey

Dancing the Edge to Surrender: An Erotic Memoir of Trauma and
Survival/ Lori Beth Bisbey
ISBN: 978-1-914-44-5040

DEDICATION

To my loved ones, chosen family, friends, and those who have travelled along the path with me, are travelling along the path with me and will travel along the path with me.

'If you go to war with your sexuality, you will lose and
end up in more trouble than before you started'
Jack Morin, *The Erotic Mind*

'One must not make value judgements, Estri, about primal needs.
One had the needs before one learned the values.'
Janet E Morris, *The High Couch of Silistra*

CONTENTS

FORWARD TO THE SECOND EDITION

As has been typical in my life, monumental change can happen in a relatively short time. In the three years since the first edition was released, the world has moved through a pandemic. During the time I spent sheltering at home as a result of being extremely vulnerable, one relationship blossomed, an organisation shut its doors, and another relationship ended.

As I re-entered the world, I became the resident specialist therapist starring in a television show helping people to open up their relationships for the first time. Then. I began touring the UK with a talk about the psychology of fetish and kink, reignited a relationship and moved to Scotland.

This new edition sees the acknowledgements change, revisions to parts of my analysis as I have gained new understanding, an addition to the erotica and a 2nd epilogue illustrating where I am in August 2023 and where I see myself going.

Over the past three years I have been reminded of the importance of alignment for deeply connected relationships, the necessity to be willing to fully examine yourself and to withhold judgement. I am humbled and filled with gratitude each day for the connection I have with my people and for their abiding love, trust, honesty and integrity.

ACKNOWLEDGMENTS

I could not have written this without the love, help and support of so many people. Some requested to remain anonymous, and I honour that request. There were many who helped me grow and heal along the way. I remain grateful to them for their gifts.

Part of my acknowledgements to many of the people who star in this book along with me are in my depiction of our story together.

So many people make my life rich and contribute in ways I have not had the space to describe. This book focuses on my erotic relationships. I also have many amazing chosen family, family and friends who support me in my endeavours and help me be fully who I am.

Many of my clients have trusted me with their journeys from victim to survivor and then beyond. I have learned from them, and hope that I have reflected some of the lessons in these pages.

Some specific acknowledgements:

To my incredible husband Terence Jerome Scott: Thank you for loving me without judgement and encouraging me always to be fully me–even when that means precious time & attention given to someone else. It is your lake.

To Sam Webster: You who have known me throughout the largest portion of his journey, thank you for being a teacher, lover, friend and companion.

To Sereth: Thank you for seeing me - fully, for coming full circle with me, for allowing me to see all of you, for doing the work and making the commitment.

To the House of Blue: My leather family. Thank you for your integrity, honesty, fellowship, friendship, and love. Mister-Blue: Sir Thank you for sharing, for the support you give, the joy and strength you share.

To Qiana Green (Mrs Blue Frost) My sister, partner and partner in crime: Thank you for the joy you bring, for being there always, for the time, patience, love, accountability, vulnerability, passion and for bearing witness to my journey and allowing me to bear witness to yours.

To Chaundra Crouch: Thank you for the joy, love and friendship.

To Empress & Pharaoh, House of Kemi-Nesew: Thank you for the inspiration, the love.

To Dr Meg-John Barker: Thank you for seeing me and helping me to bring this collection of ideas and stories, struggles and triumphs to life.

To my pre-readers and proof readers: Thank you. Just thank you.

TRIGGER WARNINGS & INTRODUCTION

Nietzsche said, 'That which doesn't kill us, makes us stronger'. This story, my story, bears this out on multiple occasions. Human beings are complex creatures. Rarely are experiences or people completely good or completely bad – black or white – instead, they are nuanced shades of grey.

Desires are complex. We often have desires before we comprehend them, and before we have internalised social conventions. When we internalise the social rules, shame is too often the result. Shame is not only unhelpful, but it is often crippling. Dr Kate Lister, in her book '*A Curious History of Sex*' says 'Humans are also the only creatures that stigmatise, punish and create shame around their sexual desires. While all animals have courtship rituals, no wildebeest has ever gone into therapy because it is struggling to express a latex fetish. The queen honeybee will shag up to forty partners in one session, return to her hive dripping semen and clutching the severed cocks of her conquests and not one drone will call her a slut. Male baboons will happily bugger each other all day long and never fear being sent to a gay conversion camp. Yet the guilt we humans feel around our desires can be paralysing and severe punishments have been doled out to those who break 'the rules'. Too frequently, we try to run from our desires, our shame, our traumas. We may change places or relationships. The problem is that wherever we go, there we are. We take our issues with us.

Some erotica in this book is intense and very challenging; when read juxtaposed with my real-life experiences, the threads connecting the erotica to some of the trauma are obvious. My sexual desires relating to submission, sexual humiliation and masochism were present from my earliest memories of arousal, long before my lover turned captor held me prisoner, raped me multiple times, and almost killed me many times. I did not consent to be raped, abused and killed. I hated most of it. Despite the situation, and to my horror, my body responded and long after the fact, some of it still turns me on.

It took me a long time to understand that some of this was due to arousal non-concordance (which is when the body produces an arousal response, but the person doesn't experience subjective arousal and is not enjoying the experience). I took even longer to come to terms with the bits that continue to live on in my sexual fantasies. Finally it was ages before I forgave myself for my sexual orientation based on surrender, to stop blaming myself for the complete experience, for the damage I sustained and for the damage done to my chosen family who got caught up in the middle.

This introduction highlights these apparent contradictions and posts a trigger warning. If you or your loved ones have experienced sexual abuse and/or rape, you may well find sections of this book triggering. Some erotica and its relationship to the story of my traumatic experiences may be particularly upsetting. It may be easier to dip in and out of the book or to skip the erotica and read the memoir and comment parts first.

Many people who have experienced trauma work on moving from feeling like a victim to becoming a survivor. I help people to work on moving beyond survivor and back into life. It is my goal to help people to place the traumatic experiences in the past where they belong and move into a fresh life. This doesn't mean forgetting the events. It means ceasing to form a central identity around the trauma and around the symptoms that have helped the person survive. In my experience and in my work with others, recovery from trauma seems to take a spiral path where layers are laid to rest, and the next level of the spiral revealed. The primary goal is congruence and authenticity, with the experience(s) integrated rather than continuing being experienced in the present. Authenticity and congruence = joy.

Many people who have experienced trauma in childhood have experienced environments where boundaries are weak and where gaslighting is the norm. These children often learn that their bodies are not their own and that their understanding of reality is untrustworthy. The gaslighting they experience makes them feel crazy and teaches them not to believe their own feelings, sensations, and senses. As a result, they look to others to describe reality for them. The impact upon their psyches and their developing identities is severe. Unpicking these issues and learning to gain confidence in my boundaries, learning to trust my own senses and instincts has been a critical part of my personal work. I have taken this into my professional work and share some of it here. Consent and boundaries are essential emotional and life skills and we can learn these skills at any age.

Gaslighting sets people up to fail in their relationships at best, and at worst sets people up for hazardous life experiences including intimate partner violence, sexual assault, physical assault and rape. If you cannot trust your own internal cues and sense of reality, it is tough to decide which relationships and behaviours are enriching, which relationships and behaviours are damaging. Part of recovery is learning how to reality test and fact check.

Consent is a crucial component to all relationships, yet often assumed or not gained explicitly. In relationships where kink and power exchange (authority transfer) feature, explicit consent is even more essential. This theme is central to my erotica, to my life story and to my work, and so reflected here. In lots of erotica, consent is implied or even dispensed with. I highlight this again later because it can feel very confusing to see fantasies that illustrate a lack of consent being sexy and positive and even healthy. Consensual non-consent are relationships or situations in which it is OK to push boundaries or to give a partner a blanket consent. This leaves the person lots of space to create sexual adventures that are edgy and risky. This can also feel confusing when things go wrong or to outsiders looking in. When things go wrong, there are three general categories of 'wrongness':

A mistake: For example, Randy thinks she will enjoy being teased with a knife. She negotiates it with Jennifer. During the scene, she realises she doesn't like this and uses her safe word. Jennifer ends the scene and helps Randy to process her experience. Randy has some trauma symptoms because of the play. It is not Jennifer's fault. It is a mistake, and Randy takes responsibility, and Jennifer is helpful in the recovery.

A consent violation: For example, Randy and Jennifer negotiate a knife scene. During the scene, Jennifer goes a little farther than they negotiate and does not immediately stop when Randy uses her safe word. Randy feels traumatised. Jennifer has violated her consent and needs to apologise and make amends.

No Consent Sought or Desired: For example, Randy and Jennifer meet at a conference. Jennifer escorts Randy home, and they have coffee. Jennifer forces Randy to have sex at knifepoint. This is rape.

Many experiences are not in one clear category; there are lots of blurred lines. My life is a treasure trove of blurred lines. Throughout this book, I highlight these messy boundaries and where lines are clear to help readers negotiate my experiences but also look at their own.

How we understand sexual orientation has changed a lot in the past 20 years. Many people look at sexuality as containing several axes now. Sari van Anders and others propose the axes include: dominance to submission, monogamy to polyamory, heterosexual to homosexual and asexual to hypersexual. My orientation is a polyamorous slave. Energy, connection and power turn me on, and gender is often irrelevant to my attractions.

My spiritual life integrates with my sexual life. I am a neo-pagan whose Gods are from a variety of pantheons and whose style of worship has always included lots of rituals and sexual magick. For people who are monotheistic, some of my beliefs and my faith can be difficult to understand and/or accept.

Finally, connection and community are essential to my well-being. As my life has been an extraordinary one, finding community has been more difficult. I have found my home in the POC (people of color) leather community and am grateful I am surrounded by chosen family, leather family and supportive friends.

Very few lives are ordinary when you stop to scrutinize them. When one is present, life takes on a richness and a multihued quality that can be hard to describe. Everyone would have something to say or some wisdom to impart from their own lives or experiences if they took the time and attention to examine them. Time doesn't heal. All it does is help people to box things up, and these boxes trigger and open at multiple times in life. Eventually, it becomes hard to keep the lids on the boxes, and the trauma intrudes into daily life regularly. This isn't a recovery narrative. It does not end with 'And they all lived happily ever after' as that is a static state and life is not static. Things move and change, and growth continues.

People who have desires that incorporate power imbalances, sadism and masochism, humiliation or other kinks often struggle with shame during their sexual lives. Some people never move past the shame and accept their desires. One goal in this book is highlighting how you can lay toxic shame to rest and helping you see the path to beginning and/or progressing that healing for yourselves. This isn't a self-help book, and so I don't provide lots of detail around techniques to do this type of personal work and healing. For readers who want a more in-depth 'how-to' book, read Dancing the Edge to Reclaiming Your Reality: Essential Life Skills for Gaslighting (and Trauma) Survivors, where I provide techniques and more to help on the journey to an integrated, authentic self.

I hope that this book will excite, inspire and open doors. There is light, no matter how long you have been in the darkness. It is a matter of learning how to kindle the flame and ignite the torch. It remains my mission to take sex and conversations about sex from the shadow to the light Everyone has shit to work on. None of us is ever truly finished – not if we commit to growth. Instead of being frightening, this can be tremendously exciting. It's all in how you approach life.

How to read this book:

Some people will find it most straightforward to read it as I wrote it.

Others will prefer to focus on the erotica or the memoir or the analysis.

Some will skip chapters they fear may trigger.

There is no right way or wrong way to read this book. Do what feels most comfortable to you.

A note about typesetting: I have tried to make a clear division in the sections by using bold italics for erotica, regular print for my story, and then italics for reflection. There is a glossary in the back where I define some more unusual terms and also personal colloquialisms.

CAST OF CHARACTERS

The reader will notice that many people in my life either stay in my life for a very long time or disappear and return (sometimes on multiple occasions). To minimise confusion, here is the cast that features in this segment of my life.

In order of appearance:

Perry: Boyfriend summer - autumn 1977. First spiritual teacher.

Sam: First love met when I was 17. Part of my first polycule and first member of my chosen family. Still part of my life.

DeeDee: Sam's live-in girlfriend. Part of my first polycule and second member of my chosen family.

Rachel: Roommate freshman year of university

Jane: Rachel's friend

Damien (Alton Cornelius Porter): The person who held me prisoner

Dave: Boyfriend around the time of Damien

Mark: Boyfriend around the time of Damien

Jimi: Friend, lover, chosen family who was killed in a motorcycle crash while I was in Damien's hands.

David B: lover 1981. Introduced me to the OTO and Aleister Crowley

Tony: Lover 1983 in Boston, Ma.

Stephan: lover 1984. Died 1985.

Kathy: lover 1984

Sereth: Master autumn 1984-1985 North Carolina, in and out of my life ever since in a variety of capacities. Master: Spring 2023 onwards.

George: lover autumn 1985 - early 1988.

Kevin: Lover and fiancé 1989. Still part of my life.

Stephen: My first husband and how I ended up living in the United Kingdom. Separated May 1998. Divorced December 2000. Died of Hepatitis C, beginning of October 2004.

Neil: Occasional lover, best friend and chosen family from September 1998 to 2022.

Son's father: Together 1999. Separated 2008 after he had a 6 month affair. Finally divorced 2014

Tom: summer 2008 - summer 2009.

Morloki: Current husband and Master. Met February 2009, accepted his collar September 2009. Married November 2014.

Martin: Partner from Portland 2011- 2013

T: Partner from 2013 - 2014.

Mistress Max: was leather family

Pharaoh and Empress: Was in a relationship with them as a couple, leather family currently

P: Was dating when this book was being finished

M: Just dating at the time of editing

Mister-Blue: Head of Household, House of Blue, husband and Master to Mrs Blue Frost, cherished leather family.

Frost: Leather sister, partner, best friend.

Some people will no doubt think I have had a lot of lovers during this period of my life. I have left out a fair few from this telling, so I have had far more than mentioned here. When I was in my 20s, I felt shame about how many people I had engaged in sexual behaviour with over the years. I could hear my mother telling me that girls who did this were sluts and inferring that sluts weren't worthy of love. These wayward girls would never have husbands and never deserved respect. My mother never said that, but there was an inference, and this is how the inference landed. At 60, I rejoice in my sexuality, my sensuality, my sexual experiences, relationships and the intimacy that comes with them. When I think about the word slut, it is as part of an edgy humiliation scene, not as a slur that takes away from my self-worth. I can be a slut and not experience others judging me and not judge myself.

I

INVOCATION

I wrote this piece of erotica when considering a new tattoo design. I chose it for this section because it talks about my spiritual connection, which intertwines with my sexuality and relationships. My spiritual learning is also the start of this journey.

I enter the dream back in the desert, in the tents that blend into the landscape. They are woven in desert colours; the weave dragging the eye to where it wants the eye to be, almost hallucinatory. I find myself on a cushion on my knees, and when He enters, I bow my head to the floor.

I cannot hold His image. This doesn't surprise me. It is often the case when I am speaking to one of the Gods. The visage changes, fluctuates. The voices stay constant, most of the time.

He starts by saying, 'And what would make you think I was happy to be part of a composite? Even in the days you studied magick, your worship moved from the composite quickly as We told you We were not happy that way.'

I do not respond, and I do not lift my head. I am trembling at the sound of His displeasure. 'Girl you know better' He continued. 'You will speak with each of Us. At least those of Us who lay claim to you.'

'Yes,' I whisper, and still, I hold my position. 'Look on me, girl' He intones. I kneel up, almost blinded by His light. I work to keep His gaze. 'I am Ra. He is Horus. In case you have forgotten'. The deep chuckle almost knocks me off my knees. 'I have not forgotten' I whisper. 'Good. Then let's begin your instruction where We left off'.

And then I wake up. My body covered in a sheen of sweat, juices slick between my thighs, ever so close to orgasm. It is 3:45 a.m.

I turn my attention to going back to sleep. As I drop off, I can feel hands on my body, moving me, and when I enter the dream, I am tied to a type of spanking bench. The padded leather-clad legs press against my thighs. Sweat gathers. The seat against my belly lifts my ass high yet holds my weight, so I am not straining. The first strike moves through me like liquid fire. I go to scream and find I cannot – I have a bit gag in my mouth. The second strike lands on the bottom Sephira Shekinah (Malkuth). I realise that He will run the paths on my back from the root up. My back is fire engine red with welts oozing blood. 'Open' I hear... 'stop fighting Me'. I take in a deep breath, concentrate on ceasing my struggle and hear His sigh as all of me, all my paths, channels are laid bare before Him. The first pull pushes me to the edge of orgasm. I hear myself raw voice, begging – though the gag distorts the words and makes them into plaintive mewls. 'Open further' I hear as He presses against my pussy and my asshole. It takes all of my will to hold my body, my mind, my spirit – everything open. The penetration is quick – I am full – stretched – all parts of my being on all planes. I scream in pain, and the pleasure follows quickly behind – intense enough to take my breath and almost knock me unconscious. I hold tight to consciousness as He moves. I have no words to describe the sensations – penetration into astral body at the same time as into flesh – at the same time on all levels. So all-consuming that thought is impossible.

As the sensations subside, He says, 'thus endeth the lesson. And now that you remember where you came from... return to your studies diligently.' I wake with His voice in my ear 'Remember.'. Hence I write this down.

This journey from acknowledging my desires through extreme trauma, PTSD and shame, through to integration, authenticity and my life today starts at 13 years old.

My parents raised me in a Jewish home. My parents were reform Jews but joined a Conservative synagogue and sent us there for religious education. I quickly took to the ritual involved. I loved the singing and the wide array of holy days that marked the year. I was Bat Mitzvah at 12 years old, traditional for a girl. Instead of leaving religious education after that, I attended Hebrew High School and continued my twice weekly religious journey.

When I was 13, I realized that I wanted to learn the mysteries of the ritual because I did not want someone to talk to God for me. I wanted to have a personal relationship. I wanted to do more than respond in the congregation. I stepped onto a spiritual path on that day. I began to understand that all beings have energy and felt the energy in myself and others. At 13, the easiest way for me to access energy was to generate sexual energy. This has never changed. Of course, I did not understand what I was doing at 13. I could not bring this up with the leader of our youth group, as he had already clarified that sex was for marriage only.

I felt compelled to raise energy. Perry & I connected when I was 14 and at Jewish summer camp. He was 18 and working there in the kitchen. Perry was soft-spoken, dark-haired, soulful brown eyes and a slightly crooked smile and he was sexy. He moved with a fluidity that reminded me of an enormous cat. I had already lost my virginity in the spring and was full of what my body could do and could entice others to do. Perry taught me some Kabbalah basics, a rudimentary shield, how to sense the energy in all things and how to identify connection between myself and all things. He warned me of the dangers of playing with forces I didn't understand, but I didn't hear him. I was too excited by the energy and those calling me to listen. It started as a distant chuntering but quickly became a cacophony of howls, growls and roars. I could not turn away from their energy. I courted the howls, growls and roars and I sang to the claws, teeth, & fur.

At 15, I asked the leader of our youth group how I went about learning Kabbalah and the mysteries. His response was, 'You cannot learn these. Women cannot study Kabbalah. You have a unique role. Men cannot even study until they are over 40.' I replied asking, 'Why are women ruled out of partaking in these mysteries?' He did not give me a reasoned reply. The following week during one of my tutoring sessions, this 50+ year old religious man put his hand on my ass while he was answering a question I had about a Hebrew passage. I pulled away but did not have the courage to speak out or to tell my parents. They already blamed me for attracting too much sexual attention. I was sure they would not believe me so I just left at the end of the year.

Jenny and I sat in the diner drinking extra thick milk shakes. I savoured the sweet chocolate so thick my cheeks hollowed out when I tried to suck it up the straw. The shake was so cold my nose crinkled and the inside burned as I inhaled the icy air. 'I cannot see the point of following a religion that doesn't see me as a full person equal to all other people. I would rather be part of a spiritual group that recognises all my potentials'. I said. Jenny replied, 'God did not intend it that way. You have read the Torah and you know that women were not meant to be learning in that way.' 'But we are as smart as they are! Why should they confine us to certain areas and certain subjects? It isn't as though learning this will prevent me from marrying and having children, if that is what I want to do. It doesn't diminish me as a woman. It just adds to me because I have more knowledge.' I said. She returned to Eve the temptress as an example. Eventually Jenny and I had to stop talking about this as we would never agree.

I collected Tarot cards and learned to read them. The imagery grabbed me as it still does today. I love to compare the differing visual interpretations of the cards. I created rudimentary rituals without knowing that was what I was doing, and I began to invoke. This was undoubtedly the most dangerous thing to be doing, with no training and no supervision. But back in the late '70s, there were few resources and no internet. One found one's teachers by chance while going about daily life. And Their call was so strong; it was ever so hard to resist. I had no idea where to find a proper teacher. I experimented holding the youthful belief that everything would be fine. I felt invincible, like most adolescents.

By the time I left for university at 17, I already had a relationship with Coyote and with Loki and was learning what life with Trickster Gods was like: Chaos moving to organised chaos. I was always tuned into the energy, and I remain so. Working with Trickster Gods requires powerful faith to get you through the sharp rises and bitter crashes. I often think it would be useful to learn to surf, as maybe that would improve my balance through the chaos waves. But presence, faith, obedience and worship provide stability needed to ride these waves and survive the falls without drowning even when submerged.

I went to Boston University and have vivid memories of the initial few days. I spent the weekend moving from the dorm to my new on-campus flat. To this day, I do not understand how Rachel and I talked the housing registrar into giving us a flat. Freshman and most sophomores lived in the dorms, not in flats. However we did it, we now had a fantastic space to share. She had the bedroom, and I turned the living room into my bedroom, so we each had privacy. Raven haired Rachel and I had much in common, though she had far more experience than I did with sex, drugs and live rock-and-roll.

Our flat was at 580 Commonwealth Ave, right outside of Kenmore Square. The Ratskeller bar was our favourite haunt because they never carded us. They were well aware we were below the legal drinking age but didn't seem to care. Rachel enjoyed drinking there to pull older guys. I just enjoyed the atmosphere. One Halloween I put on a French maid's outfit, and she dressed as a dominatrix with a whip. There is a picture of me kneeling in front of her, my hands in cuffs, reaching for her. I had to beg her to dress up like this so we could look great at the party together. I found her almost irresistible dressed in this costume, but she wasn't at all interested in girls, so this went nowhere. Every guy at the event followed us. She went home with someone she met there, and I headed back alone by choice.

Harried by the time I got to the English department, I rushed to register for my courses. I saw Sam leaning against the banister near the registration area. Long and lithe with long light brown hair, moustache and goatee-like beard. Dark poetic eyes, and a sensual mouth. At that moment, he had a pipe in his mouth. I remember his face in detail but couldn't tell you what he was wearing. He fit one of my 'types' – looking a little like a modern-day Jesus. Just the type of boy that made my parents squirm.

I am shy underneath. Most people who know me don't believe that as I appear so gregarious. I have often been deeply self-conscious, though I am less so nowadays. I taught myself how to overcome this many years ago. My anxiety rarely shows in a work setting, but it still peeks out from behind my eyes in personal situations sometimes. Back then, I was painfully self-conscious and overcame that by forcing myself to be very bold. I don't remember what I said to introduce myself, but I remember his wry smile and the conversation taking a somewhat cryptic turn quickly.

This was the old days–no mobile phones and no email. We had a phone in the flat but no answerphone. Sam and I exchanged numbers and then went our separate ways. We connected the following day. The attraction was electric, the conversation esoteric. He asked me if I knew the story of the mustard seed and also if I had ever slept with a soldier. I found him captivating; mystery speech was a turn on back then. Our sex was primal. We fit together like a jigsaw puzzle: breaking apart, fitting together, and breaking apart to start again.

We taught each other, though I didn't realise that at first. Tricksters' proteges are catalysts by nature, and I am definitely one. Spending time in each other's company quickly led to sex magick, changing both our lives and setting us both on the paths we still follow today.

I thought Sam was so mature. His eyes sparkled when he spoke, and they still do today with that same mischievous glow. When I met him, I fell for him hard. I remember the taste of him.. the intensity of my desire to suck on his cock. I remember the feel of his hands around my throat, the first breath play I had engaged in. I found the sensation intoxicating. I wanted someone to control me. The desire to submit, to surrender to the will of another – preferably male back then– who was not only physically stronger than I but who could meet my intellect at least, if not surpass me, and meet my intensity – has been present since I first fantasized about sex.

Our spiritual exploration began at the very beginning of our relationship. Sam took the lead. Here was someone who finally understood how to think, feel, and move on many levels at once. Here was someone who understood abstraction, who thought big picture. He was also incredibly sexy. There was a fluidity to him I had no words for. He moved between spiritual and material states with ease.

In my exploration, I discovered hallucinogens. Sam had the LSD, and so Rachel and I headed out to his flat to pick it up. Our relationship to that point had been a lot of come hither, move back, come hither move back. I knew he was hiding something, but our connection was so hot and so deep I didn't care.

Sam lived with DeeDee. I found out about her when we went to pick up the acid. It was my first time tripping, and as I put the tab in my mouth, I noticed DeeDee and put two and two together. I had a Jim Morrison poster above my bed at my flat that appeared to be breathing. I told Rachel that I would know I was no longer tripping when Jim stopped breathing. It took three full days while I tried to figure it all out. I adjusted to finding out about DeeDee (with difficulty at first), but DeeDee found it far harder to accept me.

Sam and I continued to see each other, but DeeDee wasn't happy with it. The relationship ended just before the summer break. It devastated me. I didn't understand why he couldn't have a relationship with both of us. I remember playing 'Triad' by Crosby, Stills and Nash repeatedly. I had the programming from my upbringing that monogamy was the only 'true' relationship model, but I had never been good at monogamy. I flipped between being upset that I 'wasn't enough' because someone would be in another relationship and wanting more than one relationship myself. I spent lots of time working on this dichotomy in various forms over the next 18 years – moving from polyamory to monogamy and back again until I finally integrated my non-monogamous nature.

Rachel had met Jane, and she became ever present at our flat. She moved into Rachel's room. Rachel & Jane were using lots of drugs towards the end of the year and living with them was becoming difficult. I started coming home from class to find drugged-out folks in my space, and it got so I couldn't even use the bathroom in peace because there was often someone sleeping in the bathtub. I told Rachel I would move out, and my parents agreed to fund me having a flat on my own. Summer was crazy, and I found people to amuse me. When I returned to school in the autumn, I was living in my studio flat in Brookline, Mass.

My father found a flat for me in a building of primarily elderly Jewish people. I often wondered if he thought this would mean I would party less and spend less time engaged in sexual activity. It did nothing to stop me, though it became awkward later on.

In September, Sam phoned, and we started seeing each other again. He would come over, and we would sometimes eat, often engage in some magick practice (often sex magick) and have intense sex. DeeDee had agreed to him spending time with me because at that point she wasn't interested in any of the spiritual stuff. I'm not sure if she realised we were fucking, but she tolerated the relationship. It was the early 80s, and we were not yet paying attention to the need for safe sex except to prevent pregnancy. She did not like all the philosophical and spiritual talk and was happy for Sam to have someone to engage on that level.

Sam and I continued our exploration of magick and spirituality. We created sex magick rituals during that period. Our arrogance was staggering. I am not sure if it came from underlying disbelief in the forces we were dealing with or only the disdain of youth–that belief that you are invincible.

The belief that you are invincible is common for young people. Some folks never lose that belief. They experience nothing traumatic, and no one close to them experiences anything traumatic on the scale that teaches us that the world is not safe and that we can experience genuinely terrifying and horrible things. I liken it to walking around in a bubble. The bubble stays intact as long as life or liberty remains secure, so the horrors of the world are always a few feet away outside of your bubble.

When an event occurs that impacts you on that large scale, the bubble bursts, suddenly, you know it is possible for you to die, that the world isn't lovely and safe, that you or your loved ones can be terrorised or victimised. You confront reality. The rose-coloured glasses disappear. Truth is in your face. You have a choice at that point – face reality and learn how to deal with the new knowledge about how the world works – or – try very hard to push the new understanding out of your awareness, stuff it back in the box and go on pretending that everything is fine.

Coronavirus-19 is a strong example of an event that is causing a lot of bubbles to burst, is causing a lot of people to see harsh reality for the first time. Many people are experiencing fear for their lives and the lives of their loved ones. Many people have already had people they know die. The virus is not predictable and not something anyone is able to control at this point. Despite how widespread this trauma is, there are still people who cling to the belief that it is a hoax and are managing to keep their invincibility bubble intact.

In 1981, at just 18, I believed I was invincible. I had experiences in my earlier years that threatened to pop the bubble. These experiences gave me a peek at the seamy underside of the world. But I could press them back into the box and continue to believe in my superhero strength. My bubble stayed intact for a while longer.

Sam and I were immersed when we undertook ritual. The ritual was intense, multi-layered and very satisfying. I remember discussing with Sam what we could do at the point at which we raised the energy to the highest. He told me to ask for what I want. His hands were around my throat as he pounded into me and I shouted 'Bring me a Master'. No qualification. No detail. Just that. I can still hear Loki's laughter and his voice in my ear, 'As you wish, girl'. How could we be so arrogant? Young, healthy, bright, curious and terribly arrogant. We had no one to look to for training. No elders. Just our intuitions, our wits, and the books we read. Later, there was training. Later there was lots of support. But then. Then there was only the two of us and our arrogance.

My sexual desires were always submissive ones. When I was 9, I created a bottle to live in as Jeannie did on 'I dream of Jeannie' to await my Master. My friends thought I was weird, but it made perfect sense to me. While my girlfriends experimented with kissing each other, I asked one to sit on my face. I wrote erotica at 12 that included being 'forced' into various sexual positions and situations. When I started having sexual encounters at 13 and 14, I manipulated my partners into restraining me or 'ordering' me or 'forcing' me. I retain coherent memories of being 15 and enjoying my 17-year-old boyfriend's hand on the back of my neck, pushing down. I discovered the 'Story of O' when I was 15 and saw the film at 15 as well. I watched 'Swept Away' (the original Lina Wertmuller film starring Giancarlo Giannini) over and over in the little art theatre in Cambridge the summer I was 16 and studying the Russian language at Harvard. So by the time I was 19, asking for a Master made perfect sense. Boyfriends could provide some rough sex. Sam provided rough sex. I even had a set of engraved gold handcuffs that Wayne, a marine I dated, had given me at 17. But rough sex and some restraint were not having a Master to serve. It wasn't just the sex I wanted. I wanted the total package of service, and I had no idea where to find it. So it made perfect sense to me to ask the Gods we invoked during ritual.

One night at 2 a.m., my phone rang. 'Is he there?' DeeDee said. 'I have no idea where he is, he was supposed to come over around ten, but he never showed up'. 'I bet he is with that blond bitch' we both said at the same time. We were both annoyed. She thanked me and then suggested we meet for lunch the following week. I agreed.

DeeDee showed up at lunch with a small bandage on her nose. They had an elevated bed, and when Sam had returned home that morning, she took a swing at him; he moved out of the way, and she ran into the bed, fracturing her nose. DeeDee was a few inches taller than I with long red hair, perfect makeup, slender shoulders, slender hips and large breasts. Sam often called me 'tiny tits' though my breasts were not tiny (B cup until I had a baby and they haven't been under a D cup since). I never understood this nickname until I saw DeeDee. In comparison, my breasts were tiny. As self-conscious as I was, this nickname was devastating, but I laughed and said nothing.

DeeDee had the figure I would have died for. I inherited my build from my father's mother: Short torso, short-ish legs, broad shoulders, large hips and a medium waist. I am hourglass-ish. My waist is not small enough for a real hourglass. My bum was more prominent than was fashionable as well. I have great legs even though they are short, just like my mom and my maternal grandmother. I got lots of positive attention from people of colour and got told I was fat by many of the boys and girls I grew up with (mostly Jewish and Italian). I worked hard to become as skinny as I could, and their attitudes helped me to create a warped body image. This has had an impact throughout my life. At that time, I looked at DeeDee and felt inferior, even though Sam found me sexy just the way I was with all my curves.

Lunch with DeeDee was fun. We had a lot in common beyond Sam. I quickly realised that DeeDee needed to be the one who had the last word. I noticed that she often talked down to me – minimising my skills, my beauty, my experience, and maximising hers. She was gregarious and had some charisma, so I let it go. Later, this came back to bite me. At 18, it didn't seem the wrong way to manage the relationship. It was easier to avoid the conflict and let her dominate.

This began a new phase in our relationship. We didn't have a label for ourselves then. Now, I would call us a polycule. We gathered a few other people who were around a lot, and these became our tribe. DeeDee always encouraged me to find boyfriends and to bring them into the group. She was always happier when I had another guy, so I brought a series of guys to join us playing dungeons & dragons, watching flicks, partying, listening to music and doing various types of magick. She was never 100% comfortable when Sam was my only sexual partner, and although we had a few sexual experiences with each other, these did not satisfy her either. Her model remained 'find a husband, get married, have children' alongside her intense career ambition. I believe she was monogamous by nature and only tolerated Sam's other relationships because she knew she would lose him if she did not. She attempted to bring his relationship interests into the fold where she could keep track of them.

They moved from the flat to a house and socialising often happened at their place. DeeDee was a gourmet cook, and the meals there were always a treat. Dungeons and Dragons was a favourite pastime and games featured in time together. Film was one of our passions so we saw all the latest releases. We were avid readers, and books were often topics for conversations. I loved the communal nature of this setup and also loved having my flat that I could retreat to for solo time. This remains my ideal set up to this day, although I have not manifested it while living in the UK to my great sadness.

Time on my own has always been important to me. I spent my alone time thinking, playing the piano, writing poetry, prose and music, developing my ability to read Tarot. Having space to myself and time to myself remains an essential theme throughout my life to date. So much so, that living with others has always been and remains a challenge. I am difficult to live with. The hours I keep have a lot to do with what projects I immerse myself in. I can obsess over a project and pay attention to little else. I love my chaos and find it difficult to tolerate the chaos that belongs to others. As long as I have time and space for myself, I can bring my full self and my total energy to my relationships and my projects. When I don't have that time and space, I tend to be irritable. Some say I am brash and one ex-husband called me controlling.

The relationship worked well for most of the school year. We finished exams in May, and we were hanging around Boston. I wasn't expecting to go back home, even for a visit until July. It was mid-May, and I had a boyfriend called Dave. We got along and had fun together, but mostly he was in my life because DeeDee would always get uncomfortable if I didn't have another guy.

This day, Dave and Sam talked DeeDee into a strip poker game. The four of us played, and it turned into one big orgy with everyone fucking and sucking everyone else. This was the first time I had the opportunity to immerse myself in eating pussy and I loved it. I loved her; kissing her was sublime. She had the most beautiful breasts; big with pale pink nipples against my smaller tits and larger, much darker nipples. We were putting on a show for the guys–finally getting my head between her legs – she tasted sweet and nutty – and she came quickly as I sucked on her clitoris. She came hard, and I could not come at all, but I loved it all the same.

I remember hoping that this would lead to more sex with DeeDee, not realising at the time that this was only strategic on her part. I only understood that years later. I remember how hot it was to watch Sam and Dave and also how uncomfortable that made DeeDee. Anything that demonstrated fluidity or was non-binary was particularly problematic for her.

One of my jobs became bringing home the unfamiliar things I discovered through the men and women I became involved with. When I found a spiritual, sexual or play practice, I brought it back to the family. I often took the first risk and then brought things home when I didn't get hurt. I was like Mikey in the Life cereal commercial from the early 1970s. The older kids brought Mikey things to try when they weren't sure about them. If Mikey liked it, they would try it. It was two weeks after the orgy that DeeDee introduced me to Damien.

Control, or lack thereof, is a central theme throughout the lives of many people who have experienced significant trauma. It has been a theme throughout my life. For many of us, boundaries between reality and fantasy, being able to hold on to and enforce our views can be especially difficult.

Some of my desires came out of an early life crucible in which my emotional and sometimes physical boundaries were repeatedly violated in seemingly small but very significant ways. I did not suffer intense physical or sexual abuse. I experienced constant gaslighting about my physical boundaries, privacy and my emotional reality. Even some of my concepts of spirit and identity were labelled 'ridiculous' or 'silly' or a 'phase I would soon grow out of'. They marked my bisexuality in this way. Neither of my parents realised the impact of dismissing things that were vital parts of me, of telling me that my reality was wrong or imagined and giving me their truth as the only valid one.

If you have trouble knowing where you end, and another begins or if you have trouble keeping your boundaries in place when others tell you their view of the world, your feelings, your actions or thoughts, you can learn different ways to improve your skills in differentiating your reality and in setting clear, comfortable easy to hold boundaries.

Think of it this way; whenever we learn a new skill, it takes practice. You cannot learn a new skill until you recognise that there is a problem with what you are doing. Sometimes it is just the way you are interpreting things and others, it is the way you respond to yourself and/ or others. I encourage you to stop being so hard on yourself as you read this book. It fixes nothing and, in fact, causes further damage. I say this several times during this book: None of us is perfect or finished. We are all works in progress. We all need to learn new skills and get rid of maladaptive patterns. We all enjoy a break from self-criticism and self-doubt.

It took me a long time to learn to create a firm boundary and even longer to learn how to stand strong in the face of pressure from others, particularly from people I was interested in or sexually involved with. The drive to please the people around me and to fit in any way I could caused me to take crazy risks. I wasn't trying to fit in with mainstream people. I knew already that though I could pass, I would never really be one of them. I tried to find the right subculture and felt an internal pressure to conform to some group's rules. Anything to feel like there was somewhere I belonged, where someone would see and hear me. I felt seen and heard by Sam, DeeDee and several other members of my extended chosen family but this didn't feel like enough in my twenties. I internalised all the messages I grew up with - from family through to culture - that said that belonging was essential to having the right type of life. Being 'normal' was important, and that was a colossal problem because I did not understand how to be anything other than what I was, and I was definitely not normal.

If you want to be normal, you have to control your thoughts, your feelings, your behaviour, your responses and make sure that these conform to the mainstream culture portrayed in the media. This is another place where control versus surrender is an ongoing theme. Social communication often involves saying little of consequence, holding back anything intimate or authentic and being hyperaware of the reactions of others to anything you choose to share. I found this incredibly confusing. I could easily see when people were saying things that they did not believe. Their expressions did not match their words. Their body language did not flow with their words, and their energy was often opposite to what they were communicating. I asked my parents on more than one occasion why people lied like this and each time they tried to explain that it was useful to fit in and important not to make people uncomfortable by communicating your feelings and this was especially true when your feelings were heavy or intense. No matter how I tried, I was useless at doing this. Inevitably, I ended up communicating how I was feeling. Sometimes I was tactful, but often I couldn't even manage that.

As I got older, I was able learn when it was appropriate and/or valuable to withhold my genuine feelings. In fact, I became exceptionally good at this and even learned how to engage in passible small talk. On an emotional level, I still don't see the value in pretending to be something I am not, pretending to feel something I do not or in acquiescing to others to appear normal. This has led to awkward situations when my feelings don't match those of the person I am interacting with. For example, recently I received a text from someone I no longer feel close to and she ended the text by saying that she loves me and misses me. I feel neither and so did not know how to respond as I know I will be seeing her in a group setting soon. In the end, I just said 'See you soon'.

In some situations, there is a value to being able to pass as a member of the mainstream majority group or as a member of the group that is in control that holds the power. Ethically, this is problematic for me as by passing, I am denying others who don't have that ability to pass - either they cannot hide their race as I can or they are not educated enough or facile enough to hide their quirks and the traits that cause the mainstream to identify them as other. There are times in life when it is necessary to consider self-care first. I rarely try to pass anymore. I am confident enough in who I am and have enough support from my chosen family to stand up tall. It took me a lot of years working on myself to get to this place in life.

II

MANIFESTATION
PART 1

The first piece, Catalyst, speaks to the path I walk. When I began my journey with Loki, he gave me the option to take a slow winding path to reach my goals or the steep one uphill, which was a faster path. I remember being told that the windy path came with more time to integrate what I was learning and less risk therefore less chance of injury. The steep path meant that I would gain knowledge more quickly. I chose the steep one. With a steep path comes a higher likelihood of injury and much higher risk. Many of us who choose that steeper path do so at a time when we do not yet understand the consequences. I do not regret my choice but do sometimes wonder how I would have experienced the slow winding path and how my life might have been different.

Catalyst

What is my job, you ask? I'm a catalyst. The spark that ignites the fires of transformation–the flames that transform or burn away, pare away the unnecessary, illuminating the core.

The Trickster Gods I serve delight in being alchemists, using me as the element in the cauldron that begins the reaction. Those whose natures are akin to mine, stay around as our symbiosis makes it possible for us both to grow. The Gods I serve feed on the chaotic energy, the fires of purification and transmogrification. We are shifters of the highest order. Our energy encourages the shift towards the most natural form for those we come into contact with.

Those whose natures are not complementary to mine move on to find their place in life. The loss felt is often bittersweet. The changes wrought can be smooth and subtle or cataclysmic.

Master reminds me that our Gods have a sense of humour. Each time I express a preference in absolute terms, they choose to remind me that in our world, nothing is absolute. There are no hard limits. All boundaries are permeable—some more so than others. As you enter the crucible, you would be wise to remember these words. The struggle can be sublime. Resistance truly is futile.

This second piece is about one of my most core desires. Brene Brown says, 'If we can share our story with someone who responds with empathy and understanding, shame can't survive.' It took many years before I could share this with anyone who responded with empathy and understanding. Maybe you have a desire that you are ashamed of? If you choose to share it, make sure that the person will respond with empathy and understanding and not condemnation. If you don't have someone in your life who can give you compassion and understanding no matter what you bring, consider sharing with a professional who has experience in these areas. This is step one to getting rid of the toxic shame. If this set of desires is not your cup of tea, that is fine. You can choose to skip to the memoir piece.

Watersports

She passes him on the way to work most mornings. She is drawn to him, and she knows he is attracted to her as every time she passes him, he is staring at her. That type of stare always results in her lowering her eyes. Each day she comes close to freezing as he catches her with his gaze. She feels trapped for a moment. Prey to his predator. Her heart flutters and then pounds. Her face flushes bright red. Sweat breaks out on her forehead and between her breasts. And suddenly, she breaks the spell - often with a shiver through her entire body, like a deer shaking off the gaze of the wolf. She walks off quickly, still shaking when she reaches her office door.

She finds herself at the same party with him. The party is in a downtown bar that has no frills. It is a local dive that hosts a band most weekends. This Saturday night, Damned has taken over the bar for a BDsM/Kink/Fetish night. The rules include no fucking in the bar, no naked cocks, no naked pussies (at least visible ones). But the bar is poorly lit, so all three rules are regularly ignored. There are safe sex supplies with the dungeon furniture cleaning supplies, so the organisers know that sex is happening.

The bathrooms are unisex. Lots of fucking goes on in the bathrooms. There is a glory hole between the stalls that has seen a lot of use over the years, two stalls and two urinals. People who don't want to pee or shit without an audience know to drink and eat little before a party there. She doesn't know the bar and so she doesn't know about the unisex loos and drinks her usual sizeable amount of water during the day. When she arrives, the first thing she wants to do is head to the loo and pee.

As she walks in, she sees two men at the urinals—both with massive dicks. They smile at her and then laugh as the blush rises over her chest and up her face. Her sleeveless silk tee leaves plenty of creamy skin exposed to turn beet red. She heads for the open stall and pulls up her leather kilt, squatting to pee. She wears no panties under her kilt, enjoying feeling exposed in this secret way.

Beth can hear people in the stall next door—the sounds of someone wanking and moaning and the sounds of someone pissing. Despite feeling self-conscious, she finally begins to pee. Someone pushes the stall door open as she is in mid-flow. She is not in a position to hold the stall door closed. He stands in front of her, grinning.

'Oh, Gods. It's him. I don't want to meet him like this'. She thinks. But she has no control as he is standing in front of her and she cannot go anywhere without acknowledging him. 'Hello,' she whispers. The blush moves quickly up her body from her toes to her scalp until she is crimson. She finds it almost impossible to meet his eyes, so she stares at the outline of his hard dick in his leather jeans. He chuckles. 'I'm Will' he says, 'and you are?' 'Beth' she replies. She finishes peeing, wipes herself and is about to stand when he says 'I need to piss'. Her pussy gushes.

Very few of her lovers know about her love of water sports. It was an integral part of her earliest submissive fantasies and has never left her. She masturbates to stories that involve being

24

made to drink piss or being pissed on, and the porn she watches often includes this as well. Will can smell her arousal. 'Unzip my jeans. Take out my dick. And unless you want me to ruin that cute kilt, put my dick in your mouth and be ready to swallow.' Will says. She moans and does as she is told.

The intense acrid flavour bursts onto her tongue. He pisses long and hard, and she has to swallow rapidly to avoid getting covered in it. She feels her clitoris pulsing with each swallow and by the time he finishes, she is desperate to come. He pulls her back by her thick curly hair and tells her to put his dick away. She moans as she carefully tucks him back into the butter soft black lambskin trousers and zips his fly. He pulls her head back by her curls, so she must look up at him. Two fingers from his right hand slide quickly into her oil slick pussy. He strokes into her a few times and then runs his fingertips over her clitoris. She moans 'please' as she is sure that coming without permission will not be acceptable to this man. She is so close she is not at all sure she can hold back if he strokes over her clitoris one more time. He knows this. She can tell. She can smell a sadist from a mile away, and he is certainly one. And he will stroke her clitoris again, but not give her permission. Will wants a reason to punish her. He wants a reason to take his belt out of its loops where it nestles around his waist and beat her with it until she cannot sit down. He wants this energy, this game with her, and he wants it now. He does not want to do this slowly, taking time to find out all about her desires, negotiating and agreeing on all the details. Will wants to take what he wants and to take it now. Period. If she chooses to be with him, that is what she can expect. She knows all this from his expression, his touch, his tone of voice, his presence.

Will runs his fingers over her clitoris again and says, 'wait until I tell you to come'. Beth tries. She focuses on her breath. Slows down her thinking. But he keeps stroking, and she is ever so close. 'Pissing in your mouth almost made you come on its own, didn't it?' He asks in a deep voice that is oil smooth. 'Yes,' she moans. 'That will be yes, Sir' he replies. 'Yes, Sir' she squeaks out. His fingers continue to slide over her clitoris, varying the pressure and sliding slowly over and around. She can no longer hold back. Her breath is coming in gasps 'please Sir please' she gasps out and hears 'not yet' as she crashes over the edge into an intense orgasm.

'Poor girl. That just earned you a beating'. He says with a sarcastic smile and he grabs her by her hair, pulls her out of the stall and towards the door. A sizeable man at the urinal says hello to him, and he replies, 'If you haven't finished yet, she would be happy to swallow your piss, wouldn't you girl?'. She moans and whispers 'yes, Sir'. The heavy butch girl waiting for the other cubicle shouts over 'I would love to use her mouth'. 'Sure Cecily' he replies 'Let's find a better place' and Cecily and the other guy, Len, follow them out of the loo. They find a space in the back room where water sports are tolerated if not allowed. 'Lie down' he says. 'If you take it all, I might not beat you as long, and I might let you come again. But I will still beat you.' He tells her.

They take Beth's shirt off and lie her on her back. A small crowd is gathering, and she sees two men with their dicks out stroking themselves hard. There is a couple playing with each other. One woman asks if she can join the queue, and Will says 'sure Rain'. Len kneels over her face and before pissing, lifts his balls, tells her lick behind, under them. His sweat is acrid and emits an odour that draws her in. She cannot get enough of the smell and the taste. It is familiar to her, and that makes it even more intense. 'Will, I want a rim job. I want to sit on her face first.' Will grants permission, and before his ass obscures her sight, she sees two more men take out their cocks and begin to stroke. She hears Will say to them, 'I want you to come on her face and chest. Let us know when you are ready, so you have an empty canvas'. Another two men join the group and stroke themselves hard. One says Will 'I need to piss first – this is a piss hard' and Will replies 'No problem, she will take it'.

Will leans close to her ear and whispers, 'Do a good job for Daddy, and I will reward you. Fuck this up, and I will hurt you. Understood? Good. You may come as often as you want to during this'. He steps back, and Len sits on her face. She buries her tongue in his asshole, and he moans as she licks and sucks. He bears down on her face so her tongue will go deeper and she comes as she licks him until he can't stand it anymore. He gets up and puts his dick in her mouth and unleashes a hot stream of piss. 'Swallow girl' he says as she gulps until he finishes. He stands up and takes his place in the circle, stroking his dick. Rain squats over her face and lowers her ass down. 'Ream my ass with your tongue first girly.' She bears down and Beth licks and sucks until her tongue is sore. Rain moves so she can piss in Beth's mouth and quickly fills her mouth full. Beth swallows and comes again.

The first three guys who arrived crowd around her face and chest as they are all about to come. One by one, they shoot hot come onto her chest, neck and chin. Each wipes his dick off on her face, squeezing the last drops of cum into her mouth so she can taste them. She can feel the hot jizz drying and cooling on her tits when the next dick is in front of her mouth, telling her to open and swallow, and the next stream of hot piss hits her tongue. She savours each dick - the small ones, large ones, thick ones, pale ones, dark ones. Some piss is almost sweet, and some disgusting. Some asses stink, but she does as she is told and licks and sucks ass. And she comes multiple times. The nastier it is, the more she comes.

The party ends with the 10ᵗʰ man shooting his hot sperm into her mouth and over her chin. Will brings a warm, soft towel and cleans her off. He helps her put her top back on and leads her to the spanking bench. He bends her over the bench, moves around so she can see what he is doing and removes his belt. It is black and medium thickness. He runs it under her nose. The smell of the well-worn leather is intoxicating. He puts the folded belt to her lips, and she kisses it. He brings his leather-covered cock to her lips, and she kisses him.

'I will beat you at least 20 times but less than 40. If you can't stand anymore, raise your left hand. OK?' She replies 'OK' knowing that she could say nothing else. The first stroke on the fleshiest part of her ass makes her jump. It cuts into her flesh and welts her immediately. Ten strokes in she has reached her happy place and is transmuting the pain of the beating into intense pleasure. At 20 strokes, she is flying, and when he reaches 30, she is in a new arc of pain and struggling to cope. He watches the changes in her body. He waits for her to surrender to the pain, and he will not stop until she does. She partly surrenders

at ten strokes and while she is in her happy place. He wants total surrender to his will. At 40, she screams, and he keeps going. At 45, he finally sees the shift as she goes limp and open and no longer strains towards the belt in pleasure or away from the belt in pain. She now accepts what he gives. He stops at 50. The swollen oozing welts cover the whole of her thighs and ass. She is bleeding from some of them. He brings the belt around to her lips, and she kisses it. He helps her off the bench and moves her to a softer area to recover. He cleans her cuts and then kisses her deeply. 'Good girl' he murmurs, and she beams with pride through her pain.

He leads her to his car and takes her home. He plans to tuck her into bed to sleep after giving her some painkillers and making her drink at least two enormous glasses of water. But she is so enticing. He slides his cock into her slowly, allowing her to get used to his length, his girth. He strokes into her. He pushes her bruised ass into the sheets, and she is moaning in both intense pleasure and sharp pain. He slides his fingers between them and strokes her clitoris as he strokes his dick into her. She is close to coming, and he takes his fingers away. 'Play with yourself as I fuck you' he orders. She slides her fingers between them and begins to rub her clitoris until she is so close to coming, she knows she won't be able to hold it. 'Please, please please I need to come please' she wails. 'Go ahead' he says, and she lets go, her cunt gripping his cock and pushing him towards his orgasm. After he finishes, he slides slowly out of her and lies with her in his arms. She is about to drop off to sleep when he says, 'Slide down to my dick and open your mouth. I need to piss'. She does as she is told and swallows his stream without losing a drop. He sends her to the bathroom to brush her teeth and then tucks her into bed with a kiss, leaving her halfway to orgasm. 'Sleep on it' he says 'Don't come until the morning'. She says 'yes Sir' and drifts off to disturbed sleep.

This part of my story is where I am introduced to the man who held me captive and repeatedly raped me over five days. I paired the erotica with it because he was the first person I could ever tell this core desire to, and he was happy to meet my passions with my consent. The first couple of weeks of my relationship with Damien were consensual. Then it changed. What happened after the change is in the next section. The gossamer line between consent and non-consent is crucial in this section and the next.

Two weeks after the orgy, DeeDee and I were at work, selling magazine subscriptions to support the special Olympics over the phone. I had started on sales and quickly moved to verification, which suited me better. The office was a cacophonous din of people trying ever so hard to convince other people that this was a good cause and they needed the magazines in their lives. There was the freedom that came with earning a bit of extra money. My father gave me the bare minimum spending money because somehow he thought restricting the funds I had would stop me from doing things he didn't want me to do – like drinking, using drugs and having sex. All this did was motivate me to get a job alongside my classes. The job paid enough for me to eat something other than rice and cream of mushroom soup, rice and cream of broccoli soup, or some of the awful food at the university canteen. When I took a sales shift, I got a commission as well, which meant money for the cinema.

DeeDee phoned me and told me she met someone on her shift that she wanted to introduce me to. 'His name is Damien, and you'll like him'. I dressed with a little extra flair that day and was excited as I headed out to work. DeeDee had told me he was 29, which seemed fucking ancient to me since I was 19. As naïve as we were, we didn't even consider he might be lying about his age (which he was. He was in his mid-30's) or about his name (Damien was one alias of many).

DeeDee introduced me as her 'little sister' which she often did. She was a year older than I. I could not keep his stare, and though I am usually articulate, I mumbled a greeting. My mouth became parched and my breathing quickened. He was about 6 feet tall, lithe, with a moderate afro and a narrow white streak of hair running through the left side. His eyes were chocolate with an amber hue. His hands larger artist hands and he kept his pinkie nail long. So naïve was I that I didn't know this had to do with cocaine use. He was wearing red and black and had a lovely ass. His skin was the colour of milk chocolate and ever so smooth. But it really wasn't what he looked like that caused my reaction. It was his presence. That man had so much charisma that Satan himself would have had to tip his hat - game recognising game.

He takes my hand as he says hello to me and draws me in closer to him until I can smell him, the smell of musk with a hint of vanilla and leather. I find the scent hard to describe but still recognise it anywhere. It is not a cologne; it is his pheromones. His scent intoxicates at the beginning and then becomes necessary for life, replacing the ordinary air I breathe as though he alone carries all the oxygen. To this day, whenever I catch a whiff of anything similar to his scent, I melt and have to fight an urge to sink to my knees. His voice is a liquid baritone.

I can't keep his gaze. I blush as soon as I say hello. He asks me out for a drink after the shift. I remember wanting to drink very little. He orders for me and I accept what he gives me. This feels like my fantasies finally becoming reality. I am content to let him lead. In fact, it is a relief. I am so paralysed by my own heat that I can't decide anything even if my life depends upon it.

We end up back at my little studio flat, and I remember the feel of his lips on mine. The taste of his tongue. His teeth bite at my mouth. His hands are deep in my hair. He tugs at my hair instead of pulling as many have done so there is no pain but a sensual discomfort that causes my nerves to fire and my clitoris to pulse. I can feel him exploring my body. My nipples rising to his touch. My pussy flooding. He lies on his back on the bed, and his cock is sticking straight up. His cock is larger than any I have ever seen before, and I have seen a fair few by then. He is long, relatively thick and circumcised at least 10 inches, more likely 12. His size should frighten me, but it does not. Instead, I am excited and anxious.

He tastes divine. I work hard to get as much of him in my throat as possible. His cock presses on my gag reflex. He whispers to me, liquid voice melting over me and causing me to melt, telling me to relax. He pushes forward gently, and I feel his cock enter my throat. I am not gagging. He lets me adjust until I cannot breathe, until he is controlling my breathing as he fucks my throat. I am on the edge of orgasm without touching myself and without being touched. He comes, and I savour the taste, sweet and acrid at the same time. I am a connoisseur of come – love to taste it, swallow it, the feeling of it warming my belly. His compares to the best I have tasted so far.

The first time he fucks me, all I can do is sob and scream. I'm on my hands and knees, and he is behind me. Sliding into me slowly at first, I cannot be still–fucking him, trying to control the pace. He chuckles and holds me steady. 'Let me' he says, and I can only sob.

He's fucking me deeply, slowly stroking my clit with one hand, and I can feel my orgasm begin. I have never cum while being fucked before. I have rarely cum from anything other than my fingers or fucking my covers. I get too nervous to let go – have a grand time but cannot trust enough to just cum. Losing control terrifies me, but it is what I want most in the world.

I love not being able to control the pace. I love being pushed to cum, not being allowed to stop myself. He fucks me until I think I can no longer move. When he comes inside me, I come again. I love to listen to him speak. I don't care what about; his voice is warm melted chocolate or sometimes liquid fire. I cannot focus on his words, but I know they are essential. In my distant mind and in my guts, warning bells are ringing, a cacophony, but I do not hear them. At 4 am, we are standing in my hall/kitchen. He is cooking me an omelette. I can barely eat, but I'm so hungry. I am drinking Kahlua and eating this omelette from his fingers and desperate for the taste of him again.

I am off balance. None of my reference points apply. I have no anchors. I have fantasised about being controlled, being a slave since I was 9. The men and women who have grabbed my interest have almost all been dominant.

I remember him telling me I can do anything I have ever fantasised about doing. I blush scarlet. I cannot speak. It feels like he is in my mind, can so hear my thoughts. I listen to him, say 'yes' in my head. I look up at him and say aloud ', but you can't have heard me' and he replies 'Why not?'. I'm still looking confused as he leads me to the bathroom, pushes me to my knees, puts his cock in my mouth and tells me to drink. I am coming as I swallow, gulping – not losing a drop. I can hear him laugh.

It is the next morning, and Dave rings. Damien tells me not to take the call. I listen as Dave leaves a message and feel a bit guilty. I don't like to hurt his feelings, but Dave never made me drip at a look from him or at the sound of his voice, never made me moan and beg for more. I have never been this turned on before, never known anyone who could make me shiver. Sex has been fun, but except for sex with Sam and a few others, less than intense most of the time.

I have never had anal sex before, and the thought of Damien fucking me in the ass makes me shake. Surely his size is going to be a problem. I am squirming. 'Let me' he says and holds my hips still as he drives in further, pulling out an inch and sliding in again slowly until I am moaning, trembling. Picking up speed until he buries his cock completely in my ass. I scream 'Please oh please fuck me'. He lets my hips go, and I am fucking him back, dancing on his dick. It feels so fucking good – pussy is throbbing and he reaches round playing with my clit and my orgasm envelops my whole body. The energy builds and shoots out through the top of my head. I am desperate for his come in my ass. His nails are scraping down my back as he fucks my ass - slamming into me – until all I can do is let him rock me. It is like riding out a hurricane. I am not sure if I am hoping I will be consumed or praying not to be consumed. He is on top of me, stroking my hair, telling me how well I have done, promising me more.

And I want so much more. I am afraid of my desire. I confront my lust head-on for the first time and find myself petrified at the intensity. Society has taught me that lust in a woman is a negative trait; that it makes me a slut, unworthy of love. I wonder if I am truly unworthy, so deep is my desire, so all-consuming. I can do nothing to stem the flow of energy, to douse the flames.

His cock is in my pussy balls deep, and his hands are around my throat, and I am coming again. His voice is in my head. I can hear him telling me to let go and something shifts and I can breathe. His hands move down to my breasts, pinching my nipples. I am gasping, and the heat is rising again. I hear myself say 'I can't' and he laughs–'Yes, you can and you will.' I want to tell him to stop, and I don't want to tell him to stop. When I finally use my safe word, he has drawn blood. He is licking up the blood that is oozing out around my nipples. He is glowing, and I am fading but so hot, so terribly terribly hot.

I have some time to myself the next day. I call friends and family, and I sound happy. I am deliriously happy. I go to class, and I shop for food. I speak to Sam and DeeDee, and Dave leaves me a few more messages, but I do not return his calls. I talk with Damien that night but don't see him. I don't see him for a couple of days, and I am pining for him. I can think of nothing else. I can feel him with me everywhere, both comforting and disconcerting.

Damien takes me out for a meal and then we are at a bar local to me. I am underage, but the bartender doesn't care. We are at the quiet end of the bar, and he is talking with me. He asks me about my understanding of Master/slave relationships. I know little except for fiction like the Story of O. I remember the tone and timbre of his voice and not the words. It is important to him that I consent. I think maybe I should ask for details before saying yes but I feel compelled to answer yes to all his questions. Spirit, 12 Dreams of Dr Sardonicus is playing in the background. His hand is at my neck, massaging, as he speaks to a man who is interested in me. It is clear this man believes I am his property. And so I am by this point. I cannot focus on anything other than his touch, voice in my head, scent, the promise of his taste. I am burning.

Consent is a far more complex concept than most are led to believe. What makes up sexual consent? Consent is when someone says 'yes'. This may seem obvious, but many people confuse the lack of a 'no' for consent. Silence does not mean yes. Consent is a dynamic process. Pay attention to what your lover is saying, the emotion being communicated and body language. If any of this seems at all hesitant or confused, check with your lover again. Ask if they like what you are doing and want you to continue.

There are four parts to consent: capacity, information, agreement/ boundary setting, autonomy.

Capacity is your ability to give consent. Children under the age of 16 cannot consent to most things, as we deem them unable to appreciate the consequences of their actions. People who are under the influence of drugs or alcohol may not be able to give consent. It depends upon how altered their reasoning ability is while taking drugs or alcohol. For example, if a person is so drunk that he cannot stand up and is blacking out, he cannot give consent. However, if a person can function under the influence of alcohol, he can give legal consent even though he may not make the best decisions, and he may regret it the next day.

Jeff and John met through a friend. On their first date, they enjoyed two bottles of wine during dinner. Jeff invited John up to his flat for a nightcap. John said yes, and they each had a glass of port. John asked Jeff where the restroom was, and when he stood up, he was weaving and stumbled. When he came back from the bathroom, they began kissing again. Things heated up very quickly, and Jeff asked John if he would like to have sex with him. John hesitated for a moment and then said, 'I rarely do this on a first date. But yes, I would like to have sex with you.' Many people in Jeff's position would make sure there were condoms and lube handy and then go back to the foreplay. After all, John has consented to sex, and Jeff is really attracted to him.

For some people, John being buzzed and also stating that he rarely has sex on a first date would be enough to make them question whether the consent was valid. Would John feel happy the next day about having gone against his mores by having sex on the first date? It's possible that John would feel upset with himself, but not with Jeff. Equally, he could feel taken advantage of by Jeff as he could think once Jeff realised he was buzzed and he had stated that he rarely has sex on the first date, Jeff should have suggested that they wait until the next time. To me, this situation is an ethical challenge. Is a person responsible for protecting their potential sexual partner from an awful decision? Perhaps, but that also could feel incredibly patronising. How does someone know if it is a good or bad decision for another person? Or is it the case that when someone is buzzed or drunk and expressing hesitancy about having sex, no sexual activity should be pursued as they are not giving enthusiastic or affirmative consent.

People who are suffering from mental illness may not be able to give consent. This depends upon the person's ability to comprehend what is being asked of them, their ability to comprehend the consequences of going through with that. If she cannot understand the potential consequences of having sexual intercourse with a man (like getting pregnant or contracting a sexually transmitted infection), then she cannot give consent.

Information: To give consent, you must understand what you are consenting to. If you don't have enough information to anticipate consequences, then you cannot honestly give consent. In medical settings, informed consent requires detailed knowledge of the procedure and outcomes. In sexual situations, people often skip this step and don't clarify with potential partners meanings of terms or details. While what a person means by a kiss may seem somewhat obvious, the definition of safe sex may not be at all clear. To some, safe sex means withdrawing the penis from the vagina during intercourse before ejaculation. To others, safe sex means using a barrier method during intercourse. For still others, refraining from penis in vagina sex defines safe sex.

If you will engage in more risky activities like BDsM, more information is necessary for consent to be considered affirmative consent. Impact play can mean a mild spanking to beating with a paddle to using a bullwhip. The pain levels, levels of marking, and potential damage caused for each of these activities is very different. Power exchange can mean only in the bedroom through to handing over every aspect of a person's life. With Damien, I had very little information. Most of what he said was seductive, some formulaic. I did not have enough information to consent to what he ultimately did to me. Even had I had more knowledge, it is likely I would have still withdrawn consent because having never experienced extreme violence, I had no way to anticipate what it would be like or what the consequences would be. He never suggested that extreme violence was part of what I was consenting to at the time I gave consent.

Agreement/boundary setting: This is the point where limits are clearly stated, boundaries described and agreement reached on these and also on also agreement on how partners signal limits and how they might break a deal. In BDSM, this is where parties agree safe words and describe them and they discuss and agree hard limits. Damien and I talked through none of this.

Some experienced BDsM enthusiasts will engage without a safe word. In these circumstances, the parties know that they are taking a higher level of risk and often are agreeing to hold each other harmless if things take a terrible turn. The people are taking responsibility for deciding to engage in a higher level of risk, recognising that this could lead to damage, hurt or a bad emotional situation. As a rule, people who work without safe words in longer-term relationships do so because they know each other's responses well, wish to push limits, and the risk does not increase as much as if they were in a new relationship. The risk still increases.

Autonomy is your right as a sentient being to say what happens to your mind, your body, your spirit. It is the foundation of consent. If you do not have autonomy in the first place, you cannot give consent. If they have coerced you, you don't have autonomy, and therefore valid consent is not possible.

Many of us have grown up without good models of consent. Thinking back, my first memory about consent though I didn't realise it at the time was when I was seven years old. I had an aunt who had schizophrenia. She was always loud, had her lipstick drawn way outside her lips and smelled kind of funny. I can remember being told to go kiss her because she would feel bad if I didn't. Before I could do so, she grabbed me, and I remember being held tight and struggling to get free. I have countless friends who tell similar stories and many friends who are parents who admit telling their children to hug the smelly aunt for the same reason.

The concept of consent has changed a lot in the past 40 years. When I started dating in the 1970s, a lot of gaining consent was unspoken. Often a man would touch a woman and see how she reacted to see if they had consent. This was the cultural norm at the time. They still taught girls to 'play hard to get' so the only actual way guys had of knowing what the girl wanted was to make an advance and see if 'no' became 'yes'. The sexual revolution was in progress, so women were given conflicting messages. If they were hip, then they should have lots of sex, but if they had lots of sex, they were branded as sluts. There were girls that you had fun with and girls that you had relationships with. The ones you had relationships with were the ones who played hard to get. I remember being confused. I enjoyed sex, but when I was honest about this, I was a slut. I wasn't ever very good at playing hard to get because I didn't lie well.

Though I usually think of this game playing as something that was most prevalent in the 80s and before, I was recently talking with a friend who told me that a woman he was close to told him he is too authentic and too nice and that he ought to play by the old rules - hesitate more, don't call the woman back, don't offer so much because women still prefer men who are a bit rough and they prefer to play hard to get.

When I think back to the examples of sexual consent in the media when I was entering the world of relationships, the first that comes to mind is Hans Solo and Princess Leia in Star Wars. He pursues her relentlessly, and she refuses continually. In the end, he pushes her against the wall and kisses her as she is refusing again! She melts, and they form a great romance. Harrison Ford forces himself on multiple heroines in Blade Runner and all the Indiana Jones movies. And all the women melt (including me). Today, we would mark this as coercive.

The message for men is that it turns women on, this caveman approach, and that eventually they will consent and melt. This might be true, but only when the man is as hot as Harrison Ford and the woman is already attracted to him. And that's the problem. If Mary has told Art from accounting repeatedly that she doesn't want to go out with him and is not interested in him at all sexually, she will not find him pushing her up against the wall and kissing her hot at all. She will see this for what it is, a sexual assault.

It isn't surprising that men feel the goalposts have moved repeatedly. With the recent mounting allegations, it has highlighted the imbalance of power when talking about harassment. If there is an imbalance of power, men are told that any suggestion of sexual activity may be harassment. When President Bill Clinton had a relationship with Monica Lewinsky, though both acknowledged that there was a power imbalance, Ms Lewinsky wrote in 2014 'Sure, my boss took advantage of me, but I will always remain firm on this point: It was a consensual relationship.' How are men supposed to walk through this minefield without getting blown up?

If I say yes because I don't want to hurt your feelings, that is consent. As long as I am free to refuse without risking some actual harm (like being beaten, killed, losing my job, my family being harmed), it is consent. It's up to me to gather the strength to refuse. If I don't refuse and I regret what I did the next day, that is my mistake, not a consent violation. This is not victim blaming. This is taking responsibility for my behaviour. To say otherwise, is to imply that women have no agency and cannot make choices - both good and bad choices. While there are certainly situations in which there is coercion, what I experienced with Damien for example, not all bad choices are because of coercion. Sometimes even the best of us takes a risk that turns out badly or acts impulsively without thinking through to the consequences of our actions.

The current narrative in the media seems to suggest that men fall into two categories: abusers or not good enough allies. It depicts few men as excellent allies to women. This is a thorny topic and often ends up making men feel that they can do no right. The thing is, we all make mistakes. In my conversation about consent with Kitty Stryker, one of the things she highlighted as being important is that there is a way for people who have violated consent to apologise, make amends and be accepted back into the community at large. We were talking mainly about the BDsM community, but we also agreed that this applies when talking about sexual harassment as well. If someone rapes a woman, a simple apology and promise not to do this again will not be enough. When someone harasses a woman in the workplace, there ought to be a way back into the workplace community. If we do not start providing ways back in when people make mistakes, and we continue to focus on blame, things will remain fractured, and the divide between us will increase.

How do we begin to repair the divide? To start, we open the conversation. All of us fail to get consent at times. Have you ever hugged someone without asking and felt their discomfort? Did you tell your child to hug Aunt Jane so she wouldn't feel hurt? We take responsibility for our part in this dynamic. Have you played hard to get or have you ignored a woman's 'no'?

Then, we express a willingness to teach and learn about consent, to look at the concept not only as a means to an end (How do I get her to fuck me?) but also as a part of how we connect, the dynamic between us.

Finally, we work on how to create real tangible ways to heal breaches of consent instead of focusing on blame so that our relationships heal and we move forward into positive relationships in the workplace, social spaces and the wider community. This is easier as we start to use our agency, educate ourselves and those around us, and take responsibility for risk assessment and the choices we make. Again, we are all works in progress.

III

MANIFESTATION PART II

*'I can bring you pain. I can bring you sudden
pleasure. Your life will only gain if your love's the
final measure.'*
Mr Skin by Jay Ferguson

I chose this piece of erotica because it deals with non-consensual sex
as hot and exciting. When read with my story, you may find it
really disturbing. Consent is many-layered, and sometimes the line
between consent and non-consent is as thin as tissue paper and torn
just as easily. In fantasy, we romanticise the aftermath of rape. In
reality, rape, abuse and intimate partner violence create emotional
havoc and often lead to mental health issues that can be difficult to
recover from. There are layers of recovery, moving back into a life
that looks to the future rather than feeling the past as ever-present.
I encourage you to remember that as you read through this chapter
and also to be kind to yourself if you find yourself as aroused by my
life story as you do by the erotica. If I find it hard to separate out the
arousing parts from the devastation and I have been living with this
for 41 years, it isn't surprising that you might too.

I would start with 'Once upon a time', but somehow that doesn't seem appropriate for this type of story (Of course, fairy tales can be dark affairs.). Instead, I will start here:

I take my time getting ready for my date. I spend a long time in the shower, clean myself carefully, enjoy the feel of the honey cleanser sliding over me. I take my time with my hair and then let the almost scalding water sluice over my body. I step out, wrapping my hair in a towel, using the deep fluffy bath sheet to dry myself. I towel dry my hair and then add the argan oil and curl enhancer, rub my favourite moisturisers into my body and face. I take time with some makeup. Unhappy with my first application, I scrub my face and start again. I grunt in approval, finally finished. I apply the hand-mixed oils, my scent, and enter my bedroom.

I put on a black shirt dress, tights and leather boots. For jewellery, I put on some ropes of semi-precious stones and wooden beads, long silver teardrop earrings, a bracelet made of lapis. I check myself in the mirror, grab my leather jacket, black leather bag and black sheepskin gloves. I head out the door. I'm not expected back tonight, and no one is waiting to hear from me.

My body tingles with anticipation. I am not sure what to expect this evening. I have been told to present myself well and to turn up at this cute little restaurant at 20:00. I am hungry but more anxious. I hope my presentation will be acceptable. I move from feeling confident to self-conscious and back, my anxiety bouncing around like the little metal ball in the pinball machine at the arcade. I hop out of the taxi in front of the restaurant and wait to the side of the entrance as they have instructed me. As I turn around, I feel a body press into me, knocking me off balance and into the wall. I am inclined to turn around and tell whoever has just knocked me over what I think, but quickly realise that I cannot move back from the wall. They knock my legs apart further, and press my tits into the bricks. I hear someone rasp 'Don't turn around' and feel the barrel of a gun pressed against the bottom of my skull. I'm shaking but try to stay still at the same time. The gun caresses my head and then my neck. I moan despite my fear.

I can feel breath on my neck and then close to my ear, hands roam my body, pinch and pull at my flesh. The leg between my thighs presses into my ass, and I have to work to stay standing. The brick is rough and scrapes my chest. I feel torn between my heat and my desire to fight. While they press the gun to me, I will not fight. I'm not willing to take that risk. I love life too much. I am pulled away from the wall and propelled into a waiting van. All the fears that come along with vans run through my head. Hippies and serial killers are the only folks with vans these days (except for commercial ventures). Somehow, I don't think a hippy has grabbed me. I am not restrained, but I can see that the door is secure, and there is no way to get out without endangering my life even further. I'm a bright girl, so I decide to conserve my strength. Bruises coming up on my hip from where I fell when shoved into the van feel tender. I slow my breathing to stave off panic. I hear whistling from the front of the van. At least my captor is enjoying himself.

I have not been in this situation before, have not been abducted. I was held captive, and I wonder if this situation will be like that one. Endurance helped me to survive. I kept my wits about me; I took advantage of the opportunity to escape when it presented itself so I strive to keep my wits about me now.

I'm directionally challenged so I cannot tell how long we drive or in what direction. We arrive at a building, he blindfolds me and brings me out of the van. I wonder what he looks like. I can smell him; musk, wood, and some spice. Despite my fear, his scent makes me hungry, and this makes me confused. 'Will you enter under your own power, or do I have to carry you in?' he asks. 'I stumble out of the van, follow him and wonder if they will construe this as consent. We go up a brief flight of stairs and enter an almost empty room. He cuts off my clothes and secures me to a chair. The place is slightly cold, and the sweat cools quickly on my body. My nipples are tight. My legs are restrained apart, my pussy open.

I smell him as he walks around me. My anxiety builds the longer he is silent. Crack! My head snaps back, and tears spring to my eyes. I am in shock. 'Do I have your attention?' he asks quietly. 'Yes,' I whisper. 'Good' he says while running his nails over my back. My intake of breath is sharp. He twists my nipples, applies clips. They feel like they are metal and slightly weighted. I groan at the bite. Sweat forms in my hairline. He attaches clips to my outer labia. I scream. 'Quiet or I will gag you' he says and flicks at the clips. I bite my lip and groan, try to breathe through the pain.

'I will release you so I can move you' He tells me as he frees my arms and legs. He brings me over to the bed, and I begin to fight. I don't know why I do this now. It makes little sense. I don't know where I am, and if I do get away, how I would get help? But I cannot ignore the urge. I kick out at him, throw a

wayward punch. He grasps my wrists, pins me down with little effort. He chuckles. 'You have some spirit' he muses. Whack! He pulls the clips off my nipples. 'Owwww' I howl. Tears run down my face, taking makeup with them. He presses me face down on the bed, kicks my legs wide apart and chains me to the bed. I hear the susurrating sound of a belt leaving trousers, feel the rush of air a fraction of a second before it cracks on my ass. He gives me ten strokes with the belt in quick succession. Welts rise; tears are running freely down my face. He shoves his fingers into my ass, spits and slicks my asshole, and quickly shoves his dick in until his balls slap my ass. I groan and try to move my hips. I haven't yet adjusted to his dick in my ass, so it hurts and burns. My legs are restrained and I cannot ease the discomfort. He pulls my hair, bending my body back into a bow. He bites my back, and I scream. I cannot help it. 'Once more and I will gag you' he growls and bites again. I bite my lip until I taste my blood and manage not to scream.

I cannot pinpoint when it changes, but somewhere it does, and I moan in pleasure. The pressure on the welts on my ass, the sharp pain and sting of the bites, the burn of the dick pounding in and out of my ass. I feel an orgasm build. He notices the changes. 'You want to come, don't you bitch?' he growls 'Yes' I beg. 'No' he growls as he pulls out of my ass abruptly, leaves me open and empty. I wail, and the slap to my face comes quickly. 'Quiet' he shouts. I sob quietly, not sure whether to feel relief that he has stopped or to beg for him to continue. He walks away and lights a cigarette. The tobacco smells strong, and I crave the smoke. He blows the smoke in my face. I inhale and then cough, which makes him laugh. The ember is close to my breast. I feel the heat and tremble. 'I could burn you' he says. I cannot respond. I freeze in fear. He brings the cigarette closer, and I smell the small hairs on my breast burning away. It feels like my flesh will blister, even though the ember has not yet touched my skin. He pulls the cigarette away and twists my already abraded nipples. He reaches down and pulls the clamps off my labia. It takes a few seconds before searing pain sets in, as the blood re-enters the area. I almost pass out. Sweat stands out on my skin. I am trembling. I can feel him watching me. I feel more exposed, as if that were possible. He leans in closer to peer into my eyes, scoops up the tears from my face and licks them off of his fingers then smiles. I manage to stay still and not to close my eyes.

I think he is attractive with his dark eyes and mocha skin. The thought scares me. I have to concentrate, or I cannot escape if I even have a chance to do so. He still stares at me; his hand runs over the welts on my ass, pinches and strokes until mixing pain and pleasure makes me sing. He runs a finger around my pussy lips, gathers the juices and chuckles. He bites my neck, holding tight as he shoves two fingers into my pussy. I work hard to be still, not wanting to highlight the pleasure this is giving me, but he can tell. My body betrays me. 'Not enough pain yet then' he states and beats my ass and back with the belt. I jump. I cannot move away as my legs are still restrained, but now I struggle. The buckle comes down on my ass and I yelp. His hands are around my throat, 'Didn't I tell you not to scream?' he says. 'Yes,' I whimper. He buckles a ball gag around my head. I hate the feel of a gag. I always think I will choke. He beats me again. I struggle until I cannot and collapse. He shoves his dick into my ass again, fucks me hard. At first, all I can do is cry, and then I rise to meet his thrusts. He stretches me, but the burn feels good. I am dizzy with the thrusts. He fucks me until he comes, leaves me on the edge of orgasm.

I hear him light a cigarette and smell the smoke. He flicks the hot ashes over the welts on my ass. I scream behind my gag. Suddenly, I feel the tip of the cigarette touch my tit - searing, burning pain and then icy water on top of it, tears course down my face again. I sob, and he collects my tears. He takes off the gag and sprays water in my mouth. I work to calm my breathing. He unchains one leg and allows me to move to relieve my muscles. 'Why don't you sit?' he says, the laughter evident in his voice. Even on the soft bed, I cannot find a comfortable place.

'I haven't introduced myself' he said. 'I'm Jack. I have been looking forward to meeting you. Fen has been talking about you'. I tremble. 'Does he know that I am here?' I whisper. 'No. But he will.' he replies. I look at him, my eyes signalling my confusion, but he chooses not to enlighten me. 'You better rest while you can' he tells me and leaves me to find a comfortable space on the bed. I surprise myself by drifting off.

I wake disoriented, needing to pee and thirsty. I sit up slowly and wait for my eyes to adjust. I don't see him. My left foot is still attached to the bed with a length of chain; otherwise, I am not restrained. 'Hello,' I say and stand a couple of feet from the bed. I don't hear him come up behind me. His hand goes around my throat, lips close to my ear. 'What do you need?' he says. 'I need to pee please and I'm thirsty' I reply. He leads me to the loo and stands over me as I sit down. I freeze. I am not good at peeing in front of anyone, but it is clear that he will go nowhere. I start to pee, and he says 'Open your mouth, I'll quench your thirst'. I do, and he shoves his soft dick in my mouth. 'Swallow and don't spill' he says as he pisses in my mouth. I swallow quickly, gulping, working hard not to miss a drop. I finish peeing, and he keeps going until I think I will choke. I manage to swallow every drop. He tells me to wash out my mouth, and I do so quickly, then he leads me from the bathroom.

'Lie on the bed, face-up' he says, and I do as I am told. He slaps my face, bringing instant tears to my eyes. He brings the cane down quickly on my tits, bringing a stripe up within seconds, wresting a scream from my throat. 'Today I want to hear you scream' he says and brings the cane down again. It feels like natural bamboo, always somewhat stingier than the nuboo canes. He lays down six stripes quickly across my breasts, the final two over my nipples. He reaches down between my legs and scoops up my juices. I'm dripping despite the intensity of the pain. 'Your body will betray you' he says as he hits me again and rubs my swollen clit. 'You will come when I want you to, regardless of what I am doing to you' he goes on and continues to manipulate my clit. I am ever so close to coming. I struggle to get away from his hand, his skilful fingers. His mouth is on my right nipple; teeth chew on it until I moan. His fingers continue to work my clit until I explode, moaning. I drench his fingers.

He gives me respite for a moment and then attacks my tits with his teeth again. I go limp as he chews and sucks. It is too painful and yet too pleasurable. He pushes three fingers into my sopping pussy, wrenching more moans from me. He fucks me hard with one hand, using his other to pinch the sensitive skin on my thighs and the sweet spot on my ass. I struggle hard, using a free hand to grab at him. He bats my hand away and moves up my body, pins my hands above my head by the wrists hard. No mild restraint this, I can feel the pain in the bones of my wrists. I try to struggle, but it is pointless. He enters me in one stroke, banging his dick into my cervix. I keen as he fucks me hard. He leans down and bites my cheek, causing fresh tears to run from my eyes. He licks up my tears and bites my ear and then sucks on my neck. He makes me come again as he pounds into me and roars as he empties his balls into my pussy. 'Don't move' he says as he climbs off of me. He crosses the room and comes back with water and tangerine pieces, feeding me the fruit one segment at a time. I moan as he does, tasting the sweet juice, grateful for the food and water. He brings over a cloth and alcohol, cleans up my welts and cuts. I wince with the pain of the alcohol on fresh abrasions. He flicks my raw nipples a half dozen times until tears run down my cheeks and scoops up my tears with his tongue.

He lays down next to me and runs a knife over me, almost caressing me with it, observing me to see my reaction. I shake, though I know that this might mean I get cut. He runs the knife over my left breast, presses the tip into my nipple. 'I will take this' he whispers. 'Pplease please no' I moan. He pushes it in more deeply until a drop of blood appears, and he laps this up. He moves the knife down under the nipple and makes a small slice. I yowl. He gathers the blood from the cut and savours it. He applies alcohol to the wound, and I screech. He places the knife at my throat, inhales, enjoys smelling my fear. Then he draws blood from a half dozen places on my body, revels in my horror, the sweet taste of my essence and the gushing juices from between my legs. He suckles from one of the cuts on my thigh and then says 'come', watching while I buck, and my pussy swells further, juices seep from between my lips.

He gets up and brings the cane down on the front of my thighs, stripe after stripe until my throat is raw from screaming. 'Turn over' he says and then brings the cane down on my ass and the back of my thighs, over the belt stripes from the previous evening. He canes me until I lose my voice. He fucks me hard and slow at first, presses into all the welts. He speeds up and pinches my tits as he pulls me to him. When he comes, I do, surprising myself.

'Your people have agreed to your release' he tells me. 'I will drop you off once the payment comes through'. I flush hot, giggle and then sigh. I find my ambivalence confusing. He continues to worry at my tits, pinch at my ass while awaiting the call that will tell him that they have transferred the money. He examines the marks he has left on my body. There are many welts and stripes, many bruises, and cuts and one burn on my tit. 'That one will scar' he says as he runs a finger over the wound. I am secretly pleased. I jump when the phone rings. He murmurs into the phone. Then he brings me my clothes and unchains my ankle. I dress carefully, wishing I had softer clothing as I have so many abrasions. He blindfolds me and puts me in the van and drives me to where I left my car. As he lets me out, he nips my neck. I inhale deeply, trying to hold on to his scent. I stumble to my car, get in, and begin to cry. I sit for a few minutes and then slowly drive home.

Master is there waiting for me and settles me into bed. He asks questions, and I find I answer quietly. I wake from a dream of my abductor, pussy dripping, nipples taught and every welt *and cut alive, the burn on my breast pulsing. My Master slides his dick into me. I moan, feeling his love and also feeling each and every welt. It is as though both of them are fucking me.*

Master checks my well-being before heading to work in the morning. 'If you need to, phone me' he says as he leaves. I am quiet and thoughtful this morning. As I move about my house, I keep feeling I am missing something. It takes some time, and then I realise I miss the chain and I miss him. I wonder if he thinks of me. I wonder if I will see him again. I run my finger over the burn and sigh as I feel the pain. I trace the welts and smell his scent. I come as I run my hands over the cuts on my breasts, tears flowing down my cheeks.

This part of my story highlights the challenges around consent and non-consent. As I had these desires long before meeting Damien, does it mean I attracted this experience? I don't think so, though I might have been more attractive to him because I already had the desires. It certainly means that I found it hard to spot danger and to assess when to run, to end a relationship or an experience. If you have experienced sexual violence, this part of the story will probably be difficult for you.

'Time to go' he says, and I cannot decide if he has spoken aloud. He calls the bartender by name, and we leave. We are ½ way down the busy avenue when he pushes me into a doorway and down onto my knees, hard dick springing out of black jeans. It is hard to concentrate. I try to press myself as far into the doorway as possible. Fantasies of being arrested for public lewdness and my parents being called crowd into my head. But I love his control. I'm sucking him, devouring him, feeling him ram his dick as far down my throat as he can . Soon all that exists is his dick in my throat, his come in my mouth, throbbing of my cunt, his hands tangled in my hair and the sound of his moan. He pulls me up to my feet and we walk back to my apartment.

I have consented to be his slave. I think. I am not at all sure what this entails. As serious as this feels, it also feels like a game to me, a form of role-playing. Perhaps it is because I am only 19 and all of my exposure to power exchange so far has been to fantasy, so I don't take the risk seriously. And I ignore the little voice inside that urges caution. I ignore the feeling in my gut that tells me genuine danger is nigh.

We are back, the door closes. Crack! I don't see the slap coming. The first strike across my face rocks me back. The shock is as bad as the pain. Tears spring to my eyes while he watches me, noticing every reaction. I am surprised when he places his hand between my legs that my pussy is dripping. I know now that this could have been arousal non-concordance—a physiological response unrelated to my genuine desire. But then, all I can conclude is that I liked the slap.

Damien slaps my face repeatedly. This is more shocking than many of the things he does to me. The slaps cut through my armour. I cannot dissociate, unable to even pull back from the physical pain, emotional pain and impact. The face-slapping is deeply personal. That sounds strange even to me. Wouldn't you suppose that vaginal rape, anal rape are more deeply personal? And yet, something about hitting my face cuts in a wholly different way. The face strikes penetrate. He knows they will grab my attention. He uses them to humiliate, to subjugate, to reduce me to nothing.

Face slapping is on my hard limits list since, and yet it has come back in my fantasies over the years. As I work on this memoir, face slapping returns to my dreams. I crave being brought back into myself, thrown back into my body without even a by your leave. Pinned down so I cannot escape the present. I crave that level of feeling. That is where my craving is coming from. A hunger to feel fully.

I am on my knees at his feet. He is lounging on the bed and talking to me. Now I cannot recover what he was saying. The next thing I remember is him fucking me, my legs over his shoulders. I feel his teeth on my neck, on my breasts, on my ass.

I haven't been answering the phone, haven't returned Dave's calls. He sends me a card and Damien opens it. He sneers at it and tells me to pee on this card. I find this almost impossible. The shame is unbearable. Suddenly, he kicks out at me because I don't respond quickly enough. The first kick lands in my stomach, and I collapse on the floor. I try to cover myself and defend myself from the blows, and I cannot. He kicks me between the legs, punches me, slaps my face. I don't understand what I have done. I am devastated. I'm in shock. I call time, shout at him to stop, tell him to leave. He laughs. He tells me I am his, and that there is nothing I can do about it. I scream for help, and he laughs harder. No one comes to the door. I know my neighbours can hear, but they do nothing. These people once telephoned the police when my music was too loud at 3 in the afternoon. I shriek 'He will kill me' and his responding laughter is just as loud. No one comes.

He does not allow me to go to the toilet by myself. He stands in the doorway. Pissing with someone watching is humiliating and stressful. I don't remember the last time I ate, and he pours whiskey down my throat. I've had whiskey and water and his piss and his come since we got back from the bar. He warns me that if I vomit, I will be licking it up. I don't vomit. I have not been able to vomit easily ever since, even when I am ill. I pull all the muscles in my throat whenever I do vomit in an unconscious attempt to stop my body from vomiting. Even now, I cannot override my automatic counter-reflex.

He lets me have a shower by myself after a day? Two days? I cannot mark the passage of time. I stand in the shower with the hot water flowing over me, crying as the water stings the bruises, cuts and my abraded pussy, ass and nipples. The water calms me, and it becomes my safe space. Even now, if I am distraught, my urge is to stand in the shower with the hot water running over me until my fingertips look like prunes.

He fucks me repeatedly, ass, cunt, throat. He beats me when he feels like it. He shoves a broomstick up my ass and tells me to clean the floor. I am lucky he does not perforate my anus. He shoves a candle up my ass and lights it and has me walk around the room - hot wax dripping on my thighs and calves. He throws things around the floor and orders me to pick them up without dropping the candle. Each time I fail, he hits me. I dare not stop until I satisfy him. There is no ritual about any of this, no consent, no play session as in 'normal' BDsM that I come to know later. Nor is there any warm-up or aftercare. There is only his will, his enjoyment, his mood, his agenda.

On day three, Damien chokes me until my heart stops. I remember looking down on my body, Damien on top of me now, pounding on my chest and feeling sparse connection to me on the bed. I begin to walk towards the colours, the light and the crowd of people I see across a small bridge. I am confused when my friend Jimi greets me and tells me I need to go back, that it isn't my time yet. I am so comfortable on the bridge, floating towards the beauty and the people. Jimi turns me around and is more insistent. Why is

Jimi there? He is alive. But I find out once I escape that he died in a motorcycle crash that weekend.

My next memory is coming back to consciousness with Damien giving me mouth to mouth. Breathing into my mouth, pounding on my chest until I cough and sputter. He looks utterly petrified and furious all at the same time. I am quiet. I have no voice as I have already screamed my throat raw. All the little capillaries in my face burst. Tens of thousands of new 'freckles' cover my face and neck. I can feel the bruising beginning on my throat. He does not put his hands around my throat again. I have a headache. I am alive again and still a prisoner, still in pain.

I don't know how long I have been in this condition. I come to consciousness, and he pulls me to him, stroking me, holding me, kissing me slowly and deeply and making my pussy overflow with juices. His kisses are so sweet. He nibbles my ears and nips at my neck, now sucks at my throat and I am coming again. I want his teeth so much. I feel so high. I can feel him sucking my energy, and I want him to take more. My heart is slowing. My breathing is deepening. He is all that exists. He is telling me about his plans and dreams. I remember him talking about building his empire. I want him to leave. I can't imagine being without him. The two states coexist.

Damien beats me again. He hits me with the bat he finds in the closet. He goes through all of my things. He laughs at some of what he sees. He grabs a belt and welts me from ass to thighs. The pace of the beating is relentless. There is no time to reach for the endorphin high. There is nothing pleasant about this, and shouting my safe word means nothing. It only makes Damien angry.

He takes me out with my record collection to Marc's shop. I dated Marc, and it has only been a couple of months since we stopped fucking. Damien has gathered up a good portion of my album collection, and we are trading it in for new wave stuff. Marc is perplexed, and I cannot explain to him what is going on. He notices a bruise on my face but doesn't feel able to ask. I am hoping he will understand my stilted speech and unusual actions and phone the police, but all he does is look worried and ask if I am ok a couple of times. Damien's hand is at the back of my neck – massaging and squeezing. There is a warning in his touch, and I can hear him in my head 'don't you dare'. I force a smile, and we leave. Months later I go into the shop on my own and Marc asks me about what was going on. He heads into the back room and takes out five of my favourite albums and tells me he put them aside as he could not believe I was selling them. I cannot say a word, the tears rolling down my cheeks as I take them from him.

My parents have called and left messages, and I have not replied. I cannot stand to listen to the messages. Dave shows up, and Damien lets him in. I tell Dave I don't want to see him anymore. Damien is sitting with his legs and arms wrapped around me. I am hoping Dave will figure out what is going on–but he doesn't. I thought I had done well, but Damien is not pleased with the intrusions, and he beats me again. I can feel him punching me, kicking me. He calls me a whore, shoves his cock down my throat. I hate the punching, but when his cock is in my throat, I come. I don't want to come, but I do. We are lying on my bed, and he pushes his ass into my face. 'Eat' He says. I have never done this before. My tongue is in his asshole, and my pussy is dripping. I lick for all I am worth. I am coming, and I don't stop until he finally lets me stop eating his ass. My tongue is sore. I hate myself for loving it so much, for loving him despite what he is doing to me.

He rips my diaphragm out of my pussy and tells me he will get me pregnant. He tears up things that are important to me and pisses all over photos of people I love. He tells me I am worthless - the only value I have is the value he gives me. I am crying, and he is kissing my tears away. The confusion is overwhelming.

Damien fucks my pussy, my ass, my mouth countless times. I lose count after 30 times. I am so raw. So sore. Everywhere. I don't sleep, and he is not feeding me. Sam and DeeDee show up. They are tripping on acid. I cannot get a signal through to them. Damien does not let me out of his sight and mostly does not allow me out of his reach except for the shower. My safe space.

He tells me to crawl, and I don't do it fast enough. He kicks out at me. We are both smokers, and he lets me smoke, but not as much. He brings his cigarette close to my pussy but only singes hair. I am sure he will burn me, but he does not.

He sucks on my breasts, watching as I try not to respond. My body betrays me, and I am moaning. He bites my left nipple, sucking and biting until he draws blood. He is talking to me about what he plans to do with me: how many marks I will bear and the child I will bear. I cannot imagine how much sperm he has poured into me already and with no birth control. I fall pregnant but still get a period. I find out when I am 14 weeks pregnant and have a termination at 17 weeks. I cannot bring his child into the world. I apologise to the spirit of the child and say that if he waits, I will bring him into the world. It isn't the right time. My son is born on the anniversary of the day of my escape exactly 20 years later.

He puts a knife to my throat, a big butcher knife. He is drawing it across my throat and scratching me, telling me not to move or he will cut me. He draws the blade across my wrists, my stomach. I tremble and am sure that he will cut me. I am sure I will die.

I have the most precise image of Damien pushing his fist into me, of screaming. It was all too much, but then suddenly it wasn't. I hate it and tremble, sweat. Will he do me permanent damage? I come anyway, and I hate myself. And I hate him. After I escape, my vulva and vagina so black and bruised that the police who took the evidence photos got sick. The doctors in the hospital have about 20 students come in to have a look, and several them have to leave to be sick.

I remember when he pushed his fist into my ass, that is how I tore the first time. I split the second time when he fucked my ass without giving me the chance to adjust to him first and the third time when he stuck a broom up my ass and told me to clean the floor with it. I didn't heal properly, but I am thankful I didn't scar too badly. In the background, Requiem by Killing Joke is playing. 'When the meaningful words when they cease to function. When there's nothing to say, when will it start bothering you? The requiem'. This refrain follows me for years.

I am paralysed by the time these things happen. I am very clear that the most critical thing–necessary to life – is to please Damien. My feelings are all fucked up by this point. I love him, worship him, am petrified of him. He hurts me physically, and sometimes I come, other times, it just hurts. He humiliates me, and sometimes I come so hard, and other times, I just feel awful. He hurts me emotionally, and all I can do is weep.

He ties my hands with rope, and the rope chafes and burns and cuts into my wrists. The gold-plated handcuffs given to me by Wayne and inscribed for my 17th birthday amuse him until he sees Wayne's name on them. He beats me until I pass out saying repeatedly that I belong to him and that he will exorcise all others from my mind, my heart and my body. I will sleep with others if he wants me to and for no other reason.

He curls up with me and tells me to sleep. Quickly he falls asleep. Sleeping with his arms around me, I cannot settle. I stay awake as long as I can so I can watch him. I am too afraid to sleep, sure that if I do, I will never wake up.

I lose more time, can barely stand. I have not eaten in 5 days. Damien tells me he is going to take care of some business and that I should not leave, not talk with anyone, be ready for him when he returns. He takes the spare key to my flat. Sam rings just after Damien leaves and I tell him to come over. He arrives, and I tell him some of what has been happening. I am packing a bag with knives, handcuffs, a picture of my family – no clothing, not even underwear. I am afraid that if Sam knows where I go, Damien will get it out of him or take it from his mind. Sam gets me to the T, and I get to Cambridge by myself. I am wandering around looking lost because I have just been told that Jimi died over the weekend. Jimi was the reason I came to Cambridge. Now I don't know what to do. A man I don't know comes up to me and asks if I am ok, and I shake my head. He looks at me and asks if I am hungry. I whisper, yes. He says, 'Don't worry. I won't rape you. Let me get you some food' and takes me into a café and buys me a bowl of soup and some crackers. It is the best food I have ever tasted. I eat slowly through my bruised lips and tongue. I am careful not to eat too quickly or too much. The man asks me what has happened and I start to tell the story. He says I should call the police and go to the hospital to get checked. I phone DeeDee, who comes and meets me at the hospital. She tells me that

Damien is looking for me and then she tells me she has called the police who will come to see me.

Emotionally I don't understand. I'm like a six-year-old whose parent suddenly disappears. The rejection, the rage makes no sense, and I'm scrambling around trying to do something to make me feel ok again. I cannot help feeling it must be because of something I did. He told me so clearly that there was nothing worthwhile about me.

I can hear his laughter. I can hear the change in the sound of that voice that I loved, the shift to pure malevolence. I remain as confused today by this change as I was then–the one thing I could never get the answer to.. why? Intellectually – I can give you a hundred reasons why. He was a pimp. He wanted to turn me out. I went on to study sexual psychopaths, for a while focused on studying serial killers. I even considered joining the FBI's Behavioural Analysis Unit. I researched how victims are targeted and the healing path for victims. I became an expert at treating trauma. I still don't understand.

Rape and abuse victims often believe that they are responsible for their abuse. Victims who experience orgasm or some form of sexual pleasure during the horror find it almost impossible to forgive themselves and usually feel an intense amount of shame because of the pleasure they experience. They believe that this means that they secretly wanted the experience (s).

Emily Nagoski asks 'Why would a person's genitals tingle or swell while reading a news story about sexual assault? The answer is a thing can be sexually relevant without being sexually appealing'. This is arousal non-concordance - when the body reacts with a sexual response (like orgasm) but the subjective experience is not pleasant, not arousal and sometimes even disgust or horror. Our sexual response mechanism is two parts - there is an accelerator, and a brake, and any stimulus can activate both at the same time. Arousal non-concordance talks about the lack of overlap between blood flow to the genitals and how turned on the person is feeling. For men, the overlap is about 50%. For women, only about 10%! Genital response is an automatic response, just like salivation. We salivate at the sight or smell or taste of food - that doesn't mean we are enjoying the food.

Predators and perpetrators often gaslight victims into believing that because their genitals react, it means that they are enjoying the experience. Gaslighting is when someone tries to manipulate a person psychologically so that they doubt their sanity, own sense of reality, individual beliefs, thoughts, feelings or all of these. Gaslighting is one of the worst forms of emotional abuse. Once you no longer trust your sense of reality, your ability to make sound judgements, and relevant decisions becomes more and more limited.

As I said earlier, gaslighting started in my early life. I learned not to trust my feelings and beliefs because I was often told that what I was perceiving was wrong or not real. 'Don't be ridiculous' or 'why do you make things up?' was often said to me when I reported uncomfortable or very upsetting feelings. When I tried to set boundaries about privacy, I was told I imagined things. As a result, I learned to look to others to tell me where the boundary should be, and I dismissed my feelings of concern, dismissed feelings that said something was dangerous, telling myself that I was being silly or imagining things. I internalised the messages the adults gave me in my life. This is extremely dangerous and is part of how I found myself Damien's prisoner. I dismissed the warning bells because I had learned not to trust my inner sense and inner perceptions of reality. When you don't trust your perception, you have no choice but to attach to the person who is doing the gaslighting because if you do not do so, you are rudderless. You have no way of steering a safe path through the chaos that is daily life. Attaching to the person who is gaslighting means living in the reality that they are creating for you. The longer you live in someone else's reality, the harder it is to recognise your truth and to differentiate between where yours ends, and other's begins.

Damien repeatedly told me that my body's responses meant that I wanted what he was doing to me. This was (and is) complicated by those desires that pre-dated my experience and that have continued into my present. These were not non-concordant in general terms but during my captivity - they were very definitely non-concordant. I froze with fear, was petrified. I was in dreadful pain and I was being harmed. I did not want any of what he did after the point that I told him to leave the first time. My body still responded automatically. The shame afterwards was crippling.

I found it impossible to describe most of what happened to me in the first six years of therapy that I undertook to try to get rid of the PTSD and depression I had developed because of the experience. It was seven years before I could talk about all the details, including my arousal, including my shame, and before I could talk it through and examine it in enough detail for my symptoms to finally resolve.

For eight years, I worked on the inner gaslighting - I worked on learning to trust my senses, perceptions, thoughts, intuition and feelings. For another three years, I had to practice and gain confidence before I could finally hold my ground. Being able to spot gaslighting, trust my inner sense, and get rid of non-productive shame are three of the most essential tools in my life toolkit. These are skills that anyone can learn at any age if they are willing to do the work. Learning that there wasn't something wrong with me - that I was missing skills and could learn these more adaptive skills - was a relief. Understanding *this allowed me to accept myself in full, to integrate even the parts of myself that I found embarrassing or painful or imperfect, and finally show up authentically in all environments in my life.*

What happens when a child does not have a safe emotional space in which to grow? Intimacy becomes impossible except in brief contacts – and only the most tenacious people will seek these out. Far easier to take on the views of that dominant parent, to learn to meet one's own needs, to expect less from others, to internalise that message that safety is not possible because of something inherently wrong with yourself.

I didn't want rape survivor to be the thing that defines me, that people remember. It was a seminal life changing experience, but there is so much more to me and more to my life. Now my identity has many more facets and a broader foundation. If you have experienced trauma, do you really want that to be what defines you in life, what you are remembered for?

I have come to believe that structure makes it possible for people to take risks. When there is a foundation to return to, then one need not panic if one's explorations or travels range far afield because the touchstone is always there. As a child, the touchstone is usually a parent – and that parent's stability is vital at a variety of points of development for the child to internalise that structure and to create that foundation internally as well. For growth and intimacy, there needs to be a safe place inside and one outside. Far too many cannot find an inner safe space, cannot hold a solid sense of self in the face of contradiction and ridicule from others. Even more, cannot think flexibly and moderate views of self based on feedback from others. This foundation is built in earliest childhood, as we see ourselves reflected in our parents' eyes. We learn whether we are worthy of having our needs met, whether we can have some agency in the world – some influence on the outcome of events. Gaslighting in childhood makes it extremely difficult to develop this inner foundation. The age at which the gaslighting begins is a crucial factor in how much internal foundation and stability a person develops. From birth to age 6, I saw reflected in my parents' eyes my value. My needs were met, and there was no gaslighting that early on. I was lucky in that regard as I created a strong stable foundation. I also learned self-soothing, which is an essential and often overlooked emotional skill. Many are not as lucky.

If you have not had the safe space to learn these skills, don't despair. You can learn them as an adult. It is a more complicated process, but all worthwhile skills take effort to perfect.

IV

AFTERMATH

It has been 37 years and I can still smell you. I still taste you, pungent on my tongue. I no longer wake from nightmares and I have not suffered intrusive thoughts for years. I don't avoid thinking about anything, talking about anything, or going places for fear of being triggered. The horror no longer touches me as though it were in the present.

The only symptom I still have is my hypervigilance. If something triggers me, I am on high alert – aware of all that is going on behind me, near me, around me. It is a useful skill, so I have not let it go. Being able to harness this is protective.

I remain drawn to some ways you used me. My hunger for water sports, intense before I knew you and before I had experienced them, far worse once you pissed on me, in me, in my mouth. This hunger has never decreased. I rarely mention this to a lover, a prospective lover, or even a potential casual fuck. The shame connected with the desire tripled after you because now I desired something nasty and also desired something that the monster who raped me did during the rape. It's the same with rimming. You were the first, and I loved it. And I hated it.

You were the first person to introduce me to anal sex. Back then, I wrote about how frightened I was—not the least because of your size. You were so gentle at first—and by the time you started to fuck me in earnest, I was relaxed and loving it. I can feel the length and girth of you, intensely hot and hard inside my ass – stretching and filling me – and the pulsing of my clitoris as you piston in and out of my ass.

You were sweet to me until you took what you wanted without consent. After that, you tore me up. I retain the scars to this day.

Your teeth left a deep scar on my left nipple. You drew blood, and I got an infection. The scar still acts up on occasion—becomes red and inflamed. Reminding me you tried to claim me. Reminding me I got exactly what I asked the Gods for when I demanded without qualifying my request and without contemplating my words. Loki's laughter rings in my ears. Loki rode you. He keeps that bite alive as His mark upon me.

I learned later that you were no Master, though that is what I wanted. You were no Master because you ignored consent. There was no negotiation and no agreement for me to give up consent. But when I first connected with you – your energy – your power – was undeniable. And my desire to surrender palpable.

I still crave that level of control. And reject it. And crave it. My ambivalence ties me in knots. Do I want my Master to micromanage me? No. Yes. I don't know. I always say no to this question and tell people that it would drive me insane. I know this because you controlled my every move, my bodily functions, even most of my thoughts and feelings for five full days and that seemed an eternity, and I cannot imagine choosing to let someone do that again.

And yet.

I crave strong structure. I crave being a prisoner–at the will of another. I crave. I know my cravings are fantasy and that I would not enjoy any non-negotiated situation and where I did not give my consent. Since I started working on the memoir, my fantasising has increased. My desire to be torn apart returned. My desire to feel at such an intense level paramount. The ache unsated. The burn felt all the time. I burn with this desire. It is literal. Visceral. The flames climb through my body from the base of my spine to my sacral area, through solar plexus and then to heart. There is a steady burn that is potent enough to be distracting.

I can hear you saying 'Open. Open your mouth' and watching pornography this week suddenly heard a man say it that way. I come just thinking of you saying, 'Open your mouth and swallow. It is all you will get to drink.'

And that's the rub–a part I hadn't allowed in, at least not profoundly in. That I loved Damien. Oh, I said it enough when telling the story. But feeling it – well, that's not something I have wanted to do. I have actively avoided it.

I could never integrate the two parts: The love I felt and experienced & the hatred he expressed when he took me. I acted 'as if' a lot. Doing what I was told to do — doing what was right. I didn't want to die. But without him, I didn't want to live. And that persisted for far too long. I was told this was Stockholm Syndrome or a trauma bond, but that doesn't account for our prior relationship.

Retracing my steps in Boston brought up this unavoidable memory of the feelings I held before. Of walking together down the road. Of enjoying a drink and a meal. Retracing my steps reminded me how vulnerable I was. How vulnerable I stayed in the aftermath. It's rarely straightforward, and this situation was ever so complicated.

I recollect the hunger for all he did in the first two weeks, even the things that pushed what I thought were my limits. He was positioning me. Moving me towards what he wanted me to become. My shock when he turned was fierce and swift. I couldn't comprehend what had happened. I quickly understood that obeying him might keep me alive, and disobeying was likely to get me seriously injured if not killed.

And yet, the horror did not make the hunger dissipate. To my enormous shame, after they locked him up, I woke as often to erotic dreams as I did to nightmares. These endured for years, and I spoke to no one about them. They disappeared after I did some major spiritual and psychological work in 2009, and that last bit of shame with them.

Since I began this journey, they have returned. I can no longer see his face but I recognise his scent, his energy & and his presence. These are not nightmares. They are dreams filled with hunger, with craving. And when I wake, the hunger continues. This hunger has a power that makes me vulnerable. I am taking care to watch myself. It is at times like this I draw danger to me to attempt to sate the hunger. I am more impulsive. I am grateful that I have a Master, a structure, that helps to keep me in check and sadistic yet safe people who I can seek to sate this hunger with without worrying about dying or being harmed (which is permanent as opposed to hurt which is temporary).

The ambivalence that comes with desiring the very things that horrified me, that damaged me when Damien held me prisoner pervades my life much less often now. I have integrated my desires, accepted that my desires did not cause Damien to kidnap, beat and rape me. My passions added to my vulnerability, though. Unintegrated, these desires place me at risk. If I am ashamed of my desires, I am far more likely to act on the impulse to get them sated without scrutinizing them, and without weighing the risk. The ambition is to get them sated quickly and without thought–as fast as possible so one does not feel the shame. Once I worked through the shame, the risk level lowered.

Shame comes with all rapes. Varying levels impact on a victim and a survivor of rape over time. We are taught to be ashamed of many of our desires. To be ashamed of any desire for sexual pleasure. They still teach us in a host of overt and subtle ways that sex is for procreation with a spouse. Wanting sex and especially craving unusual sexual acts stokes the fires of shame.

Though some shame is constructive, most of us would want people who commit atrocities against others to feel shame; this type of shame gets in the way. It does not serve a definite purpose. Becoming authentic, accepting all of myself, got rid of most of my shame. That was a long road of intense personal work. The work is never done. We are all works in progress and I am grateful for that. The pressure to be perfect produces tons of shame. Being comfortable with being imperfect and being able to be vulnerable is an antidote to our shame-filled world.

To work on shame, we need a safe, judgement-free space. We need a witness to remind us that we are acceptable, loveable even with all our quirks, oddnesses, faults and foibles. It is usually easier to do this work with someone you are not in a personal relationship with because you don't risk being judged by someone whose opinion matters to you and/ or losing an essential connection which is what many fear will happen if they expose their hidden desires to their partners, lovers, spouses and playmates.

V

AFTERMATH
PART II

This first piece highlights the intensity of the need for surrender and the severity of the loss when that is taken from me or given up by me.

Surrender 2.0

There is that moment when all of my walls dissolve, when I am no longer capable of thought, can do nought else but respond and feel. That moment of surrender in the purest form. Words leave me when I try to describe what that feels like to me, how essential that surrender is to my being whole, how fractured I feel when the walls return.

The people close to me, those whose opinions I trust and respect, believe that crying is good for me right now. I guess it doesn't matter what people think as I don't have a choice. I no longer have control over when and whether I cry. I can no longer shut out my feelings, nor can I shut out yours even when you believe that I'm not reading you. All I can do is surrender.

For all my intellect - my accomplishments and achievements - relationships and feelings matter most to me. That I am a woman and can feel myself female - happily, gloriously female is precious beyond words. To have even one safe place: I cannot express what that is to one who has spent so much of her life safe only on her own.

There is that moment: The first time I hear your voice, the first time I see you, the first time you touch me — that moment when my joy and my gratitude light up my soul. There are the moments when the desire to rest at your feet is overpowering. That is where I was always meant to be.

There are the moments in my day when I am acutely aware of drenched pussy, aching nipples when orgasm overtakes me without warning. Moments where the fire rushes through my body and moments where the waves wash over me.

There are the moments when your presence floods into me. When I can but bow before your brilliance. Moments when your strength - physical, emotional, intellectual, spiritual amaze me - I revel in you and your masculinity, your dominance.

Moments when I feel your possession of me so acutely: Your nails dug into my ass, your cock buried in the ass you have claimed, your hands in my hair, when you gather all of my arousals from the past, the present and the future - from all sources and claim that energy for your own... and then feed it back to me... setting me alight.

Moments when your intellect, perception and vision astonish me, and I bask in the light that is you. Moments when your capacity for life staggers me, and I hold on tight because I know (and you have reminded me) it will be a wild ride.

Moments when the laughter overwhelms me - when I no longer take myself so seriously. Moments when all I can do is grieve - your losses, my losses. Moments when your sharp edges cause the hair to rise on my body and my pussy to flood. Your ability to keep me dancing on that razor blade, over the abyss is exquisite.

Moments when your ability to pluck the thoughts and dreams from my head astounds and terrifies me, and when I rejoice that you have this power and that you find my thoughts and ideas of interest. Moments when I am aware of your desire, when I know I am pleasing to you - fulfil me, make me tremble and cause me to sigh with relief. And the ones when I have displeased you bring me to the depths of despair. I love you. All I want right now is to come home.

This piece is a meditative piece I wrote exploring what surrender is to me, means to me and why I find it so difficult to give up control. Some people may find this an interesting statement as I am engaged in a relationship where I willingly surrender daily. Being a control freak is not a choice for me. I became a control freak to deal with how out of control I felt when people rode over my boundaries, gaslit me, denied my very existence. Control was my attempt to adapt to my environment, both internal and external. It worked very well for a time. But then I had to take more and more control to feel safe and to feel I had a voice. Eventually, I controlled myself into a corner. The desire to surrender has always been there. The flexibility of a need to control and surrender is ideal, and I am still a work in progress. Therefore, I have no sexual relationships that do not involve some measure of authority transfer, control and surrender.

Surrender has always been a challenge for me. Surrender requires faith. I learned to have limited faith in myself and insufficient faith in others. I have faith in my Gods. Sometimes, my intellect overrides my faith. Because of my first profession and my upbringing, I focus too much on mind and neglect intuition. When I am in touch with intuition, with my faith, with my gifts, with my Gods, then I do the best work — both in my vocation and my avocation. When I can let intuition guide and intellect inform, that is when I truly fly. When I can let the energy move me and guide my focus, that is when the fire blazes — when I become a creative inferno. This is when I am in flow.

During my pregnancy, I learned how difficult it is for me to yield, to cede control to another. My growing child took from my body without my consent. We created him, and I consented when I became pregnant. He caused a wide variety of physical and emotional feelings. His consciousness was present early on, and I had no privacy. He had more access to what is me than anyone had ever had before. I had no choice. I did not understand when I chose to go through with a pregnancy that doing so would be the last trigger for a collection of chronic autoimmune diseases. Please don't misunderstand; I have no regrets. It is an example I return to that highlights for me that giving up control is just that. Once the step has been taken, many consequences — all unforeseen by the person yielding — can come into play.

To surrender, I must let go. I must turn over control to my Gods, to my Master, to Ones who am I serving. To surrender, I must trust. Surrender is a choice I renew daily. Surrender brings more profound and deeper levels of connection. The more complete my surrender, the richer the rewards.

In my reading, I read descriptions of surrender to the Divine that talks about how sometimes the effort at surrender, in and of itself, can be the individual attempting to control the relationship with the Divine. The person talked of being pushed into or taken into surrender. It was as though someone took him there. Perhaps it is easier for me. My Gods take what They desire, and any illusions I have had of 'control' have long since disappeared. They have wrought changes in my consciousness, my spirit, my intellect, my heart, and my body. Their imprint can be seen upon me.

Master, I give myself into Your care. I yield to Your Will. All that I am You own. I bring You all I have been, all of my potentials, my energy, my will, my intentions and dreams. You will do as you see fit. Perhaps I will even manage to learn patience...

In the aftermath of Damien, I continue to feel completely out of control. Chosen family do much in an effort to 'heal' me or keep me safe.

In the hospital, DeeDee is with me until the doctors and nurses want privacy to do the rape exam. The doctor comes in and introduces himself and his junior. They put me into the usual stirrup position: Legs bent at an unnatural angle, the pull in my hamstrings brings me close to cramping. Frigid air hits my vulva, and I shiver so hard I almost come off the metal table. I am aware of the ice-cold metal stirrups on my heels and the dull ache in my belly. I have always wondered if there were another way to do an internal exam on a woman that wasn't so awful. The position itself is uncomfortable, no matter how young and flexible you are. The stirrups are always cold, and heels on them always provoke a leg cramp. There is no comfortable way to move your bottom forward and stay there while the doctor uses a metal (now plastic) torture tool to open you up. Even with lube, it is never pleasant.

On that day, it is excruciating. I am so bruised that my vulva and perineum are black. I don't even look purple. My vulva is swollen and the blue-black of some Africans. When the doctors see how bruised I am, they invite a group of medical students in to look at me. The fluorescent lights are white hot, and there is a crowd in the room, all staring at my damaged cunt. I am too freaked out to do anything about it. There is no consent sought, and I cannot give real consent. The anal exam is worse than the vaginal one. I have tears that are still raw. They take swabs from everywhere and comb my pubic hair to see if any of his is still there. This seems bizarre to me since Damien would never deny fucking me. He would claim I consented to everything. I wonder what the cops will think if he tells them about the handcuffs and worry they won't believe me. I forget that the CSI people will comb through everything that is in my flat.

The nurse assigned to help rape victims comes back to me and tells me she has called the police. 'Are you happy to talk with them?' she asks. My reply is a whispered 'yes'. One of the detectives is about 5'11", stocky, with salt and pepper hair. I am sure he is Irish. The other detective is shorter, also stocky but more muscular. Both ask if I will come down to the station so their photographer can take pictures for evidence. They are soft spoken and handling me gently. I wonder if either of them has daughters my age.

They ask me to ride with them while they look for Damien so I can point him out. No identification parade where I get to be behind glass. They want me to finger him. Today this would never happen. It is preposterous. I am petrified, so petrified my mouth is bone dry, and I cannot swallow. What if he sees me? I don't want to be even miles from him, let alone a few yards. Being in a cop car doesn't make me feel any more secure. At this point, I know that Damien can see me, feel me if I am ever near him. The detectives tell me that another car will join us so that when I point him out, they will take me to the station and take Damien in a separate vehicle.

I am not sure where Damien can be found so we first go back to my flat and he isn't there. The flat is trashed, and the detectives tell me that the print team will need to come and dust for prints. It takes ages to get the dust off things once the CSI people leave.

The team is there, and we hit the streets to find Damien. I am not sure how I know where he might be, but I follow my intuition and there he is. I point him out as we approach the area. They pick him up and whisk me away to the station to have photographs and give my statement. Hours and hours of questions. The same questions repeatedly. I still have not had a proper meal. Soup and crackers after five days of starvation are not enough to keep me fuelled so I can go over things again and again. The photographer looks at my vulva and excuses himself. I hear him vomiting. He comes back into the room and continues documenting my bruises, cuts, scrapes and the petechiae all over my face and neck. Every capillary burst when Damien strangled me. Petechiae are pinpoints of blood which look like freckles to the uninitiated. I already have quite a few freckles and the petechiae highlight my fair skin even further. My fair skin is significant. Had they had not perceived me as white and he black, it is likely that Damien would not have stayed in jail for the time awaiting trial. They deny him bail because they see him as a clear and present danger to young white girls.

And then they release me. They keep Damien in jail. The police detective tells me not to worry, Damien is not going anywhere. I am released to DeeDee and Sam and go home with them. I am relaxing while dinner is being prepared, and this woman comes up to me, screaming. She is older than me and is not wearing her age well. She has some wrinkles, blond hair and long, sharp nails she is using to try to claw my eyes out. Debbie is Damien's live-in girlfriend. I had no idea he had one. He never mentioned it. He never mentioned wanting to be anywhere else other than with me.

Debbie shouts that she would be happy to take anything from him – to lick his asshole, to be beaten until she bleeds, and ultimately to give him her life and demands I explain how I dare send him to jail. I am barely managing to say anything. I am standing outside my body, looking at myself. It feels safer that way, as I cannot feel as much. I am in shock, dehydrated, with infected cuts, and fevered. I am shaking like a leaf. DeeDee leads her away and then comes back and apologises and says, 'Debbie has nowhere else to stay'. I respond quietly, 'Neither do I.'

In 2020, as I read back some of my fantasy and think about the things I have re-enacted, the acts I still desire, can I understand where Debbie was coming from? That line of consent/no consent is so terribly thin, like tissue paper easily torn. And yet, I did not consent to Damien's systematic destruction of my being and my body.

Lying in bed at night, hand between my legs, fingers drumming rhythms on my clitoris as I bring back the memory of him pissing down my throat until I scream with the intensity of my release, I wonder. Forty-one years later, the strength is no less when I bring that scene to mind. All my senses still experience it. No flashback this but coveted reality.

To be owned in fantasy is not the same as to be owned consensually is not the same as to be owned in reality. Damien no longer invades my dreams, my waking. He no longer walks through my mind, my thoughts, my fantasies, my memories unbidden.

A couple of days after I land at their home, Sam and DeeDee drive me to my parents' house so I can tell them what has happened. My grandmother is visiting, and the first thing she asks is if anyone is hungry. She is cooking spaghetti and meatballs, and soon there are big plates of food for everyone. Sam eats heartily, and DeeDee barely eats. The conversation is light. They want to support me but don't want to be in the middle of any family drama that arises. They leave after the meal, and I go to talk to my parents.

My parents freeze. They are both in shock. And they both respond to the trauma with anger at me. This pattern is familiar. When they could not make things better for me, when I was in pain, that feeling of inadequacy leads to anger. Then they turn the anger on me. My mother shouts about my choice of boyfriends and points to Damien's blackness as a reason I am in this situation. I am horrified by her racist statements and horrified that she is blaming me.

They decide my father will drive me back to school and help me clean up and deal with the court case. I experienced my father as intrusive during my adolescence, and this situation is all about sex. I don't want to talk with him about any of this. It feels like a further rape being pressed to talk about details with them. I do not wish to share the intimacies and the deepest parts of the crime or my desires or fantasies. The pressure is to talk as they feel they somehow have a right to the details. I stand my ground and eliminate some of the most intimate details.

My parents want me to leave Boston. I look at Sarah Lawrence College to see if I can transfer. I still have to return to Boston for the prosecution. I decide to stay and finish my studies. I change majors from broadcast journalism to special education with a psychology minor, and I stay.

We return to Boston. The apartment is a mess. There is clothing strewn everywhere, fingerprint dust on all available surfaces, sex toys on the floor, erotica and pornography lying around. My father looks at things while we clean up. He tries to start a conversation, but I refuse to talk. I am utterly humiliated and not in a pleasant way. Sam and DeeDee invite us for dinner. I am still staying there, and my father is at a local hotel.

After dinner, Sam passes around the long pipe that always reminds me of a peace pipe filled with marijuana. I take a small toke when it reaches me. My father takes the pipe and inhales deeply. I am thrown. I know that he has smoked occasionally in the past but I thought he and my mom tried it with friends, and that was that. I think he is trying to fit into this group. Instead of making me more comfortable, it makes me extremely anxious. I don't need a friend now. I need a father who has solid ethical boundaries. Sam and my father are discussing altered states of consciousness and Sam brings up LSD. I am whispering under my breath 'Guilt by association Sam', but he doesn't get it. I am relieved when the topic shifts and when my father leaves, and I can crawl off to bed.

There will be a probable cause hearing before the grand jury. I have to testify at the and so does Damien. I wrote a poem about this.

The Trial
1982/1983
I'm so frustrated and tired
So tired
The waiting – the anticipation – bated breath
It will kill me.
Seeing him again.
His eyes boring through me like a high-speed drill
Leaving holes all over me
Telling me, commanding me to understand that
Nothing.
Nothing had changed.

My throat parched
Losing control of muscles, feeling lost
Alone with him in the room
Scenes flash through my mind
As I hear them lock him in that cage
A prisoner.
I feel myself still a prisoner of his will
And somehow it resembles a ridiculous, clumsily choreo-
graphed dance
Poorly directed play
B Budget X rated film
Me in my innocent, low key, brand new finery
Plaid skirt and penny loafers
Thinner, demure, a shy little girl.
Him in his newly tailored light coloured suit, greased
hair all in place

Small, neat freshly grown moustache
Not a long fingernail in sight
An ad for the United Negro College Fund

We are all cleaned up while being asked about base things. The Judge refuses to allow the photos that the police have taken into the hearing as evidence as he calls them 'obscene' and I am furious as I cannot understand how the images are more obscene than what Damien did to me. The whole situation was obscene. If evidence is excluded, how will people understand how bad it was?

Despite this and the intense cross-examination about my sexual experience, my sex life and my desires, the Judge decides there are a variety of cases to answer, and it goes to grand jury. The Judge says there are 35 counts of rape, 2 counts of assault with intent to kill, 2 counts of assault and battery and 2 counts of assault with a deadly weapon (his hands). He does not add false imprisonment, though he acknowledges that I was not free to leave.

The prosecutor phones us a week or so before the grand jury. He is not sure that he can get convictions on the rape counts. It doesn't matter that my vulva was so black that it took weeks to heal from the bruising. It doesn't matter that there were cuts, bites, and bruises all over me. He believes that the jury might think I consented. Even though I have witnesses, who will say they couldn't reach me, that there were people who heard me screaming for help, screaming for mercy. I was promiscuous; the prosecutor says in front of my father, and I had some desires that might lead the jury to believe that I consented. After all, I had consensual sex with Damien more than once. That meant the jury would have trouble finding that when I said no, I meant no. It didn't matter that they were charging him with assault with intent to kill because he choked me until my heart stopped and the breath left my body and all the capillaries in my face and neck burst. Or that I came back to consciousness with him pounding on my chest and giving me mouth to mouth, freaking out. His relief when I opened my eyes quickly turned into fury because I frightened him. And because it frightened him, he beat me until I passed out again.

The prosecutor explains to my father and me. Mostly he talks to my father. He explains that Damien will plead guilty to a couple of counts of assault and battery, assault with intent to kill, assault with a deadly weapon and take a sentence of 4 years with credit for his time served and good behaviour while he was serving the time so he would be out in another few months. In the end, he spent just over 15 months in prison. 'The 35 rape counts will be kept on file. If he ever does anything again, these will automatically be brought back into play. There will be a restraining order so he can't ever come near you again'. I am overwhelmed. A family friend had recommended that we hire a lawyer to protect my interests. My father said no because he believed that this was the prosecutor's job. It was my father's naivete coming into play. He believed that the state's interests and my interests would be the same. The prosecutor is there to represent the state, not the victim. So we find ourselves presented with a fait accompli. My father thinks it is a good idea to accept this strategy, even though asking us is just a formality. The prosecutor doesn't need the victim's permission to accept or offer a plea bargain. My father thinks it would be better if I didn't have to be on the stand, giving evidence when the courtroom was completely open and in front of a jury. The plea bargain goes ahead. I cannot stand against these two men who are trying to protect me. I am just never sure if they are protecting me from further hurt or trying to enforce their view of what is best for me.

The restraining order is not even worth the paper they print it on. Damien has to keep 200 ft or yards away from me – I cannot remember which measurement it was, but what I can remember is that he kept showing up at one end of the bar when I was at the other, and he was just about legal. He stalked me for the rest of my time in Boston. I knew he was always watching me.

My boundaries were already a mess, and this made them worse. He attacked me in my home and I was still living there, so nowhere felt safe. My hypervigilance increased. I would pace around the small studio flat, check and re-check the door. I was always aware of all that was going on around me, never sat with my back to a room if I could control where I sat. If someone got too close to me in a public space, I had to restrain my desire to move them physically. I almost ended up arrested when a man invaded my space on the T and brushed against my breast repeatedly. I elbowed him in the guts.

Many people who have experienced sexual violence are re-traumatised by the medical professionals whose job it is to help them heal and also help them make sure that the abuse never happens again. Sometimes this happens because the professionals haven't been well enough trained. Other times, they are focused on the evidentiary aspect of their job and they forget that there is a live human being with thoughts, feelings and fears in front of them. To make matters worse, people in this situation can rarely advocate for themselves. They are often in deep shock and significant pain. Some of them dissociate completely. Dissociation is a psychological defence. It helps a person separate from the horror, trauma, intense physical and/or emotional pain in a situation so they can survive the situation and continue to function. People describe it in a variety of ways, including: standing next to themselves, looking down at themselves, 'going away in (their) minds', 'leaving the scene'.

Most of us experience some minor dissociation during our lives. For example, have you ever been on a journey and cannot remember how you got from A to B? You may have been driving or on public transport, but it feels as though you have lost that time. When you are learning to drive, you have to focus on every single step. When you are experienced, you may not even realise you are driving because you focus on your music or a conversation you are having.

Dissociation takes a few forms: the mild form as I just described, the more pronounced type where you feel you are separate from your body, even more pronounced is a fugue state where a person loses a large chunk of time and may not even remember significant parts of their life. Finally, there is dissociative identity disorder, when a person develops multiple separate selves specifically to deal with various aspects of life. Not all people who have many selves are dissociating. This can be a healthy adaptation, or it can be because of spiritual practice. Sometimes it is dissociation in an effort to survive.

Dissociation is a very useful defence. It only becomes problematic when it stops us from feeling and experiencing life any time there is a trigger. It often happens when sexual violence survivors are having sex or in any intimate situation. This can make orgasm almost impossible. Or sometimes, orgasm is something that happens at a distance, so they do not feel the pleasure. When dissociation stops us from living fully, then it is useful to address it with a therapist.

Orgasm requires letting go of control and trusting another human being. Many women who have experienced sexual abuse and/or were raised where boundaries were poor have trouble reaching orgasm with a partner. Some have trouble reaching orgasm at all because they cannot surrender control even to their own body's process. One of the lasting effects of being taught that your body does not belong to you but is instead community property is a desire to control everything in an attempt to keep safe. This extreme level of control does not help. It does not allow us to stay safe. It does not help us discriminate between relationships that are healthy and ones that are not. All it does is exhaust us and keep us from being fully present, embodied and experiencing full pleasure. The first steps to being able to let go of control come from learning to be present. Being able to stop dissociating and become embodied is part of the process. Once a person is ready to be fully embodied and chooses to step in to the body, learning orgasm can become easy.

Hypervigilance is another defense that comes out of experiencing trauma. It can also be trained into a person and is frequently trained into emergency service personnel and soldiers. It is an instrumental skill. When you are hypervigilant, you are spending a lot of energy being aware of all that is going on around you. You are at heightened alertness. People who experience this often check the perimeter of their homes repeatedly, rarely sit with their backs to a room or the exits, will always first see where the exit is. Some identify routes of escape and others identify weapons. All are hyper-observant. High levels of hypervigilance seriously interfere with life. When my hypervigilance triggers, I get little sleep. My body is telling me I am not in a safe environment, and I must keep aware. My adrenalin and cortisol levels are over the top. If it stays this way for too long, physical damage can occur.

Hypervigilance that is not triggered but is turned on when appropriate (so it is a skill) is very useful. As I have found it so, I have not sought to rid myself of this skill. However, I still get triggered by circum-stances in life sometimes, and then my hypervigilance can interfere with my level of enjoyment and wellbeing.

VI

CHOSEN FAMILY

Long before 50 Shades of Grey, I wrote this poem in the winter of
1982

I am
Shades of grey
Abstract voids
Green envy streaks painted through
Shades of grey
Purple passion pulling pieces from depths within
Shades of grey
Rampant red raging anger emanating out of
Shades of grey
Blinding blue billows of burning tears bursting from
Shades of grey
Slick, sinister silver slinking through
Shades of grey
Warm, loving, caring orange opening-up
Shades of grey
Offbeat, tie-die aqua and mauve mixing and

arranging
Shades of grey

And in June 1983, I wrote this poem:

A year later
Spiralling faster
Blackness comes to meet the dawn
And out from the tornado, I strut
Tall and proud
Down and dirty
Knowing I am world's above you and your dangerous
games
I've made it
Freedom
Liberation
Or should I say libertine?
No, but no
I am above all that
And yet still strains hit my ears
The ringing overpowers me
'I'm into you like a train.'

Sam and DeeDee joined the OTO (Ordo Templi Orientis) and pursued initiation. I introduced the group to the teachings of the OTO after meeting David B in the summer of 1981. First to Sam and then eventually, DeeDee took an interest. I read The Book of the Law for the first time while tripping my brains out. Everyone talked about joining a lodge and taking initiation. They expected me to join them on the trip south. I did not feel a need for an artificial initiation; I experienced initiation with Damien in real life.

Once initiated, I attended gnostic mass as a member of the group rather than as a priestess. DeeDee finally succeeded in taking my place with Sam magickally. I came to see the family various weekends, bringing along whomever I was fucking at the time. The dynamics shifted from week to week.

I felt a wall between us. I had full-blown Post-Traumatic Stress Disorder and did not feel understood. The first hurdle after the preliminary hearing was finding out I was pregnant from Damien. I thought I had no choice but to terminate. I could not bring his child into the world. I could still hear him telling me I would bear his child and that he would bring the child up to enforce his will upon the earth. The night before the procedure, I told the child who wanted to be born that it wasn't time for him to come into the world yet, but promised I would have him someday. I did not realise that it would take 20 years before that came to pass. The cramping after the procedure felt like someone had reached up inside me and was squeezing and twisting my uterus. I went to bed for a few days until it all subsided.

Sam and DeeDee connected with Jen and Marc, who lived in Providence, Rhode Island. They brought me down for a variety of rituals and parties, and they became part of my extended chosen family. Dave and Mary were also part of this group. Everyone had different ideas about what they could do to help me move past the PTSD. The group was fond of the therapeutic effects of various hallucinogens. I took mushrooms several times with this group with exciting results. I have vivid memories of being bathed by Marc to wash away my pain on one trip and spent another in ritual. Now there is research and proven protocols for using hallucinogens for treating PTSD, but back then it was not at all sanctioned.

DeeDee introduced me to a man she met at a festival called Black Eagle. Eagle was a Viet Nam veteran who suffered from PTSD and also had a long-term heroin addiction. I don't believe that DeeDee knew that he was an addict. In some ways, we were still all very naïve, having had pretty protected upbringings.

I was comfortable with Eagle. He felt familiar. I understand now that part of this was the PTSD. I had a series of relationships with Viet Nam veterans who had varying degrees of PTSD symptoms. They were all between 16 and 18 years older than I and all smelled right to me. They seemed to understand me better than my peers did now, and I felt protected with them. I also found their edges irresistible.

I did lots of hallucinogens with Eagle, created lots of rituals, and had lots of almost sex. Male heroin users often have trouble achieving and maintaining erections. I didn't mind. It made him safer to be around until I was ready for more. The relationship didn't last very long because he lived in New York City, and I was in Boston. I began to take more risks. My symptoms interfered with my daily life and my judgement. I was lucky not to end up in situations that caused too much damage. My next relationship was with Tony.

The cashpoints in the bank are in a front hall that is octagonal. I see Tony there, and he leaves before I can say hello. I'm wearing a red and white check halter top, jean shorts, sneakers and it is sunny out. I'm running to catch up with him. It takes almost ten blocks, and I am out of breath as I get alongside him. He is laughing at me without a sound. What must he have thought about this little pale freckled Jewish girl chasing him?

I say hello, and so does he. He finally slows down, and we end up sitting on the grass near BU and chatting for a long time. Tony is 6'2" of medium to large build long legs with semi-sweet to dark chocolate skin, a fairly closely cut afro that is barely receding, eyes the colour of Hershey's chocolate kisses, a nose that is more Caucasian straight and high rather than broad and a beautiful smile full of straight white teeth. He has sparse chest hair, though he has some. He has a circumcised cock, 9 inches or so, thick but in proportion with his length. His ass is lovely, slightly high and round. His hands with lovely nails are relatively soft. Most of the time, we spend talking, eating food that we have cooked at home and fucking. He takes me places to increase my education. He enjoys playing with my emotions at times but ultimately shows that he cares for me. He is well educated and erudite. I love conversing with him. He has a partner and a child at his home in Roxbury. He spends a few nights per week with me. During the time we are together, I see my friends less frequently. When he takes me out for meals, he takes me to fine restaurants. I eat well when I am with him. We frequent Legal Seafoods in Cambridge, have breakfasts at a fantastic Jewish deli near my place, wait in the queue at Steve's for original mix in ice cream.

I lived in a building of condos of mostly elderly Jewish people. These folks are the ones who did not phone the police when they heard me screaming for my life - heard me begging for my life, ignored me because I was with a black man, because they were frightened, because each one thought someone else would or had done it. That day we arrived after having been out for brunch walked through the lobby and an old man half stooped, bald egg head holding two shopping bags approached Tony, my lover, who dressed in designer sweats. My lover who was the first black man to attend Marist Academy in Georgia; who had a Master's in Public Administration from Harvard and worked for the city of Boston, who owned his own home in Roxbury - a brownstone if I remember correctly. This old Jewish man approached him and said 'carry these packages upstairs for me will you boy?' My mouth dropped open as I lost my breath. It confused me - this could not be real - could not be happening. I caught my breath and protested as Tony put his hand on my arm and said, 'Certainly, Sir'. He took his bags, and we rode up in the lift with the man who gave Tony $5 at his apartment door. We descended the lift to my apartment in silence. 'Why' I began to say. 'To show you' Tony replied. This was only one lesson Tony taught me in our time together. I was angry, and I was also ashamed to call myself Jewish. I remember the taste of Tony and that I called him Papa, and to this day he is the only man I have ever referred to as Papa. He was the first man I fell asleep on top of after sex. He challenged me to tell my parents about him. I did, and my father became upset about it. I challenged him, 'You taught me all people are created equal. You didn't say, 'all are created equal, but you don't fuck some of them.' My father went to slap my face and then pulled back. In the end, Tony never came home with me. He just wanted to see if I would stand up to my father. We saw each other less when I reached my senior year, though we continued to talk.

After Sam and DeeDee graduated, off they went. DeeDee headed to Los Angeles, California as had always been her plan and Sam ended up in New Mexico. I was lost. My relationships were strange. I had almost relationships with a couple of women, Kathy being the most memorable. She was ever so soft and had lovely breasts. I was slow to pick up signals from women, and I was shy with them as well. Kathy and I went dancing at a gay bar that allowed lesbians in on a couple of nights a week. There was one night that was women only, but we usually went on the mixed nights and danced our asses off. They had only one bathroom. I remember the first time I went in, there were a bunch of guys at the urinals and in the stalls, and two started conversing with me. Blushing crimson, I tried to engage as though it wasn't a bizarre situation. Eventually, I got comfortable and could converse no matter what else was going on. This place had sawdust on the floor, and the stalls had wooden half doors like stable stalls. There was a disco ball, red and white checked paper table-cloths, pitchers of beer and peanuts with shells on the table. There was a popcorn machine in the corner. Kathy and I spent a few nights together exploring each other. She was careful with me because she didn't want to scare me off. She tasted sweet, and I enjoyed sampling all of her. Kathy introduced me to Stefan, who was a friend and her connection for substances.

Stefan was at least 15 years older than I. He was rail-thin, smoked Djarum clove cigarettes and wore a black cape. He lived in a house with at least 30 cats. He was a bass player in a band and had been a session player for years. He smoked dope constantly and also used heroin. The straight community had not heard of AIDS yet and although I was not straight, I was sleeping with straight men (and gay men too). Things were just heating up in the gay community. We took few precautions. I was fortunate to have remained healthy.

I remember waking in Stefan's place in the dim morning, the smell of cats, marijuana and Djarum cigarettes ever-present. There were always a bunch of folk crashing there. I remember sucking Stefan - I can feel his hardness in my throat, his pale blond soft pubic hair tickling my nose. I can taste him even after all these years, spicy as though the clove from the cigarettes was being secreted through his pores. Stefan was safe. He was always available if needed. He didn't flinch when I had a flashback and was careful of my triggers. He held me when I cried.

Stefan told me one day that he was moving to the mountains in North Carolina. It devastated me. I stayed at Kathy's place that night, crying in her arms. Graduation was soon, and I didn't know where I wanted to go. I knew I could not cope with living with my parents. I wasn't ready for graduate school and thought I might want to go to medical school. If I went to medical school, I had to make up undergraduate science and maths as I had avoided taking these classes during my BSc. I decided to move to North Carolina and go to the University of North Carolina - Chapel Hill. They had an excellent medical school and a good psychology graduate program. If I lived there for a year and took undergrad courses, I could establish residency and lower the fees significantly. I went with my parents to visit North Carolina and found a flat in a town called Carrboro, which was near to Chapel Hill. The complex had a gym and a pool and a games room. I agreed to move in the 1st of August. I was to start classes early in September. I registered for organic chemistry, physiological psychology and psychopathology - diagnosis using the Diagnostic and Statistical Manual of Mental Disorders - III.

Before heading to North Carolina, I headed out to Wisconsin to attend Pagan Spirit Gathering. PSG is a week-long clothing-optional pagan camping trip in the woods of Wisconsin. There was ritual, workshops, a fantastic market place and social time. I was excited to see Jen and Marc, who were en-route to California to join DeeDee. I agreed to drive out in my new to me car, the family Honda accord, which was my graduation present from my parents. Roland was joining me to share the driving. All the women loved Roland, lithe with long ebony hair, dark sparkling eyes and olive skin.

My mom didn't want me to go. She asked, 'When will you grow out of this?' I replied 'I am unlikely to. I have been pagan since I was 16.' She scowled. A week before I was heading out, my left breast began to hurt, and a pocket of fluid developed on the underside. This was where Damien bit me, it had been infected on and off since. 'Mom, I need to see the doctor' I said and then described that was wrong. 'Your father can look at it' she answered. 'No, that feels funny to me. Just take me to see the breast doctor' I pleaded. 'Don't be ridiculous. Your father is a doctor. There is nothing wrong with him examining you.' my mom insisted. My mother called my father down, took off my shirt, and he examined me in the kitchen. The tiles were cold under my feet, and I was crying as he felt my breast. Both of them believed I was crying because of the pain from the infection. I was crying because I felt violated.

Neither of my parents ever understood why I felt violated. My mother was furious that I suggested it was inappropriate for my father to examine me. I could not stand up to my parents and as a result the examination went ahead. It felt like an assault. It is easier for others to understand why examining my breasts was inappropriate. However, even examining my arm would be inappropriate if I said that I didn't feel comfortable with my father doing this examination. What should happen in a situation like that is the parents honour the boundary set by the adult child. Instead, my mother gaslit me into allowing an examination that triggered many other symptoms. I didn't even realise how strange this examination was until I told two female friends about what happened and it mortified them. Mary's father was also a doctor, and she said that he would never do an intimate examination on anyone in the family or even family friends. What struck me more intensely was when Mary said that her parents would respect her wishes if something felt uncomfortable and that they wouldn't question whether her feelings were right or acceptable or tell her she was being ridiculous. They would simply respect her feelings because she had them. This was a revelation to me as I was often required to justify my feelings, and even then my feelings were often dismissed as wrong or ridiculous or made up or dramatic.

In the end, my father said there was an infection, and I would have to see the breast specialist. This was obvious. Even I was aware there was an infection as my breast was swollen and there was an area filled with liquid that was hot to the touch. I did not need my father to examine me. I simply needed a referral to the breast specialist. My mother took me the specialist the next day. The doctor took a needle and drained the fluid out, which hurt terribly and put me on antibiotics. I was told to keep it covered, which led to me wearing a fur sash and a short skirt during PSG instead of going topless.

Roland arrived to meet me at my parents' house and off we went. The drive to Wisconsin was a lengthy one. We were speeding on the Pennsylvania Turnpike when Roland told me we had a pound of marijuana and several ounces of magic mushrooms in the car's boot. I almost had a coronary on the spot. We drove more carefully for the rest of the journey. Outside of Chicago was an accident and the entire motorway came to a stop. The night was beautiful, balmy with lots of stars initially, and then it rained. We stood outside the car and looked at the stars for a while. We must have been there for a couple of hours before the accident cleared and the road was open. The police pulled us over in Wisconsin because I had feathers and charms hanging from my rear-view mirror, which was illegal in Wisconsin. I held my breath the entire time, but they merely warned us and sent us on our way. We took a nap on the side of the road, an then finally arrived at the campgrounds.

I ended up camping opposite Rodney and his family. Beautiful man with a lovely wife and two gorgeous children. I still have the piece of rabbit fur this six-year-old gave me when we went on a walk in the woods. He told me it was magic, and it would protect me.

The gathering renewed my spirit. Marc dancing Pan is impossible to forget. Time spent with the fairies was incredible. At one point, we were stoned and had a blow job contest. I won against a gay man for sucking off another gay man. At the time, I had mixed feelings about doing this in public. Now my pride and comfort with myself would allow me to revel in the environment. Then I had fun while it was happening, but I felt guilty and ashamed afterwards.

We had a potlatch gifting at the summer solstice circle. Each of us had been asked to bring a small gift, wrap it and place it in one direction in the circle. We were all told to pick up the gift that called to us during the ritual. I picked a gift wrapped in purple velvet. It was a shell on a string with an ankh carved in it. The note said 'This shell was picked up on a beach in the outer banks North Carolina' and talked about the carving. To me, this was confirmation that my move to North Carolina was the right move, a move along my path.

During the week, I tripped on mushrooms and enjoyed myself until I found myself alone. When I was alone, Damien was there, menacing and enticing. I could not find my way out of his world. I wandered until morning came and I could find my way back to where the people were.

Sam was running around with Oz at this point. He had come by way of New Mexico and what Oz could teach. DeeDee was in

California working. Her fantasy of marrying Sam and having twins not yet fulfilled. I said goodbye to my chosen family and headed back to my parent's house to get ready to move to North Carolina. My people kept asking why I wasn't coming to California with them. All I could say was that it wasn't time yet. I still felt separate from them. My symptoms interfered with my daily life. I spent at least half of my time partially in the past with regular flashbacks, nightmares and intrusive thoughts. My chosen family had been wonderfully supportive up to a point. I sensed that everyone was waiting for me to be better finally. I no longer felt comfortable talking about my thoughts & feelings fully with anyone.

Looking back, I don't blame any of my chosen family. We were all so young, and none of us had experienced trauma at that level before Damien. Sam and DeeDee were involved in the whole situation. DeeDee introduced me to Damien. They came to the house during my captivity and yet didn't realise there was something wrong (through no fault of their own). The experience left a lasting impact upon all of us.

Back on the East coast, I was ready to head to North Carolina. The first person to call me in my new flat was Tony, wishing me well and making sure that I knew he still wanted to spend time with me. My grandmother bought me my first proper furniture: my first wood headboard, double bed, pine planks and a good mattress. My electric typewriter on the dining table and a new two-seater couch. It thrilled me. This flat was a one-bedroom, a step up from the studio flat I had in university. Lesley came up from downstairs to introduce herself. She pointed out that our building was the building that had all the blacks and Jews. Welcome to the south. It amazed me. Thus far, I'd had no real experience of Anti-Semitism. We went out to a diner to eat, and the guys at the next table were talking about how Jews have horns. I ran my fingers up through my curly hair and wiggled them at these guys, showing my horns. I appreciated that it was clear where people stood, unlike in the North.

I needed money, so I started applying for part-time jobs, jobs that wouldn't interfere with classes and would provide enough money to live on. I got a job on the swing shift as a psychiatric technician. I was to work 20 hours a week, and I got overtime if I worked more. My starting salary was $5.25 per hour. When I left a year later, I was earning $5.77 per hour.

I was excited to be working in the psych field. The inpatient psychiatric ward was in the county general hospital,. Most of the folks were there voluntarily. Some were there under section. It was an adolescent and adult ward for men and women. I had my first experience with psychotic people working on this ward and learned how perceptive people who were experiencing mania could be. I learned all the basic skills I would need for therapy in the future. Swing shift played havoc with my social life.

People gravitate towards each other for reasons that are not always obvious. If we don't figure out our patterns, we are doomed to keep repeating them or some harmonic of them. I gravitated towards people with an edge - somewhat dangerous people. I still do. I own this desire now and make better choices. I risk assess and take responsibility. But in the early years after Damien, when my PTSD was the strongest, I was in no position to risk assess accurately. My Gods protected me from further extreme harm, and for that, I am eternally grateful.

We choose the people who smell right to us. Often they smell right because they are similar to what we have previously experienced. Damien was the first addict in my pattern of choosing addicts. I didn't know he was an addict. I just knew he had an edge, charisma and was compelling. He was the first in a long line of addicts that moved from actively addicted to family of addicts finally to clean and sober for long periods. I tell people that in the past if I were in a room full of people who had never been addicted to anything, and there was one addict, that is the person I would find attractive. They would smell right. Though this has changed in the last 20 years, I still seek for that edge. I now understand far more about the type of edge – the sharpness, the thickness, the type of material it is made from.

Because I have accepted my desire for that edge, I no longer feel shame about it. My risk assessment is better because I am not trying to hide my passion. I am less attractive to predators because I am integrated, and my boundaries have improved. I have developed keen intuition, and I trust myself. I have excellent communication skills and the confidence to set and enforce limits. These are skills that anyone can learn and develop. There is no need to remain at the mercy of the perception of others.

VII

NORTH CAROLINA

'Hate and love are like pain and pleasure, lady, at
times one and the same'
Janet E Morris, The High Couch of Silistra

I wrote this next piece when Sereth and I reconnected after a long separation. Though I am at the beginning of the story of my journey with Sereth, it well describes the tone & tension between us.

Persuasion 2.0 (with a nod to Richard Thompson's song Persuasion)

The small hairs on the back of my neck rise and I feel the muscles along my spine stiffen. Almost imperceptibly, I straighten my spine, attempt to square my shoulders and lift my chin. At the same time, I can feel the defiant expression appearing on my face and that all too self-righteous anger rising. I bite my lip before the words, not fully formed but born on a wave of jealousy and ire, leave my lips. I'm not angry anyway – just frightened and anxious – as I always am when first confronted with your presence. No matter what weapons I arm myself with, no matter how good my camouflage, in your presence, I am stripped bare by one look. My defences seem to me, useless faced with your persistence. I am glad this is so. It would be a shame to go through life able to control almost all of my encounters – to be able to manipulate all my lovers without ever being held to account for my behaviour, thoughts, feelings or most of all, my desires.

I shiver – you are closer now, I can feel your presence clearly as you enter a room and more intensely as you advance. Having been self-possessed and confident up to that point, I am now incredibly self-conscious. I have gone silent at the wrong time in this conversation, and my companion looks at me. 'Are you all right?' he asks frowning. 'Fine' I reply in a tone that comes across as dismissive. The noise in the room seems louder suddenly and the tinnitus I live with since Damien repeatedly hit me in the head has become intrusive as it usually does when my anxiety or arousal rises. I wish I had put in my hearing aids, but as usual, when I know I will be in an overly loud environment, I did not. I work hard to read my companion's lips. Unfortunately, he doesn't really enunciate well and I don't have my glasses on. Internally, I sigh at my lack of preparedness in relation to my disabilities.

I take in a sharp breath and forget to let it out, as I usually do when I am on edge. My breathing pattern deteriorates. I smoked for 26 years, in part, to regulate that breathing pattern – particularly when stressed. I miss smoking at this moment, intensely: The feel of the smoke flowing into my lungs, that deep inhale and holding of the smoke for a moment, the nicotine flooding my body, and the release as I exhale.

'You've truly disappeared'. My companion remarks with a wry smile on his face. I shake my head and smile, 'No, just

drifted for a moment. You were talking about some dates in November for that conference....' I re-enter the conversation with enthusiasm – giving no ground as I discuss the pros and cons of a November conference in that location – and the possibilities for programs and tie-ins with other events. 'I can provide the content if you can provide the venue and enough attendees to make it worth our while to travel that far.' I am saying as your hand lands on the back of my neck. I startle at your touch, and you chuckle. As you begin to knead my neck, my body softens, and I relax into your touch. Well, I relax as much as I can. I'm trembling; my nipples have become like diamonds under my sheer blouse and my vagina hot and viscous. I am sure that you can smell my arousal and know that if you can, so can others. Your hand moves lower, tracing my spine until you reach the cleft at the top of my buttocks. I'm in danger of sighing with pleasure as you stroke me and know that if I bite my lip, my companion will notice. I'm sure that you are enjoying this – knowing my arousal – knowing my anxiety – knowing my body so well that you can trace every effect in minute detail. 'I need a drink' my companions says 'What are you two drinking?' he goes on. 'The lady will have Macallan and water – in a tall glass, lots of water. I will have diet coke' you reply and off he goes to get our drinks.

We are suddenly alone amidst this chaotic lounge – three or four languages being spoken in all tones around us. My back is still to you, and you hold me in that position – pressing into me, pulling me to you tightly – one arm, encircling my throat and a finger running around my collar. I cannot breathe, and I am afraid that my knees will not hold me up much longer. I lean into you and can feel your arousal pressing into my ass. My eyes close as I push back into you. 'Evening Estri' you whisper in my ear, the tenor of your voice causing my body to vibrate. My body becomes your instrument – reacting to your touch, your breath and your intention. I move to turn around and greet you face to face. This lack of eye contact is disconcerting. You hold me in place, strumming me slowly, warming me up as you would a bass before a gig. A moan escapes my lips and I colour quickly, cerise cheeks highlighting the colour of my hair.

My awareness has become focused on your presence and your touch. Jack's voice cuts into my space, and this time I startle. 'So, when do you think we can confirm this program?' Jack asks. I can feel your amusement at my hesitancy. I have not yet gained my balance and colour even more deeply as the moment stretches out. 'You haven't yet told me what areas you are most interested in.' I reply. Jack grins 'Exploring romantic and sexual relation-ships that involve power exchange' he replies. 'Fine' I reply in a somewhat strident tone, and you chuckle again as you tighten your grip on me. 'Won't you excuse us?' you ask Jack politely, 'she will call you early in the week'. You don't really wait for his reply but smile and guide me through the crowd, hand on my back, ever so lightly, until we reach the entrance to the reception. 'Are there any other goodbyes you must say before we go?' you murmur in my ear. I shake my head. 'Good, drink up, and we'll go.'

Out we head into the damp night, the smell of fresh rain is strong and I wrinkle my nose. I have always referred to this smell as 'worm smell', and I have disliked it since I was a child. At home, after the rain, many earthworms littered the ground.

I always found the sight of them and the smell repulsive. With some alcohol on my stomach and anxiety singing through my veins, the nausea is stronger, and I fight for control. I am no longer cerise, but rather an interesting shade of chartreuse. I usually manage nausea with deep breaths, but since it is the smell that has caused me to become queasy in the first place, I grit my teeth and keep walking. I focus on the feel of your body close to mine, your hand on my neck, my back, the sound of your breathing and your footfalls as we walk to my car. We get in, and I am still silent, waiting for you to tell me where we are going. It amuses you. It always delights you when I am speechless. It is such a rare occurrence.

You direct me to an old Victorian townhouse in a town not too far from your home. The CD player remains on randomise as we drive, and the song choice seems ironic as always. At various points during the drive, you reach over and touch me – pinching a nipple, running your finger over my lips, pulling on my hair, stroking my thigh. I am trembling and struggling to keep as much of my attention as possible on the road. The smell of my heat rids me of the last vestiges of queasiness. Squat, the Goddess of parking smiles on us, and I find a spot very close to the house. I'm curious, but I keep my own counsel and await your command. You guide me to the door and ring the bell.

An immaculately presented man of indeterminate age answers the door. He greets you by rank and I raise an eyebrow. A brief glance from you keeps me silent as he ushers us into the elegant hallway. 'Will you be dining first General?' the man asks and you reply 'Yes, James, thank you.' 'Good Sir, this way'. He answers and leads us up a staircase two floors to a private dining room. The table shines with starched linens, elegant crystal and china, silver and candlelight. You pull out my chair and seat me and then seat yourself. 'Drinks Sir?' James asks. 'Just some sparkling water, thank you, James' and he excuses himself to see to it. He has not done more than glance at me and has not said a word to me since we arrived.

Theory and fantasy are one thing – one can attempt to predict one's responses – emotional and physical, but it is only an attempt. Reality is tangible rather than virtual. I find this situation disturbing – more so than I would have predicted. My body trembles, my mouth is dry. I find it challenging to manage your gaze, let alone meet it. 'If I did not mind feeding you, you would be closely bound now. But I do not feel like feeding you tonight so that will wait until after we have eaten.' I lower my eyes and try to still my shaking limbs. I know you are waiting for a response, and yet I cannot bring myself to speak. An eternity passes, and I whisper, 'Yes, Master'. My face is scarlet. 'Look at me' you breathe. I look up and meet your gaze and am glad that I am seated, as were I standing, I would have fallen. Our first course arrives – an exquisite looking salad with langoustines. I force myself to focus on the taste and texture of the food though my appetite has fled. I know that I will need my strength for later.

We discuss current affairs and music during the first two courses. Yet my awareness keeps returning to the feeling of the silk velvet of my dress against my bare skin, the weight of the silver chain running between my nipples and down my stomach, encircling my waist and then down through my nether piercing, between my legs and splitting my buttocks, and back to my waist. I clink and jingle ever so delicately as I move.

The coffee arrives, and I savour it – the bitterness combined with the richness – the warmth of it as it slides down my throat, the heat of the cup in my hands. Trembling again, fear and excitement combine, producing the jingling. You smile and rise from your chair, moving around behind me. You slip a velvet blindfold over my eyes; I moan. You whisper 'shh' in my ear as you help me rise. You slowly remove my dress. The chill air causes me to startle as goose bumps rise on my skin. You bring my arms behind my back, binding them behind me, just high enough to set me slightly off balance. My legs are shackled around the ankles with about a foot of slack between. My trembling now produces clinks, clanks and soft tinkling. 'Shh,' you whisper again, the feel of your breath causes me to tremble more violently. I hear the door open.

'I'd like to display her in the library, James'. You say, and I cannot believe my ears. 'I'll see to it, Sir' James replies and attaches a leash to my collar. I bite my lip to keep from moaning and hope that the tears that have quickly formed in my eyes do not soak the blindfold. You say nothing more as I am lead from the room. There is plush carpet beneath my feet and then icy stone and finally more carpet. The room is relatively quiet – the sound of rustling pages and a crackling fire are the most obvious noises. The scents of wood smoke and sweat are pungent. I am led to a pony and chained into position – facing the central bar – hands tied together above my head, legs spread wide and ankles secured to the bottom crossbar. The leather between my legs is quickly hot and slick with my body's arousal.

111

I am in this position for eternity. I sense a presence next to me, but before I can think anything about them, I hear a crack as the crop connects with my exposed ass. I cry out in shock as much as pain and jump as the next strike lands. Ten blows in quick succession, reddening the whole of my bottom into the creases underneath. And then the feel of a gloved hand stroking the abraded flesh. My moans are plaintive – pain and desire fighting for supremacy. Ten more strokes with the crop – the wielder is expert – lifting each cheek – catching sweet spot each time – wrenching gasps and moans from my throat. Ten more and I begin to beg, to plead, but I've no idea with whom I am pleading and what I am begging for. I hear my voice – ethereal, as if from another far less tangible world. 'What do you want, little crell?' you ask. 'Stop please, I cannot – no don't, please release please' I mumble hoping that I have given enough detail to get my needs met – whatever they may be. I am no longer sure. My body is burning from the roots of my hair to the tips of my fingers and toes. The pain is sharp and the pleasure is jagged and rising. There is a leather-clad hand is stroking my ass again and slides between my cheeks. I rise to meet the hand as best I can bound in this position.

The leather-clad hand strokes the bottom half of my face – fingers parting my lips. I kiss them impulsively, trying to suck them into my hungry mouth. I hear you chuckle. I feel your hands in my hair and moan. 15 more strikes of the crop – hard – bringing up welts until the last strike draws blood. At the last strike, I scream. I don't know that you have drawn blood until I hear someone commenting on it. My body still aflame through the pain – transmuting the pain to ecstasy.

112

I am left alone. Tears run down my cheeks. I taste the salt as they flow over my lips. I can feel the bruises rise. Then there is someone in front of me and they present the crop to my lips. I kiss the crop and then I kiss the gloved hand, my tears falling on the leather. 'Leave her there for 15 minutes so the others can see if they wish', You command. 'Yes, Sir' James replies.

I am aware of at least one person's gaze. My body sizzles as his eyes traverse me noting the colours of the emerging bruises and the criss-cross pattern of the welts. I can feel the heat rising whilst his silent appraisal continues. At last, my ankles are unbound and my wrists released and I am helped to rise slowly. I move slowly, stiffly and with great care as I am led, still blind-folded, from the room.

James dresses me gently. The silk velvet on my welts is alter-nately irritating and comforting. I am left alone in the room for a time. Hands reach around and stroke my breasts, pulling on the rings and then pinching tightly. A whimper escapes my lips. You remove my blindfold and turn me to face you, gathering me in your arms and kissing me deeply. Your hands knead the new welts and bruises on my ass. I whimper steadily as your tongue probes my mouth, leaning against you, as I can no longer support my weight.

My orgasm takes us both by surprise, quick and intense – the energy rising from the base of my spine up my body and out through the top of my head. 'There will be punishment for that later' you whisper, though I can tell you are pleased with me from your energy and the self-satisfied expression on your face. 'Yes, Master' I whisper, still working on catching my breath.

I get into the car carefully, wincing as my abraded ass contacts the seat. 'Too bad we didn't request the club to provide us with a ride home, then you could have said 'Home, James'. I laugh. I've always wanted to say that.

I was not prepared for living in North Carolina. Moving to a society where racism is overt from one where it is covert was more than a bit confusing. After a while, I learned how things worked. It was OK to socialise and be pleasant at work, but locals frowned on dating and socialising after work across colour lines. I had never paid attention to these rules, and I ignored them when I was living in North Carolina. Swing shift is a nightmare for your social life, especially if you are in your 20s. My shift started at 16:00 and ended at 00:30. I had to leave my flat by 15:15 to get in on time. By the time I left the hospital, I had enough time to grab one drink at a local bar before it was closing time. People who work swing shift usually socialise with other people who work swing shift. We get home around 02:00 at the earliest, get to bed at 03:00 and then get up at 11:00 or 12:00. So we have about 3 to 4 hours to get things done before work the next day. Thankfully, I wasn't working full time, though I took overtime when possible. But between classes and swing shift, I didn't have much of a normal social life. At 21, this was a problem.

I met Sereth my second day at work and I took an instant dislike to him. In fact, I almost hated him on sight. That is not a usual response for me so it took me aback. I could not put my finger on what was bothering me. He was my supervisor for the night, so I had lots of contact with him. I ended the night still having potent feelings. He was tall, substantial rather than slender, with a thick mop of wavy salt and pepper hair, pale skin, moustache, lush lips and piercing eyes.

I have always loved some facial hair on men. My godfather had a fantastic big bushy moustache for years that tickled when he kissed me. Perhaps that is the genesis of my love because my father did not have a moustache or beard. Many of the men I have loved and still love had moustaches and/or beards. I suspect part of my love comes from my love of varying textures, tastes and smells. Hair usually provides all three.

On our second night working together, I didn't hate Sereth as vehemently. I still had a visceral response. He knew his stuff, and I was learning a lot from him. His energy still had my hackles raised, though. Towards end of shift, a group of us were sitting in the nursing station, and I asked if anyone wanted to go out for a drink. Of course, Sereth said yes. I didn't want to be rude, so I didn't back out, and off we went to the local watering hole. I have always suspected that he was well aware of the ambivalence I was feeling towards him and that it amused him. Recently he confirmed that this was true.

I have always been a cheap date: One drink or one toke and I am tipsy. I pushed past my limits in university and hated getting sick, so determined never to do this again. As a result, I rarely have over one drink when out and even when I am in, two drinks is a rarity. When I met Sereth, my alcohol of choice was usually a Kahlua and cream. Sweet drinks that hid the alcohol flavour were my favourite choices back then. Sereth drank bourbon.

My memory of that night is patchy. I had more than one bourbon with him. He asked me lots of questions about myself and teased out all my deepest, darkest secrets. He had a captivating style of interrogation so I didn't even realise I was answering questions that usually would have provoked me to say 'none of your business'. The next few times we worked together, we repeated this pattern. I became more comfortable. I rationalised that he was safe because he was married and because I wasn't attracted to him.

One night instead of going to the bar, I invited him back to my flat. I was off the next day and didn't have class until 14:00. I had scotch in the house and offered him a drink when he arrived. I remember talking until dawn and then he left. I went to bed turned on and frustrated. The hatred had revealed itself to conceal an intense attraction that felt very dangerous. Perhaps, I thought, I hated him because of the intensity of my response to him. I felt vulnerable, and to a control freak vulnerability is death.

Thus began our 'friendship' or rather thus began his seduction of me. I shared more and more about my desires, fears, past and hopes for the future. He took in every word. He questioned me closely about my fantasy life, the things I was always afraid to disclose. He was so skilful I always gave more than I wanted to. I have known him now for 39 years, and he remains just as skilled. He revealed some of his life but kept much under wraps. He was mysterious and fascinating as a result. His mind was sharp and his intellect more than matched mine. For me, this has always been an incredible turn on. I love people who can out-think me. I haven't met all that many, so when I meet one, I am always instantly switched on. Relationships with people who can out-think me or at least match me are exciting and full of energy and inspiration. I also love people who can teach me new things and provide fresh perspectives. Often this has meant that my partners have been older than myself, from a different culture or both. I define sapiosexuality as being sexually attracted to intellect and/or the human mind. Sereth widened my music horizons, engaged me in philosophical, intellectual, strategic discussion. He challenged me to contemplate and analyse life and myself (and he still does).

I found Sereth's refusal to touch me maddening. It wasn't as though I asked him to do so. I couldn't even admit my attraction. He just didn't take the next step. We were spending hours talking about authority transfer based relationships, BDsM, my fantasies, the magnificent experiences I had had and the diabolically bad ones. I was in a constant state of arousal around him. And he did not take the next step. He pointed me towards Janet Morris' Silistra series, which remains one of my favourite series of books to this day. I devoured these and noted the relationships and how authority transfer played out in these books. On some level, I knew this was a seduction. It was a seduction of a sort I had not experienced before. Sometimes I could see the situation transparently: Sereth was learning all there was to know about how my desire worked. He was learning my rhythms, my acknowledged limits, and by learning so much about me, he could determine which boundaries he could push. Sereth was handling me, expertly, deftly, and so skilfully that I didn't see the cage until I had waltzed into it and the door had shut behind me, locking securely.

I became frustrated and annoyed. Why would Sereth avoid touching me? I was attractive, was I not? Surely he desired me. But nothing happened. Each morning he would leave me hot, frustrated, and so completely bothered that I couldn't sleep without masturbating multiple times. I hatched a plan to draw his attention, or at least to bring things to a head. Sereth had taken to coming to my apartment after his shifts, even when I wasn't working. When I brought a date home, I would always make sure they left by midnight so there would be no crossover and no awkwardness. I stopped doing this. I began to invite Sereth in as I was almost kissing a date goodbye. I answered the door in less and less clothing – sometimes without even showering off the juices from my lover. One night, we agreed to watch Purple Rain together. He arrived, and I had the video cued up. My boy of the moment was leaving as Sereth arrived. We had a drink and started watching the film. The film over, Sereth got up and said goodnight. He walked out the door and started down the stairs without hugging me goodbye. Though it wasn't what I truly wanted, I craved his touch, so a hug was better than no touch at all. I stood at the top of the metal stairs in my short silk robe, barely belted, hands on my hips and shouted, 'Hey wait! Where is my hug?'. My tone was strident, posture challenging, and the robe left little to the imagination. Sereth turned, looked me square in the eye; I could see the challenge in his face. I wondered if I had pushed him too far. He came back up the stairs and grabbed me. He kissed me so thoroughly there was no breath left in me then let me go and left. I almost sank to my knees on the stairs. I was up the rest of the night, overthinking everything as I finally allowed myself to admit the full extent of my desire for him.

Some short while later, Sereth laid out the rules of this power exchange. I do not remember the details of the consent conversation. I remember talking limits, none of which have stayed in place to the present. Over the years, he has pushed most of them with my consent. I remember him asking me what I wanted most, and I was clear that watersports and humiliation were extreme turn-ons for me. I had engaged in neither since Damien and felt particularly shamed by my desire to have someone piss down my throat. Whenever I fantasised about this, it was Damien I saw, and that usually stopped the fantasy dead in its tracks. He had yucked my favourite yum (ruined my favourite turn on). Orgasm had become even more elusive since Damien. As I found it easy to come with him, and he ripped that from me, it was now difficult to let go of control at all. I masturbated but anything that required me to let go of control with another human being was tremendously difficult.

The next time Sereth and I met up, we agreed to go to a party after work celebrating a co-worker's new baby. I held the baby, and she tried to suckle and ended up with a wet spot on my dress. It was a purple and grey cotton short dress. I was wearing it because Sereth told me to. I also had on heels, which was never easy for me. I could never walk in heels, and any hope to look graceful disappeared as soon as I tried. I was always too self-conscious to be anything but clumsy. These days I don't even attempt heels as to do so with my psoriatic arthritis would lead to torn ligaments. I am known for my collection of Dr Martens® boots. But in those days, I still tried to wear heels. The more comfortable I have become with myself, the more grace I have gained, but I am still not the most graceful of people, especially when I am anxious.

Going to this party together was risky, since people Sereth had worked with for years knew his wife. I had the sense that no one would deliberately throw him under the bus, but if she were to ask, they were not about to lie. We agreed that he would meet me at home after we made our polite excuses. The hostess had noticed us leaving together, though we weren't yet aware of this. We got back to my place after 01:00. When we walked in the door, he pushed me to my knees and told me to unzip his trousers, put his dick in my mouth and be ready to swallow. I sank, hands shaking, barely managed to open his pants and get his semi-hard dick in my mouth before he began to piss. I gulped and with each gulp my pussy clenched, clitoris twitched and by the time I finished I was on the edge of orgasm. He looked down at me and said, 'You may' and the floodgates opened. My whole body spasmed in pleasure. It felt as though it went on for hours, though it was probably only a minute or two at most.

My face was beet red and burning. I stayed at Sereth's feet, on my knees, until he helped me up and brought me to the sofa. He had a small bag with him and removed a variety of chains of varying weights. There were locks, keys and lengths of rope. I had never much enjoyed being bound, and he wanted me that way so he would secure me. He had just finished restraining me the way he wanted when my phone rang. He released a hand so I could answer. It freaked me out that the phone was ringing at 02:00. I had a brief flash of DeeDee ringing me to find Sam when I answered the phone and heard a woman's voice. She asked for him by name and I responded that he had just walked out the door after seeing me home safe, if she held on a moment I could probably catch him. I took a minute and then handed him the phone. There was a brief conversation and then he hung up. I was shocked and asked how she had gotten my phone number. He replied that the female co-worker had passed it on when she told his wife he had left with me to see me home safe. That ended the evening. It was the worst timing as it left me in turmoil, without feeling at all grounded. I had expected him to stay over as we agreed, but that would not work. It never did while I lived local. In fact, in all the years of our intimate relationship we spent only a handful of nights together because of each of our other relationships. My partners always knew about him, and his partners never knew about his actual relationship with me.

That night ended with me sleeping bound, but so I could release myself in the morning. Despite being interrupted, it was exciting. I could not stop thinking about this relationship. I had such difficulty surrendering to him. Sometimes I am sure I drove him to distraction.

Sereth was drinking during the first part of our time together. He was the first alcoholic I had a consensual serious relationship with. He is also a Viet Nam veteran and 17 years older than I so he fit the pattern of people who smelled right, had that edge and understood my symptoms and my desire to take risks. Damien was a cocaine addict, though I didn't know it at the time we were together. I spent time later trying to figure out why people who were addicted, family of addicts or now sober addicts were so attractive to me and it was only then that I discovered the patterns in my family of origin though neither of my parents were addicted to substances.

The edge and the charisma always drew me in and the lack of emotional availability always frustrated me. People who are actively using substances are not emotionally available. Some of them are downright abusive though Sereth was not. Since I was entering relationships that were emotionally and physically intense, the lack of stable emotional connection was devastating and left me feeling adrift with all the feelings that arose from the sex we engaged in. As I wasn't able to own fully my emotions and my boundaries were still a mess, I felt a need for someone to help me contain all of this chaos. The structure of a power exchange combined with a strong Master should have enabled me to do this, but in this case, Sereth's actual unavailability because of being married and his emotional unavailability meant that the internal and external chaos raged.

We spent many nights together drinking, with me smoking cigarettes and playing backgammon. I did not think twice about his drinking at the point. We always bet and usually played for time and who would be in control of that time. I still had the hope I would win some time that I had control over so that I could ask for what I desired. I rarely won and by the time I left for California I am sure I owed him a several months. He always suspected that I let him win and when the relationship began, I did. From Sereth, I learned about being bound tightly. I learned what it felt like to sit at the feet of my Master. I made progress with my surrender (though I am still a work in progress and am likely to always be). I learned to take some pain because that is what my Master desired though I repeatedly said that I did not enjoy pain. I now know that I am a masochist and an edge player (someone who plays at the extremes of pain, danger, sensation). I need a bit of a warm-up to get into my stride. Then, I knew that I hated the crop and yet I shivered when I saw it in his hands. I despised the gag but dreamed about it.

Sereth also provided a safe space for me to explore parts of my upbringing and the impact it had on me. Being with him often calmed my PTSD symptoms, but I was never sure why. Looking back, I believe that this arose from two directions: His trauma experience and understanding matched mine in places, and somehow this helped create the eye in the middle of the storm. He was (is) a good therapist and could hold a safe space, ask good questions to provoke insight and accept what I placed before him without judgement. When we met, my symptoms had me pacing the flat often for hours - checking the windows and door. My symptoms kept me up at night, and when I slept, Damien inhabited my dreams. I was often triggered and more often dissociated. I could not calm the chaos inside quickly and often not at all. He helped me learn to manage the symptoms and to function despite them. He taught me the value of hypervigilance. He began the extensive work of helping me to stay in my body, stop dissociating and become present. As conflicted as I often was about our relationship and as angry as I often was at him, I owe him much.

Sereth attempted to teach me to move with grace. It was an utter fiasco. The more I tried, the more self-conscious I became and the more clumsy I was. He attempted to teach me to walk in heels. I never mastered this skill. I did not know I had psoriatic arthritis, and perhaps then it had not yet manifested fully. I always had issues around twisting ankles though and trying to walk in heels was beyond painful. My self-consciousness was a nightmare. The internal critic raged the more I tried to be graceful for him. To this day, moving with grace often eludes me. If someone I am serving does not draw attention to my movements, I am much better at being embodied and moving with some rhythm and in a pleasing manner.

During the time we were together in North Carolina, Damien continued to stalk me. Sereth had resources and after a time made sure that this stopped. My relief was palpable, but the hypervigilance did not disappear. It was a very long time before I could get rid of Damien's shade.

Our relationship both fed me and was never enough. I was very symptomatic during that time, and there were frequent triggers. I had repeated breast infections that fall stemming from the area of the scar. These had to be drained in hospital. Sereth often talked with me about piercings, marks, and wearing chains under my clothing, and this I found compelling. I took my classes and did well in all but organic chemistry. I all but decided to apply for clinical psychology PhD programmes instead of medical school after the fall semester. CSPP- San Diego's application process was still open, so Sereth convinced me to apply as a trial run. He helped me to compose my personal statement and edited it. I sent in my application and was surprised when I received a call two weeks later that there were still three places for the fall of 1985 left and offered an interview. I flew out to California and had the interview. They accepted me for that fall.

I had not intended to leave North Carolina that quickly, but acceptance to a clinical psychology PhD programme was so difficult to come by, so I dared not turn it down. Once they accepted me, Sereth and I both knew we had limited time left together in person. My last months in North Carolina were bittersweet. I wanted all the time I could have with Sereth, and it did not get any easier. My frustration at the limitations his situation imposed upon us was often apparent, and that meant that there was more conflict between us than I would have liked (and definitely than he would have wanted). I was experiencing FOMO (fear of missing out) though we didn't have that term then. In attempting to pack everything in, the chaos level rose.

When I was most frustrated, I would take my African speaking drum out to the woods, sit on the trunk of a humongous weeping willow tree and drum. Or I would write in my journal. I wrote poetry, fantasy, letters, tirades. Then, I would cry.

I left for graduate school and to live finally in California, where I had always wanted to be. I still nominally belonged to Sereth. Our power exchange dynamic continued on and off over many years. Though I was often conflicted about it, the depth of our friendship and connection was less contentious, and we have sometimes endured closer and sometimes more distant (emotionally) from each other, but we still have a relationship to the present day and this connection still enriches my life. Though I did not expect us to ever be in an authority transfer based relationship again, we recently re-negotiated and this has brought me the balance I have been seeking. This time, everything is above board and he is emotionally available. I have stopped running.

When Sereth wasn't available, my impulsivity would surface. I often got myself into dangerous situations that I needed rescuing from and he was the person I would look to for my rescue. That brought his attention firmly back to me - or pulled him out of wherever he was inside himself. I was lucky that I did not end up injured or dead during that time, that he could rescue me. This coping strategy was not healthy. Even so, it took me some years to learn a new, more adaptive way to express my needs and cope with his unavailability.

Trauma survivors have a strange relationship to chaos. They both despise it because of the symptoms and the instability and often court it because serenity feels alternately dull and like they imagine death would feel. If they are lucky, they connect with people who can help them work through the chaos, minimise the actual physical and emotional danger and learn to not only tolerate but enjoy periods of serenity. They discover that they can still have a taste of the delicious chaos or rather controlled chaos without being swallowed up and disappearing and/or without losing their minds, without losing their lives.

A sense of foreshortened future is one symptom of PTSD that often people misunderstand. People who have this symptom do not wish to die. They are not planning to commit suicide. They don't believe that they will live a long, full life. This is a disturbing symptom to the people around them. It is a way of attempting to move from the past into the present moment, though this rarely works. Instead, people move from the past to the future and bounce back and forth, betwixt the two.

Combine a sense of a foreshortened future with considerable chaos and that often sends a person looking for someone who can help understand their reality which feels so very different from the norm. Most of us grow up with a narcissistic bubble around us that tells us that no matter what we observe in the world, it won't happen to us. Danger, violence and all the negatives are at a distance - even if only a slight gap. That bubble is burst when real trauma intrudes (for some very early on and for others, not until they are in their teens or young adulthood or even later). Once the bubble is burst, and the person sees the reality of the world - that there is danger, that some of it is random, that bad things happen to good people - that they have far less control than they believed - they never recover that sense of omniscience again. Adjusting to this alternative view of the world, much more in tune with reality, and adjusting to the fact that most of the people that surround them don't see reality complicates things. Hence they seek people who get it. Of necessity, these are often also people who have experienced intense trauma and have similar damage.

Many people who sustain intense trauma turn to substances to manage the feelings, the intrusive thoughts and flashbacks, and also to sleep. Substance use often becomes abuse and sometimes dependence which complicates the trauma picture. Alcohol remains the most seductive substance to use, as it is still socially acceptable to have a drink to manage 'a hard day' or a challenging experience. The substances increase the level of chaos rather than helping it to subside. Many co-dependent relationships form between sexual violence survivors and substance abusers. They replay the cycle of abuse over and over emotionally with someone who is not emotionally available, is chaotic and obliterates boundaries at every turn.

We keep our coping mechanisms because they worked even if they no longer do. Even when they become maladaptive, we continue to use them because we know no others. Remembering that we were not choosing to behave in a fucked up manner that made our lives and the lives of others worse but instead of trying to manage or cope with a difficult and sometimes an impossible situation is essential as we strive to grow and forgive ourselves for real and imagined transgressions. Most of us do as well as we can at any given time.

VIII

CALIFORNIA

This piece was written much later but has the feeling of my transition to California. I moved from Sereth before I was ready. I went to a brand new situation, and that always made me feel anxious. I am much better at walking into an unknown group of people now, but still don't find it easy to silence my inner critic. At the time of this transition, I tried to tell myself that I could have a 'simple' mainstream relationship. I wasn't ready to embrace my needs entirely. I wanted to fit in.

The top of my back piece was showing in the sleeveless dress, and the man commented on the tree of life and asked if I was a kabbalist. I explained that the kabbalah was one of several paths I interact with. He noticed Erzuli's tattoo on my arm and could even pinpoint that it was Erzuli Freya. He saw Ogun's cauldron. I showed him Papa Legba's piece on my thigh and Thor's hammer. I could hear him silently ask 'What are you?'

And my response, also silent: 'Property. I am property. I always have been. The Gods make use of my body, my talents, my labour as they see fit. The relationships that work for me all involve a full power exchange. Where we all understand that I am property, that my job is to surrender, and that is all.'

Daily work on staying present is necessary to fulfil my role. Being property means understanding that my wants and needs are secondary to the Great Work. I cannot be a pure vessel and I cannot do their Will if I am not present and embodied.

Please don't misunderstand. This is not an ascetic role. My Owners need my energy and kindle it in the most natural way possible: by tapping into my sexual needs and desires. My embodied owners now have a road map to follow, and all they need do is trace the paths etched into my body. They open the channels, and the energy flows. I become the vessel, the container, the repository of the kindled fire and then the torch wielded by those who light the way.

The sight of Others overtakes my vision. My Will is their Will, and I am the voice of their Will, their words in the world. I can be a precision instrument or a targeted weapon.

Self-care is essential. I walk away from relationships that don't feed and nurture me. They demand much of me, and I cannot be depleted when they call on me to do my work. When not fully used, I am bereft.

I was the second youngest in my graduate school class at 22 ½ years old. My chosen family (DeeDee, Sam, Jen and Marc) were all in the Los Angeles area, and I was a couple of hours south in La Jolla, just north of San Diego. Having a bit of distance was helpful. I felt I needed some separation. I thought they didn't understand what I was experiencing and disapproved of some of what I was doing. But they were still my bedrock supports, and I was happy to be much closer, to be able to see everyone, to be able to touch everyone. In reality, they feared for me. They were unclear if I could make better decisions and I was still walking the edge I had walked when I met Damien. They were no better at figuring out who might be safe in the sexual worlds I was inhabiting, so they could not help me to reality test.

I found the programme exciting and challenging. My symptoms were still through the roof, and I started into therapy quickly. I went twice weekly for most of the time, I was working with this therapist. Our programme also required that we experience group therapy as we were to be taught how to do it, so I spent 2 ½ years as part of a therapy group. I grew a lot through this experience and highly recommend it. One advantage to group is the therapist can see your interactions with others in real-time rather than have to extrapolate from how you interact with them and what they tell you. At that time, I drew risk to me. I was not aware of the energy I was putting out and didn't understand why people responded to me as they did. It was helpful to learn how a variety of others perceived me, so I could change if I wished.

My father bought me my first desktop computer for graduate school, complete with a 300/1200 baud modem. It was the autumn of 1985, and computers mostly had dual disk drives and CGA monitors. My parents also bought me a townhouse to live in while I was in school. It was an investment for them and meant that I didn't need help with my rent. Even with that, my student loan debt was through the roof. The sound of the 300/1200 baud modem connecting was the sound of connection to the world outside of my house. I signed up for CompuServe and spent many hours conversing with others who engaged in BDSM, kink, and fetish. There were no photos, no emoticons. All we had were our words. I connected on a couple of bulletin boards as well. At first, I met no one local via the internet. I didn't know where to find people who had desires like mine, and I was swamped adjusting to the unfamiliar environment and demands of graduate school. Besides, I still loved Sereth.

I started taking T'ai Chi within the first six months of moving. I trained at a fantastic place called the Academy of Martial Arts. Parker (the owner) provided a variety of karate and T'ai Chi classes and styles. I haven't seen a place in the UK that teaches T'ai Chi cane form, sword form, and two-man form. I loved the atmosphere there. All training included the internal disciplines; learning to work with chi. T'ai Chi was not taught as a simple exercise. They taught the real deadliness of the form. I had not been there long when I met Carroll and George. Carroll was a surfer - tan, blond curly hair, blue eyes and a fantastic grin. I found him instantly attractive but did not believe he would find me attractive. I did not have much confidence in my looks at all then. George was olive-skinned, dark-haired with a little extra weight, sparkling dark brown eyes with a wit and intelligence that was captivating. I liked George but wasn't super attracted to him.

After class one night, Carroll took me out for sushi. It was the first time I had encountered sushi, and I loved it and the experience. We had fun, and when I left, he asked me if I wanted to have dinner the following week. I didn't think it was a date because I didn't consider Carroll would be into me. Carroll and George shared a place. When I arrived, Carroll was asleep. He had been working long hours and wasn't feeling that well. I hung out with George for a while to see if Carroll would wake up. George was smoking marijuana and offered me some. I got pleasantly high as we talked and listened to music. I discovered that George was a chief petty officer in the navy. We ended up heading out to eat together, and then he came back to my place. Talking became kissing, and somehow we ended up in bed. George was the first man to go down on me with enthusiasm. He loved to eat pussy, and he was superb at it. I discovered that I could come reasonably quickly from having my pussy eaten well. The women I dated up to this point were not terribly oral, so I had not experienced good cunnilingus. Though as I was (and am) oral, I had eaten a lot of pussy. George was amazing.

Once I had slept with George though, Carroll was no longer a possibility because they were best friends. Carroll expressed some disappointment, and I was surprised to realise he had been interested in me. Their lease ran out about two months after George and I started sleeping together, so it made sense to let him move in with me. George was the second alcoholic I had a long-term relationship with. Our relationship lasted almost two years until I could no longer deal with his attitude and one day he came home to find the stereo blasting 'Would I lie to you?' by the Eurythmics with me singing at the top of my lungs while packing his stuff into boxes. George was part Mexican, part Native American, and also a John Birch Society member. I could never understand that level of self-hatred. He was a survivalist and taught me how to shoot a gun, helped me buy my first gun (a Beretta 380 semi-automatic 16 shot), taught me to shoot a rifle and used to put me through drills where I had to prove I could shower, dress, grab my gear and be ready to leave in less than 15 minutes. We spent long hours designing a house built into a mountainside, and he taught me how to make a homemade radiation counter. When he left, there were many kilos of sugar, flour and bottled water amongst other supplies still in my garage.

Parts of my relationship with George were unhealthy. He was extremely critical of me, especially when he was drunk, and my self-esteem was already low. His drinking made all things worse. He wasn't physically abusive when drinking, but he could be emotionally abusive. There were times he insisted on having sex when he was drunk, despite me telling him I wasn't interested. I didn't see it as rape or even coercion because he could usually talk me into sex. The worst experience was when he passed out while licking my pussy. He lied to me, and when I confronted him lied again, furthering my knowledge of gaslighting. Other parts of my relationship with George were incredibly healing. He taught me about relaxing during sex. He enjoyed my oral fixation and so would encourage me to spend long periods rimming him, sucking his dick, kissing him, and sucking on his nipples. He was another man who was extremely intelligent and despite having had no advanced schooling, could keep up with me and in some areas run circles around me. He was the first of several not formally educated, brilliant men I had relationships with. George and I had a sort of traditional relationship. He was an alpha - ish male. I was submissive in the bedroom, but we didn't talk about this formally, and though we had quite a bit of rough sex, some of which was seriously hot, there was never a real power exchange.

During my relationship with George, I was working hard in therapy and confronting the trauma that was from my childhood. My symptoms gradually got worse, and I eventually developed severe clinical depression. George would head out to sea for periods of a few days to several weeks. One night I found myself with my Beretta in my mouth seriously contemplating blowing my brains out. I had agreed with my therapist that if I were ever suicidal, I would call him before I acted. I put the gun down and phoned him at 2 am (the only time in 4 ½ years of therapy). He referred me to a psychiatrist to take antidepressant medication. It was 1988, and they prescribed me the newest drug, Prozac. I had a severe allergic reaction: broke out in hives, my throat started to close. They switched me to the old-fashioned imipramine. I hated the side effects, but it probably saved my life. I was on it for seven months, when I discontinued it, I was no longer depressed though I still had PTSD. I have never experienced clinical depression since that time. It was when I was on the medication that I found the courage to leave George.

I was still in contact with Sereth during this entire relationship. Sometimes the communication was infrequent. Other times it was intense. At times, it confused me. Sereth would often make promises and not keep them. I found this maddening but could not stay away from him permanently.

The medication had caused weight gain, so when I came off of it, I went on an extreme diet (a medically supervised extended fast) and for five months ate no solid food. I lost the weight and was at the gym regularly. Doctors diagnosed me with Hashimoto's Thyroiditis, which is an autoimmune disorder. My thyroid was slow, so they started me on medication, which also improved my mood and my energy levels. Therapy was proceeding, but I still had symptoms and was finding it a bit frustrating. I noticed a handsome man in my therapist's waiting room one day, but I couldn't get the courage to say hello. And then one day I was using the stair master at the gym, and he got on the machine next to me.

At this point in my life, I was one of the walking wounded. I had very severe PTSD and clinical depression, and yet I managed a full-on graduate school course and was seeing clients as part of my internships. Most people who met me did not know how I was struggling. There are walking wounded everywhere. These are the people who have moved from victim to survivor but have not been able to move back into life. Their trauma remains part of their daily lives as though it were still ongoing. They re-experience the trauma regularly through intrusive thoughts, through nightmares, through flashbacks and through the survivor identity that they have built.

Survivors often develop a trauma bond with their abusers because sometimes their emotional needs are met and sometimes they are abused. It is because these cycles are intermittent that they cannot predict when the abuse will occur and can be lulled into the belief that the positive experiences will someday be a central part of their relationship with their abuser. The abuser is intermittently cruel, threatening, and intimidating alternating with treating the victim/survivor as though they were royalty.

The predator entraps the victim/survivor by starting the relationship with a ton of love, admiration and adoration and the victim/survivor believes they have found that perfect partner until the cruelty begins. These days we call this love bombing. Damien did this with me. The first two weeks of our time together, he smothered me with love, met all my needs and desires and made me feel as though I were the most incredible woman in the universe. Then he turned and became vicious Even during the time he was brutal, he would switch and be caring and express adoration. It was confusing. I got to where I would do anything for the positive stuff.

It is important to note that this cycle institutes a neurochemical cycle as well. Adrenalin, cortisol, oxytocin (the bonding hormone), serotonin and dopamine are all involved in differing complex ways during both parts of the cycle. This chemical storm is part of what makes it challenging to break the bond.

IX

WHIRLWIND

This morning I find myself crying, which is definitely outside my comfort zone on a train. I woke missing you and wondering when my finances will change enough for me to hop on a plane without thinking about it again.

The ache is far more intense than I planned for, and that phrase makes me laugh at myself. As though I can prepare for how I will feel. As though I have that much control. As though I would ever want to.

This control freak enjoys the times she doesn't have control more than anything. Those are the times where defence and pretence disappear, where she is stripped down, naked and authentic to the core. I crave that I – Thou connection and the time to pursue it without interruption.

I struggle with time. I feel I am getting less of what I want and more of what I require. I must pull myself together before this train ride ends – before someone notices the tear sliding down my cheek and asks if I am OK — some uncomfortable British stranger who feels an obligation to ask but desperately wants to avoid emotion.

I remember noticing him in the waiting room and finding it hard to look away. There was a sense of the ironic meeting someone there. 'At least he is working on whatever his issues are', I thought, thinking about the other men I had been involved with who had significant issues but would never have considered therapy.

I can't say what grabbed me first – but I remember he reminded me of Kiefer Sutherland, except that his exquisitely intelligent blue eyes made him far more attractive. The relationship was a whirlwind. I had never fallen in love that hard and fast before, and it had been long since I joined with someone whose sexuality fit mine like pieces to a giant puzzle. Everything about our relationship was intense. Nothing was ordinary: from sucking his dick in his office under his desk to being whisked off for the weekend.

When Kevin proposed, it shocked, excited and frightened me all at once. It was the first time someone proposed to me and I knew I would say yes. Earl had proposed previously, but I knew I would not marry him. When we got back from our weekend, I called my best friend and told her I was getting married. She was quiet on the phone. 'Are you sure?' she said. 'You have only known each other such a short time'. 'I'm sure' I said. I brought it into therapy. Our therapist looked upset. It confused me as he had expressed no opinion in the 3 ½ years we had seen each other – even when I wanted him to. He said, 'It is not a good idea'. It floored me. And angered me. He would not give me a reason because of patient confidentiality.

The high when I was with Kevin was tasty as any high I experienced in a relationship, during sex, or on drugs. I had wings and I could do anything when I was with him. Our conversations captivated me. His intellect was (is) staggering. When Kevin touches me, my body sings. He learned my body quickly and coaxed responses from me I had not felt in a long time.

When it ended, it was quick. I tasted the cocaine on his nostrils when we were in the shower together. I confronted him afterwards. I remember my devastation. I remember how hard it was to stay separate from him. I can touch the dull ache I carried with me for years. I could not make sense of the end of the relationship.

I was rigid about not being in a relationship with someone who was abusing drugs or alcohol, having been devasted in my relationship with Sereth and then George. Kevin wasn't clear about what was going on with him. There was another woman in his life and he was unclear where he needed to be. Recently we spoke about what was going on for each of us at that time. Shortly after we broke up, he became clean and sober. Had I known that he would embark on a journey of recovery, I might have stayed. I ended up in a relationship with an active alcoholic who never stayed sober and so was embroiled in the same lessons as the ones I sought to avoid by leaving Kevin.

Once I had agreed to marry – I needed to marry. I met Stephen within months of the end of the relationship with Kevin. I went to a conference on Traumatic Incident Reduction and then experienced it, and my PTSD symptoms disappeared. I ignored the warning signs with Stephen and jumped into a relationship. Stephen was an alpha male, but not at all interested in BDsM. Like many vanilla marriages, we negotiated no contracts – the marriage contract was the standard one. There was no discussion as to what structure our marriage would have.

The pressure to follow through with a significant change once you have decided often leads to poor choices. There is an impetus that is hard to deny, that pushes you forward without time for reflection. Sometimes this is purely psychological, and others there is a hormonal or chemical element.

High levels of emotion, unspoken familial and societal expectations set many of us firmly on the relationship escalator, moving towards a lifetime commitment before we have even explored whether that type of commitment is what will bring us joy. This urge is even stronger in people who have experienced significant trauma, particularly sexual and relationship trauma. We rarely consider the consequences of these decisions. We rarely look at the legal aspect, the impact upon others in our environment, and sometimes don't even consider the effect upon our occupations.

When we do this, we bring all our unexamined, undigested expectations and project them onto the relationship and the partner. It continues to amaze me that any of these relationships turn out well.

I encourage all my clients to stop and breathe before making a lifetime commitment. I encourage them to examine their expectations, beliefs and goals for relationships. Which needs are you hoping to meet in your romantic relationships? Where will you seek your other needs to be met? I realise how difficult it is to step back when you are in the maelstrom's midst of emotions, and your body is awash with chemicals. I urge you to try so you have a better chance of making a decision that will bring you sustained but joy.

X

MOVING & MARRIAGE

Marionettes
Boxed in
Isolated
A lone star
Far away galaxy
Language always misunderstood
Never seen clearly
Never known for self
Exploding
Imploding
Cast out
Sucked in
Dragged away
Pulled towards
Manipulated, manoeuvred
The players marionettes of wood
I – a marionette of flesh
A visitor
A spectator even in participation
Caged
Hard walls, no windows
Just strings
Always strings...

Stephen was about 5 foot 11 inches, thick dark brown wavy hair, a thick moustache, deep brown eyes that sparkled, chiselled nose and chin, pale creamy skin, and a brilliant smile topped off with a posh English accent. I melted the first time we met. Our intellects connected first. We spent hours talking about trauma and trauma resolution, about the problems with conventional therapy, about the need for structure and an open-ended safe space. The first night of the conference we went out for drinks and then ended up back in my room. I was tipsy, but he didn't seem at all affected by the alcohol, and he had been drinking all evening. That should have given me pause. I dismissed the inner voice of warning and powered forward.

Stephen was the first uncircumcised man I ever saw. In the US, circumcision was routine for most baby boys at the time I was growing up, so most of the dicks I encountered were circumcised regardless of culture, race or religion. 'You look different' I said once I got over my shock. 'Haven't you ever seen an uncut cock before, darling?' he asked. I said that I hadn't and set to exploring him. We had lots of fun, and when we finished, he said 'That was nice'. I burst into tears. To an American girl, 'nice' is a word you use when you cannot think of anything good to say about someone but when you don't feel there is anything too bad to say about them either. To Stephen, 'nice' meant he had really enjoyed himself. It was like saying 'great' in American. Throughout the beginning of our relationship, the American-English language divide was the source of a lot of laughter. As George Bernard Shaw said, 'The United States and Great Britain are two countries separated by a common language'. I spent less than a week with Stephen before he went back to the UK. I went to visit him three months later, and within a week he proposed. I dismissed my misgivings about his drinking and our already flagging sex life and said 'yes'. We planned the wedding for the 13th of October.

It shocked my parents when I told them about my engagement, but they planned a wedding for us. I had a beautiful white wedding dress made by a local seamstress. I picked a venue and organised a caterer. My mom had invitations made up, and we sent them out. I even had a bridal shower despite the scant lead time.

Stephen arrived six days before the wedding. He looked awful when he arrived. He was pale and sweating. Within 24 hours, he was vomiting up blood. I finally rushed him to the hospital. By the time I got him there, he had lost so much blood that the doctors said had I not brought him in when I did, he would have died within a couple of hours. The doctors took him to intensive care. Soon, he was in full delirium tremens and didn't recognise me. It was terrifying. He was shouting and swearing at me. I called my closest friend from the hospital and asked her to call people. There was no guarantee that Stephen would make it and if he did, we would not get married on the 13th. My family arrived, and I had to tell my parents. They were furious. There was a lot of yelling at me. I was in no condition to take in the anger or any advice. I loved Stephen and was desperate for him to be OK. I wasn't even angry yet that I didn't know how bad his alcohol problem was. I just thought he drank a bit too much. He was physically dependent and an alcoholic.

I told Stephen that I would leave him if he didn't stay sober. On the day that was supposed to be our wedding day, I went to my first Al-Anon meeting. Stephen went to an AA meeting. He never engaged with the program - another red flag that I dismissed. Despite my father telling me he would disown me, I moved to England and still planned to marry Stephen. The transition was awful. The culture shock was tremendous. The phone charges were really high, and we had no money. Stephen's financial situation was far worse than he had told me. I moved into a big Victorian house with my fiancé and three male lodgers. I had always either lived alone or with a partner, except for my first year at university. Living in a house with four men, three of whom were total strangers, was not a simple change. I found it hard to feel safe in that environment. I couldn't work on my fiancée visa, so for nine months until we married, I depended on Stephen for everything. I found this extremely difficult to manage. I was already a moderate control freak, and I had control over very little.

If you have never been around a newly sober addict or alcoholic, you will not understand how crazy they often are and how hard it can be to be around them. Take away the substances, and it leaves the person with all the stuff they were using the substances to cover up or push away. Stephen smoked more cigarettes and ate tons. He had stopped eating much when he was drinking heavily, like many alcoholics. Now he was eating for England. Our first Christmas I remember him eating his way through a 5-pound box of chocolates. Stephen had no libido either, and this was definitely difficult for me to manage. He blamed me for his lack of desire, though I could never figure out what I could have done. The first two years together were downright awful. When we disagreed, Stephen would shout, stomp around and once in awhile throw things near me. I barely recognised him when he got angry with me. He would tell me that if I did not agree with him, I was the enemy and therefore he felt justified to do anything he needed to do. I married him anyway. I could not figure out what else to do. I loved him. I had moved my entire life to be with him. When we got along, it was great. We would talk about therapy and counselling techniques. We wrote workshops and organised three international conferences together, and we worked on a larger research project together that I designed. If we had been friends and done business together, we would have been great. Instead, we got married.

We had sex about a dozen times in the 8 ½ years we were together. I never understood why he refused me. He began drinking again after just under three years of sobriety. Life with him became more chaotic. I repeatedly talked myself out of my perceptions. He did not hit me; therefore, he was not abusive. He wouldn't touch me. He told me this was because I was overbearing, domineering and busting his balls by asking for sex. I waited for months before I approached him again. It was still too soon. A year went by, and he never approached me. Then he told me it was because I had gained weight. I lost weight. Another year went by. Later I came to find out he was having multiple affairs. The Gods protected me, though. Stephen had hepatitis C, and we did not know this while we were together. He wasn't diagnosed until about ten months after I left him. I did not catch hepatitis C. Most likely because we didn't have sex. The last time we had sex, I fell pregnant and then had a miscarriage after eight weeks. I was grateful, as I did not want to bring a child into the atmosphere of our marriage.

Stephen's drinking became worse. I was away at a conference and met someone. As I had agreed to monogamy for this marriage even though it really didn't suit me, I decided to leave as soon as I realised how badly I wanted to be with the man I had met. I rented a house and planned the move. My parents wanted me to come back to the US, but I had a practice and didn't know where I would settle if I came home. I decided to stay in the UK.

During this time, I was trying ever so hard to fit into the relationship style I saw growing up. I knew it didn't sit well, but I still felt a need to try. My parents were married for 55 years when my father died, and my mom had never had another partner. Somewhere inside me, that was the model I recognised even though I had known for years I was polyamorous and for even longer I was bisexual and a slave. None of that was compatible with a monogamous marriage like the one I was in. The family script was so strong that it was extremely hard to resist.

After Stephen, I met Neil when I went to get a tarot reading from him. We became occasional lovers and excellent friends, and he remains chosen family and bff to this day. Neil reminded me what fun felt like. Our conversations have always been incredible. They are far-ranging and intense. I trust Neil always to have my back, and he will tell me what he thinks even when he knows I won't want to hear it.

When I met Neil, I had just started dating. At 35, dating was wholly different from it was in my 20s. Dating in the UK, even more so. The first few dates were disastrous. One person came into my living room, saw my bookcases filled with books and asked, 'Have you really read all of these?'. That was the end of the date. The next guy turned out to be a 28 year old virgin. He had never kissed a woman. The whole date was awful. I couldn't get out of that fast enough.

Neil and I explored a little swinging together. It was fun to meet people with him. I got high with him, and it was the first time I had been high in years. I enjoyed feeling so relaxed and having my inhibitions reduced. We took to spending some weekends together at my place. One weekend, we got high and had some hot rough sex. I was so high that the rhythm got lost and I banged my nose on Neil's forehead. There was an almighty cracking sound, and we stopped for a second. 'Are you OK?' he asked. 'Yeah' I said, and we kept fucking.

The next afternoon, I was talking with my father on the phone, and he asked me if I had a cold. 'No, I banged my nose last night.' I replied. 'You need to go to the hospital. Your nose is broken.' my father said. I went to the hospital on my own after saying goodbye to Neil. The triage nurse asked me what happened and I replied 'I was dancing, and I banged my nose' I was too embarrassed to tell the nurse what happened. It is clear the nurse didn't believe me. The senior house officer approached me next. She started by trying to make me comfortable and then looked for details about how I did this while dancing. After about ten minutes of questioning me, she finally asked me if someone has abused me. I turned scarlet and laughed. 'I will tell you the story, but I don't want everyone here to be laughing about this tonight'. She reassured me she would keep this private. I didn't believe her. I have worked in a hospital, and I know what it is like. I told the doctor that I was fucking my lover and banged into his very hard forehead. The doctor burst into hysterical laughter. I couldn't help but laugh with her. She examined me, and they sent me off to X-ray. After I saw the consultant, they told me I needed surgery to reconstruct the bone. I was booked in for the following week. For years, Neil did not want me to tell this story because it embarrassed him. I kept telling him it is badass to break someone's nose while fucking.

When I hit 35, my hormones kicked in. Neil and I had talked about whether I would have children. I remember saying I wasn't really planning on it. And then my hormones took over. My son's father and I had very little in common besides a love of reading, particularly science fiction and fantasy. He wanted to be a father. He was 12 years younger than I. We weren't even sexually compatible, but my hormones were raging. I never believed the stories about how strong hormones can be and that they can impact judgement. Now I understand. I became pregnant accidentally within six weeks and had a miscarriage at nine weeks of pregnancy. This was my 3rd miscarriage. I got engaged to my son's father and set out to find out why I couldn't carry a baby.

I married my son's father, and they discovered that my blood was sticky, so there was now a plan to help me keep a pregnancy. My son was born in June 2002. It took one try to get pregnant. I had an agreement with my son's father to be non-monogamous. The deal was that each of us had the right to say no to the other person's choice of partner. Early on, I found out he lied to me. I should have ended it then. But I had internalised the idea that having two parents together raising the child was best. So I didn't end it.

Stephen died of hepatitis C when my son was just over 2 years old. This had more impact that I thought it would. I found the grieving difficult.

The first poly relationship I had during the marriage was with Sereth. He contacted me while I was pregnant. It was as though no time had passed. Finally returning to my core desires was a relief.

Most of us take on cultural messages and familial messages about relationships. If you are being raised in a heterosexual family, this usually means the Disney version of happily ever after. Even when we manage to examine these structures and desires and see that they don't fit us, they still act upon us at a deep level. Many of us find ourselves captive in that fairy tale without even realising that is what we have done. I call this the monogamy hangover®. All the tenets of modern monogamy determine the pattern of our relationships. We meet, we get on that relationship escalator, and each step runs right into the next until we get married and have children.

If we don't thoroughly examine our patterns, it dooms us to repeat them. Recognising the patterns can be unusually difficult. The second serious relationship looked so different from the first in the beginning. They didn't physically resemble each other, or they were from two different walks of life. Their histories differed and yet they turn out to have the same issues as each other. Both relationships are failing for the same reasons because they fit the same pattern that we have been repeating.

As I said earlier, I have often told people that if I walked into a room of 100 people and only one was an addict or alcoholic, that is the only person I would find attractive. I went from Sereth's alcoholism to George's alcoholism to Kevin's addictions, to Stephen's alcoholism, to my son's father having the same qualities without the active addiction. It wasn't until my current husband that I moved squarely on to people who had been sober for an extended period.

Examining our patterns to change them means doing the deep work necessary to move from recognising the pattern to unearthing the things that keep us stuck in them to change the things we find. The work requires a safe space, courage, and an understanding that we are all works in progress. The more of this work you do, the more likely you are to create the relationships that truly feed you.

The other part of genuinely creating a conscious relationship is knowing what is possible. Do you truly want to live with your partner? Perhaps you prefer to live alone and have multiple partners who you visit or who visit you or both. That is solo polyamory. Do you want to have one partner you live with and others you see regularly? One partner and other play partners? Or maybe you are genuinely monogamous? All possibilities are equally good as long as you are making a conscious choice and you can only do this when you are aware of what you have internalised of the patterns, rules and judgements from your parents and your culture.

XI

RECOLLECTION

After my son was born, I spent a lot of time in contact with Sereth. I journaled for him as I did when we were first together. I wrote this piece in 2003 after an intense dream.

We are somewhere in the conflict, one step removed. I am training people in trauma management. I spend the evening before you arrive attempting to decline politely a powerful, dangerous man who finds me spirited and is determined to add me to his collection. I am loath to mention your name – preferring to handle the situation myself, which given the culture is ridiculous, really. As a result, I end up in the debt of another man who makes my relative position clearer. He tells me to give you his regards, but for the life of me, I cannot remember his name.

The locals escort us around some structures. To call them buildings is misleading. It implies modern dwellings. These are more hollow and haphazard and blend well with the sand. One is still smoking, reminding all who are with us that this is not a safe environment. The adrenalin junkies in the party and I count myself as one, find it all fascinating, terrifying, adrenalin can make you both high and nauseous – a potent mix.

As the only aware woman, I am attracting some attention. Respect is something many of these men do not apply to women. As you surmise, I find this problematic thus leading to my run in the previous evening. We are at a meal with tables low to the rugs on the floor when you arrive. You have no trouble spotting me. Despite my attempts at modest local dress, my body posture and animation in conversation give me away. I am having a heated debate (muted by my usual standards)with the man who rescued me last night. There is a crackle of flirtatious energy in the air, a veneer over his aggression. His desire to own me he keeps in check out of deference to you. I feel you arrive as you come up behind me and your arms go around me, cupping my breasts, pinching my nipples and pulling me firmly into you. A squeal of pleasure escapes my lips. I know better than to turn around. You hold me tightly. I press my buttocks back into you, delighting at the feel of your stirring cock, the pressure of your arms around me, the feeling of sinking into your body, and being enfolded in your arms embrace.

I am still in a bit of control until you begin to manipulate my nipples. My breathing becomes ragged. Colour rises to my face as I notice the gazes of several other men and women gathered. The locals appraise my responses and your command of me. Those of my own culture appraise a variety of other things. I feel most shamed before them. Their lack of understanding and acceptance burns. Most of them see me as a bold and independent type. Though they are not aware of what they now view (they see it as blatant sexuality which is coarse or common – not worthy) I am aware they see my submission, and by this, I am ashamed and also proud. The mixture of emotions and reactions are confusing as usual. You greet your associate and thank him for looking after me until you were free.

He makes comments about my behaviour and the 'mishap' of the previous evening, and at first, your face darkens. I shiver to see that look - even with my back to you. When all the details are revealed, it amuses you. 'Poor little crell – you are unused to these rules which likely chafe as much as heavy crell bracelets and chains'. You march me to a place (with limited privacy) where we can recline and press us both to the ground – continuing to arouse me – pinching my nipples, moving to stroke my clitoris – finding my pussy soaking wet. I am moaning steadily, but you still have not let me touch you, turn around, kiss you. I struggle in your grasp to turn – 'Be still'. I moan and press against your now hard cock. A small moan escapes your lips. I grin, having managed at last to provoke an audible response. My body is warm liquid – honey, olive oil – viscous, flowing.

You turn me – lifting my chin – gazing into my eyes, my soul, my heart. You take a kiss from me. My heat rises higher. You hold me close and ask me to tell of what happened the night before. I begin to explain about touring the abandoned stronghold. My comments about planning – offhand – not meant to cause any reaction. I was thinking out loud. I describe our guide's response, spluttering an apology to one of the local men at the front of our party. One of the western reporters ribs me – winding them up – and presses me again about why I am there and what I hope to accomplish. Several men are laughing at this point. My temper rises. I am not a team mascot, nor am I there as a token. I have a brain and am accomplished, earned my right to accompany them – my analysis is sought after, valuable and so on. I have shut them all up, and my face is now burning red. I know better. You asked me not to draw attention to myself. I'm humiliated, angry, and frightened. Worst of all, I fear your displeasure. I apologise to the local contingent gracefully and then stick my tongue out at the western media boy.

My watcher is none too amused. The local 'chief' has decided that I am worth a second glance, however. What can I do? I am polite, deferential – as best I can be – I do not want a second glance from this ruthless man who can see me as nothing but chattel. I have enough on my plate – do not need more discipline (though I suspect you will beg to differ hearing this). I have no desire for a second master. Right now, I can only manage the one, thank you. I will do what you will. Should you wish me to serve him, I will do so, and I will do so well.

We move onto the next stop on the tour. Somehow they press me to the front – near to the chief – his hands are on my arm as he describes something. I stiffen. He kneads my arm. I will myself to relax. If I am polite, maybe I can get out of this with no one losing face. My inner commentary is scathing.

He asks my opinion with a look of amusement, one that tells me he is playing, that a woman with a view is an oddity to him. With appropriate deference (or at least an attempt), I state my opinion. He laughs out loud and his hand moves to my ass. He gives me a resounding slap and I fight to remain in control of my temper. The western boys double over with laughter, waiting for me to explode. I am aware of the consequences of exploding and am keeping a handle on my temper – if only barely. He is now kneading my ass. Any movement on my part seems to increase contact rather than decrease it. My discomfort amuses him. He leans into me and nibbles my ear.

I almost slap him. His laughter is resounding, booming as he sees my struggle. My watcher rescues me at this point. He politely explains that I belong to you and I listen, shocked, as they discuss whether or not you would consider selling me or at the very least loaning me out. 'Feisty' he says and grins. I am both enraged and petrified, fighting for control of my temper. I'm determined to behave well, at least from now, as they have mentioned your name. The stakes have risen. I do not want to devalue your name. This is suddenly no game.

At last the tour is at an end. I politely bow my head, lower my eyes, and express my pleasure at meeting him, unfortunately, through gritted teeth. The watcher translates his response. 'A well-trained slave would kneel at this moment'. I reply that to ask me to do so in the circumstances would be an insult. I realise I have taken liberties and cannot find a way out. He is right – I should kneel regardless of the westerners surrounding me. Both he and I know what I am. My watcher silences me with a look. I do not know what he has promised this chief, but he is not pleased.

My tears land on my thighs as I finish the story. 'I will punish you' I nod my head. You gather me closer into your arms, inspect the chain at my ankle, explore me again as is your right, and a sigh escapes my lips. Your hands on me always produce – I don't have the words- all others pale in comparison. I am shaking, sobbing in your arms – with grief – with relief. Then you discuss my punishment. The chief requested the loan of me – and when you respectfully declined – demanded at least to see my punishment – so much did he desire to teach me my place. He offered you one of his so you could compare. When you tell me this, I freeze, grief-stricken. I hold my tongue. 'What, no response?' you muse. 'your Will, Master' I whisper once again tears raining from my eyes. 'I agreed to punish you in front of him only. The rest we shall see'. The next hour we spend resting in the heat. At the appointed hour, he arrives with two young beauties and a young man who he quickly sends away. The boys had noticed my absence. So they send a message. I am assured it will amuse them.

I remain on my knees; eyes lowered when they arrive. I will not disobey you further. My behaviour interests the chief. I stay deferential, and it is clear I am not pretending. It occurs to him, he muses, that I respect you. I do not speak, though that is bait – surely. I want so badly to answer. 'You may speak' you allow. 'Thank you, Master' I reply, softly, with respect. 'Of course, I respect him, Sir. I could not serve him if I did not' I breathe, eyes lowered appropriately. 'It seems your training may be sufficient' he comments. I am aware of the insult and incensed for you – which I am sure you find amusing. You can read my rage in my carriage so well do you know me after all these years. Steam is virtually coming from my ears. I shift on my knees – one sharp look from you stills me.

The chief slowly walks around me – 'splendid carriage despite her size' – still incensed but proud – despite my size – culturally I know I am not unusually large – still self-conscious. 'Would you care to examine what I have brought with me?' he challenges, and you nod your assent. Though I know you can do no differently without losing face, I am devastated. I also know you would enjoy the loan of these beautiful girls – as much to enjoy my jealousy as of what they were. You would find it a delicious tribute as long as I was not in too much emotional pain. You always have. The women disrobe and kneel before you. They are gorgeous – thick black hair, midnight eyes – lovely dusky skin, well rounded with pert pear-shaped breasts, beautiful hips, waists that are not small but not large – in proportion to the rest of their frames. I used to have proportions like that before childbirth. I aim to have them again – but am not there yet – nor am I as resilient as I was when I was as young as they. I know you remember me when I was almost as young. My heart is in my throat, and I bite my lip to avoid crying. I will not compare myself to them. I note that you are watching my responses as you run your hands over one girl and see me shudder. She is responsive. The chief watches me with pleasure as he too can see my upset mirrored in my body. He sees me fight for control of my emotions and it impresses him that I keep my place with my eyes lowered, keeping silent despite my obvious pain. I will not disgrace you by doing otherwise.

You finish exploring the girls and remark on their beauty, carriage and behaviour. By now, I am bright red from anger and also from shame. I keep silent still. You call me to you, and I crawl over, bow my head to your feet and stay there ten beats until you raise me to my knees. We had discussed this, and I did not hesitate, though I am indescribably embarrassed to be crawling in front of you, let alone anyone else. The sight of the crop sets me shivering. In all the heat, I am suddenly iced cold. It has been years since I endured this, felt this. I have only done so at your hands. There were other implements at the hands of others, just you with the crop. I remember the first time. My fear was insurmountable – how impossible it was to stay still, to accept the blows. I wonder how much better I will fare now with an audience, with your reputation on the line. '10 strokes, we have agreed it' I hear you say. 'I will start and deliver the first nine strokes, leaving you the last one. Unless you prefer to start'. I freeze further, if that is possible. I am prepared for you to start, but I do not know if I can be still for him. He looks at me and then smiles brightly. 'I will start' he declares. I pale. For a moment, I might faint. You bend down in front of me, look into my eyes. 'Do your best for me' I nod my head as I do not trust myself to speak. I lower my head and wait – trembling ever so slightly. I feel the rush of air as the crop comes down, just before contact is made with a resounding 'thwack' and the sharp stinging pain. A cry escapes my lips – I can hear him chuckle behind me. My eyes focus on your feet. A delay and then the next one – higher on my ass than the first – a cry and a moan torn from my lips – my nipples tingling – my ass stinging, hurting, throbbing, liquid at my centre. I don't understand my response – I know that it is a deep, thorough response – from my heart – from my soul – from my core – the next blow rains down harder – tears run down my cheeks. I hear him chuckle. I have not moved away, and I have not begged for relief or mercy. So far, I have accepted this as punishment due me. I am determined to perform well for you. I notice your hands are on one of the women, teasing her – but your eyes focus on me – observing my response. I move to invite you. I plead with my eyes. After the fifth stroke, you move to take over. The chief runs his hand over my welts before surrendering the crop. I cry, moan and press my buttocks back on to his hand. He dips his fingers between my legs, drawing out hot nectar. 'Good' he says, having measured my response. I am deeply shamed – red-faced, burning – wishing this over – craving the rest – more frightened and less frightened that you will deliver it. The first few strokes come in quick succession with no time to recover. The pain is overwhelming.

I invite you but scream as the last stroke rips into me. I feel a soft hand rubbing oil into the welts and am trembling again. The final two strokes are harder and placed on top of the welts. I moan, bow my head lower so they cannot see my tears. 'Thank you, Master' I whisper. You motion me up and kiss me deeply. I can feel your pleasure with me in your touch. I know I have done well. 'She is well trained. She is also truly yours'. I sigh, thinking myself safe from further humiliation at his hands. For the moment, I am. What you will do later is unclear.

I know that there are enormous pressures on you. You will – what – take your pleasure with me, use me to de-stress, use me as a tool? It is your will – that I am clear upon – I am determined to please you, to make you proud, to make you desire me. I am committed to being yours.

I finally went to see Sereth again in February 2003. We met in Washington, DC. The meeting brought back my desire in full. I was clear that I no longer wished to settle for a vanilla relationship. My relationship with my son's father was challenging and had been since I went back to work after my seven-week maternity leave. We had no intimate life. He spent time with friends and then had an attitude when I returned home from work, as though it entitled him to even more than I was providing. He talked to strangers on the internet, and I soon found out he invited a woman to come to our home while

I was away for work. When I found out about this, I made sure that it would not happen. He didn't even consider any of the horrible things that could happen if the stranger turned out to be criminal and didn't think exposing our son to this might be a problem.

I met El when I attended my second Extreme Wicked party. I was nominally collared to Sereth then. I drove up to Surrey for this party, wearing a corset and short skirt, leather collar and my gorgeous silver lead. The party was in a private home with lovely grounds. There were a variety of play spaces, mostly dimly lit and there was beautiful outdoor space - a patio, a pool, lawns and trees.

When El first saw me, he commented about a lost slave. My reply was 'I'm not lost, I'm just loose'. He replied, 'Not any more' and picked up my lead. His energy was enticing. He led me outside so he could smoke a cigarette. He briefly introduced me to his wife, V - blond, statuesque, lovely but ever so cold. I remember little of the initial conversation except that I told him the limits I had negotiated with Sereth - which included no fucking. I had limited permission for oral sex, but Sereth would have preferred that I restrict myself to non-sexual play. Slut that I am, I found this exceedingly difficult and determined to go to the limits of the permission he gave me.

After the smoke, El led me to the cross and tied me up. He started with a flogger and worked me over well - building slowly until I was writhing beneath the stroke and a hairsbreadth away from coming. I felt his fingers between my legs and heard him laugh as he gathered my juice. I was ashamed that my desire was so apparent.

We watched some action and El told me that as a present he would top his wife in public. Since she was a pro-domme, this was very unusual. He asked for my help during the scene. El brought her out blindfolded and tied her to a massage table. His first request was that I help him get hard. I was on my knees and sucked his dick. Quickly, he was hard. I kneeled next to him while he fucked his wife, alternating fucking with beating, pinching, biting. About 30 people were watching - many men were jacking off as they watched this woman get ravished. It was exciting to be so close to the action and yet not to be an active part because I did not have permission. There was something so objectifying about this position. It is, was, and remains one of my most intense fantasies.

I remember he finally exploded inside her and then pushed me forward saying 'Clean her'. I dove in, eating her pussy until she screamed with orgasm. I was coming as I ate her, one hand between my legs rubbing my clit until I was in a frenzy. I finished, and El untied his wife and cuddled her, leading her off for some aftercare. Before he left, he said 'Stay there'. I don't know how long I stayed kneeling on the floor in the middle of the playroom. Mostly I was aware of the sensations in my body, my arousal, the ache in my knees.

When he returned, he lifted me. V talked with her fans, and then we all went to the changing area. El gave me their card, and I gave them my details, got changed, said my goodbyes to the host and hostess and walked to my car. I remember two guys trying to pick me up as I was leaving and feeling flattered but tired and aware I had a lengthy drive. I left feeling exhilarated but confused about what I would tell Sereth how I would describe the scene and the players. I spoke with Sereth the next day and told him all lest I leave out what he wanted to know.

In the summer, Sereth came to visit me. After the first night I spent with him, my son's father exercised his veto power and said he wasn't comfortable with me continuing the relationship. At the end of the trip, I ended the relationship. It tore me apart, but I agreed to this rule, and I aimed to keep my word.

Sereth made plans to come to England to work for me. I was not sure if this would go ahead. By this time, I knew he had re-married and we were again in a relationship that was being hidden from his partner. I felt better about the relationship ending as I didn't wish to be part of an affair. I engaged in ethical non-monogamy only.

I continued to spend time with El, V and their girl C. I had an absolute blast running with these pros. I served at events and attended parties at their place. In December, I travelled with them to Paris to attend a few days event, and at that point, it was the largest public BDsM event I had ever attended. Dungeon time was exciting. Helping them with their performances was hot as hell. I came back from everything revitalised and happy to dive back into work.

I found it hard to refuse Sereth when he told me he still plans to come and work for me. He planned to come over first and have his wife join him. I agreed to work together but clarified that we would not be in a power exchange relationship. My son's father had been clear about how he felt, so I was clear that I couldn't have an intimate relationship anymore. This was very difficult. Sereth and I had a relationship on and off for many years, so it was difficult to resist falling into old patterns. I wanted to re-negotiate my agreement with my son's father but he had no interest and was adamant that he didn't want me to renew this relationship.

We worked well together at first, though I realized he chafes at having me as the boss. Neil shared the office space with me, and unfortunately, Sereth and Neil did not get along well. We managed the work together, despite my concerns for two years. Then Neil reported that Sereth was erratic at times and I was suspicious about alcohol use. His reporting time slowed, and I could no longer manage him well, so I ended the working relationship. This was one of the hardest things I had done to that point in my life.

Afterwards, Sereth worked for himself and took a significant chunk of clients with him. I had little trouble filling my time and still had too much work, so I hired another psychologist to work with me. As a result, I wasn't upset with the clients moving over to Sereth. We talked less frequently but were still on reasonable terms. It was more comfortable with me no longer being the boss.

It was only after I divorced that I discovered my son's father believed that I continued to sleep with Sereth until Sereth left the country. He said nothing to me, and so I had no opportunity to set him straight. He lied so often to me he assumed every one lied as he did.

Ethical non-monogamy requires transparency and superior communication skills. But as I said previously, people can find it hard to shed their early life conditioning so when they come up against the need to be honest even when it might hurt a partner, they often find it easier to lie. Lying is one of the hardest things to get past in relationships. Many people work on the adage 'It is better to ask for forgiveness than to ask for permission'. This adage is almost guaranteed to cause strife in a relationship. It goes along with things like 'what x doesn't know won't hurt them'. Doing something that you know will upset your partner without being willing to negotiate in advance almost guarantees the conflict you are trying to avoid. That idea that lying doesn't impact a partner if they don't find out is wrong. When you are keeping secrets, you are withholding a part of yourself from your partner. When you are working to withhold a part of yourself from your partner, they will feel the distance.

XII

KISMET

This piece highlights some desires that were at the forefront when I sought someone new who might help me satisfy them.

Moving Tales for Predators

1

    Cinnamon. Cloves. Blood. These are the scents emanating from the kitchen. Spicy sweet metallic tang. I start to drool as I approach. I'm late, and I try not to trip as I cross the threshold. I look around the kitchen as I enter and see no one there, just the aromatic scents drawing me forward. I know better than to call out. I sink to my knees by the table and wait. 'Lift your hair' breath hot in my ear. I lift my hair high onto my head, exposing my neck, and within a fraction of a second, your teeth tear at my throat. The shudder runs through me as I struggle to stay on my knees. I am pressing into your mouth, juices beginning to wet my thighs. I moan loudly until you take my mouth, devouring my tongue, taking my breath. I breathe with you, through you or not at all. When you let go, I am limp with desire.

The timer rings and you remove the cinnamon bread from the oven. The aroma is overpowering, sweet, spicy with that metallic bite. The secret ingredient is only for our special guests. My thigh aches where you bled me earlier this evening. You prepare a tray of slices of the warm fragrant bread, a jar of comb honey, some fresh churned butter and a second tray of small glasses with a bottle of 21-year-old rum, lime wedges, mint leaves and sparkling spring water. I take the tray of drinks through first and hand the plate around to the pack assembled on the couches and chairs scattered throughout the great room. Many lounge on the deep pile furs on the floor covering parts of the broad flagstones in front of the walk-in fireplace. Hands stroke my naked thighs, run over my flanks, pinch at my ass, run up into my wet folds and pinch. I sigh, moan, jump, and the low chuckles of greeting make me even weaker. I almost forget my task. I can hear you in the kitchen, awaiting my return for the second tray. I quietly excuse myself once everyone who wants one has a glass. I pick up the humidor from the table before leaving, opening it and handing it to R, who takes the first cigar. The humidor is being handed around as I make my way back to the kitchen. The low rumble of conversation ripples the surrounding air.

I return to the kitchen and before I can grab the second tray, your arms are around me, pressing me back onto the cleared oak table. The grain under my back is rough and cold. You ravage my throat, moving to my breasts, biting and suckling until I am writhing beneath you. Your fingers gather my salty-sweet slick juice and press into my mouth as you suck harder. I suck and lick my juice from your fingers as though I am starving. You plunge your fingers back into my pussy, fucking me until I am screaming with need. 'Please, please,' I wail. You growl in my ear, 'come then'. My orgasm roars through me, drenching your fingers. You pull me up quickly, smack my ass and hand me the tray. I wobble a bit and then stroll into the great room again, trying to bear the plate with grace. My cheeks are a deep red and the smell of my sex thick, clinging to my skin and the air around me.

I offer the sweet bread around with the butter and honey. I am halfway around the room when R rubs butter on my left nipple, coating it well before sucking it deeply into his mouth, teeth nipping as he sucks the butter off. He pulls me forward, sucking my breast in deeper. Fingers spread my ass cheeks, and I feel the warm butter begin to meltdown my crack. I am bent over R's knees, ass sticking in the air, butter dripping down my crack and into my softening hole. I jump as someone's tongue plunges in deep. I open my mouth to scream and smell fiery dripping pussy in front of my face. My tongue flicks out over someone's clit. I am gathering up the juices. Pussy fills my mouth. I cum almost immediately as I lick, suck and nibble. Hands in my hair hold me, so my face is making full contact. My face is being fucked as I eat sweet pussy, gasping for breath and pressing in deeper. Fingers replace the tongue in my ass. First one plunging deep. Then two, deeper and faster. My pussy rubs against R's thighs as someone opens my ass further and I continue to devour the pussy pressed to my face.

I moan as I feel dick pressing into my ass, sliding in hard, pulsing. I am opening further, that burning that I only feel when being ass fucked. It is like I become warm spicy oil with each thrust. I crave more, and I am held in place with each body pulling me until we finally set up a rhythm together, the three of us moving as one. The orgasm begins as the dick fucking my ass explodes. The orgasm runs through me into the pussy in my mouth and then back through me again, wave after wave of energy moving through the three of us until we collapse.

Your hands are at my lips, pressing a piece of cake into my mouth that melts on my tongue. You give me a sip of the Mojito. The taste of rum, lime, mint, sex, cinnamon, cloves, blood and honey flood my mouth. The smell of cigars, cinnamon, cloves, blood and sex permeates the room.

2

The air is fresh after the rain. It has that autumn rain scent on a backdrop of burning leaves and twigs. The colours run together. As I walk through the wood, I inhale deeply. Though wet, the leaves still crunch underfoot. The air is chilly, and I pull my jumper closer around me, pulling up the hood, tying the scarf around my face. The cashmere on my face is soothing – warm and sensual both. I walk under the old oaks and rowans, newer pines, taking my time, following the leaf and wood smoke. The light is filtering through the trees, creating patterns on the moss, ferns, leaves and bark. My mind drifts from sensory data to snapshots of memory as I walk. Taking my time, refocusing on the surrounding beauty, I take out my camera and take a few shots.

I enter the clearing and pause, taking in the scene. You are chopping wood in a vest, weapon in a shoulder holster, legs encased in worn blue jeans. The fire is contained in a well-con-structed pit. The dogs are relaxing in the shade. The crackle and pop of the fire seem loud in the quiet. 'C'mon over here' you say, and I make my way across the scant distance. I'm not surprised you heard me enter. Your senses are finely tuned. I kneel next to you. You put the axe down and ruffle my hair. I bend to kiss your boots, inhaling the smell of wood, smoke, leather, oil and your musk. You lift my chin, grinning 'Get some food on'. I head into the cabin to start a meal. There are sweet Italian sausages, fresh rolls, peppers and onions. I prepare a new potato salad and some coleslaw. There is fresh tomato sauce and mozzarella cheese. There's beer in the fridge and fresh lemonade. I put the sausages on a rack and bring it out to roast them over the fire. I put the peppers and onions in a frying pan with a little olive oil and set them sweating. I heat the red sauce slowly and grate some mozzarella. I feel you come up behind me and press your sweat covered body into mine. Your scent is arousing. I moan and push back into you. I am slowly taking the pan off the heat. You reach around and pinch my nipple, increasing the pressure until I am standing on my toes, pressing into you. You keep pinching until my gasp turns into moans, until my knees buckle. I can feel your excitement. You let go suddenly. 'Let's eat' you say. I bring you a plate of food and wait while you taste it. You grunt your satisfaction and motion for me to get some for myself. We eat in silence, enjoying the flavours, smells and the sounds of the wood.

Having finally lost the weight I gained when I was on high doses of steroids to manage my autoimmune disease; I seek someone to explore power exchange with again. I agree to seek someone in the US so that my son's father doesn't have to come face to face with one of my lovers. I was unaware at the time that he had already begun an affair with one of the other mothers in the class. Rather than seeking to connect with someone who I won't run into, he decided on someone who spoke to all the people she could at the school, so everyone knew about their relationship except me. However, I did not yet know about this when he asked me to seek someone out far away.

I met Tom online and it was clear we clicked. I agreed to meet up with him for a meal when I visited a friend in Los Angeles, as that is where he lived. I had decided to stay in a hotel so if I wanted to do more than have a meal, I could do so. Initially, I was being logical and safe. We agreed to meet for a meal but ended up in my hotel room and eating room service in the wee hours of the morning. The connection was immediate. The sex was fantastic. By the time I left, I surprised myself by accepting his collar. It was July.

In August, Tom and I were on the phone when my son's father entered the bedroom and told me he needed to speak with me. He told me to make sure that Tom would be available to me after we talked. 'I will call him you in 30 minutes'. He said 'I will be here.' My son's father told me about his affair, assured me it was over. I asked why he was telling me then, and he told me the woman's partner was going to tell me. I was gutted. We agreed to practice ethical non-monogamy, and he had been lying for eight months. There had been a few incidents: I found used condoms in the wastebasket, and he insisted it was for masturbation, which I knew was absurd, and I told him that. I found a g string that was not mine, and he insisted it was. It was smaller than I had ever been as an adult, so he knew that was also absurd. But he stuck to his lie. He had slept with this woman in my bed and my home. For a brief period, I agree to try to keep the relationship together if he attended therapy. He did this for a short period and then stopped when his therapist had to stop working due to a family emergency. He chose not to find another therapist. But by this time, the relationship was over. There was no coming back from the multitude of his lies. The more I looked, the more lies I found. I asked him to move down into the space he was using for an office until the annexe work was done and then to move in there.

In the autumn, I ended up in the hospital for ten days because I developed septicaemia from a skin break on my bum that didn't heal. It became infected and spread. In February, I headed to a spiritual conference in California that I had attended for the previous two years. I met Morloki there. I was wearing my collar and arrived all excited about the event. My suitcase was closed with zip ties, and the front desk of the hotel had no scissors to lend me. They suggested that I go to information and ask there.

I bounded up to the information desk and came up short as I noticed him. His energy hit me first full of challenging heat and sharp edges. I could not look at him for more than a moment without flushing. He was using a pair of wire cutters on a piece of jewellery. Time for my professional persona. With more force (and volume) than I meant, I asked, 'Does anyone have a pair of scissors I can borrow. I need to cut a zip tie from my luggage'. He told me I could borrow the wire cutters. 'I promise I'll return them as soon as I can.', I said as I grabbed them and looked for a quick escape. 'Yes, you will' I heard Morloki say, hearing the humour in his voice 'You don't want the bad karma if you don't return them'. I took off into the crowd, the hair on my neck prickling, a deep chuckle at the edge of my hearing. I shook my head as if to rid myself of the sound of that laughter. Anyone watching saw me shake as though I was shaking off an entity – like a dog shaking off after a downpour.

Back in my room, I worked to steady my breathing, shook my head to clear it again and picked up my cell phone. I rang my play partner, who was busy, so I left a message. I was cross. I was horny and in need of relief. It surprised me how agitated I was. Again, I tried to clear my head. I rang one of my sisters and arranged to meet for dinner in 15 minutes. Snipping off the zip tie, I rifled through the suitcase and dressed to attract attention as per Tom's instructions. Tom told me to practice my skills, to get comfortable with the attention he said that I routinely attracted because I was a submissive pain slut. I was almost out of the door before I remembered to grab the wire cutters. A trickle of sweat slid down my back to the hollow above my ass.

I settled down with my sister at a table in the café restaurant for a needed meal, though I expected nothing genuinely palatable. We were catching up on the week's news as I spied Morloki walk by. I shouted 'back in a minute' and practically lept the café wall to catch him, out of breath and touching him on his shoulder, handed the wire cutters and said 'I told you I'd return them ASAP.' (It was sometime later before I realised that I had reached out and touched him – despite the general 'don't touch' sign. I am usually cautious about not invading physical space.) I didn't take in his response. I was away too quickly, back to safety at my sister's table. My hand was tingling. 'You must have run quickly' she said. 'Why?' I asked, and she replied, 'You are so flushed.' I was practically panting and my panties were soaked. I tangled my fingers in my collar. I fobbed my sister off with a line about being out of shape. And in the distance, there was that laughter again.

When I finally returned to my room, sleep would not come. The weekend progressed and I spent more and more time at the information desk. I could see Morloki had well developed that 'harmless' facade but in a room full of people who were supposed to be able to see – why was no one noticing those delicious edges and the tongues of fire? Again, I heard the laughter and shook my head. Morloki raised an eyebrow as if to ask 'problem?'. I smiled and blushed. Off I bound again, conscious of his eyes on me. By this point, I had learned his name, and the next time I checked in with Tom, I mentioned him.

And so the weekend continued. I found myself drawn back to the information table when he was there. I was aware of at least one woman's angry and disapproving gaze, but this made no real impact. I finally hooked up with my play partner for a quick session (which was rough as he was none too pleased to see me collared by another and his access to me changed and controlled by another). Again, I found a reason to be at the table. I brought down my jewels to show him – custom-designed slave chains – made with moldavite, hematite and large pearls, a second set made of blue topaz, larimar and pearls. His appreciation was obvious, and I found myself drawn further in, flames licking around me. I have no idea what our conversation was. I remember commenting on the jewellery he was making – apart from that, I am on autopilot – babbling no doubt – noting his scent, the variety of chocolate tones to his skin and my desire to touch, to taste, the flames, his humour and that ever-present edge – so tempting, so enticing.

I remember that someone who was offering me a treat asked me what kind of chocolate I liked – milk or bittersweet or dark, and I replied 'Yes' as I imagined what he would taste like. I should have admitted then I was playing with fire.

One conversation I remember ever so starkly. Morloki was alone at the desk, and as I approached, another beautiful black man approached. He joked about people being nervous after all, two black men congregating was cause for nerves. Without missing a beat, my response was 'In my world that is a smorgasbord and cause for great celebration'. I am sure I turned crimson while both of them laughed.

We exchanged contact details. I knew that he understood my collar, but he never said a word. I remember being so cross that he didn't mention it as I did not feel I could mention it first. The subject never came up, and I left the conference feeling that the contact was significant and distinctly unfinished. I returned to Tom with permission to correspond and hoped that I would hear from him again soon. I received a thank-you note upon my return home that warmed my heart and made my pussy wet. We both joined Facebook at the same time and began to chat. It quickly became apparent that he knew my collared status and the conversation turned to discuss this – along with an intensified flirtation. We quickly got to a point where I knew that I needed Tom's permission to go further.

I headed back to Los Angeles in May to see Tom. I stayed at the Erwin Hotel in Venice Beach. My relationship with Tom was often challenging. He had a girl he wanted me to play with, but he had not told her about me until after he collared me. Not surprisingly, Eve hated the whole situation. It made everything more cumbersome, and Tom was no fun at all when he didn't get what he wanted. He alternately blamed me and blamed her.

Morloki invited me to lunch and Tom agreed to allow this. We met at an Indian restaurant. My response to him was just as intense as it was the first time we met. We were sitting and awaiting the food when his face changed and Loki talked to me about what happened with Damien and about the contract I entered with him (Loki). I was stunned. There was so much information pouring out of his mouth that he could not have known unless Loki was talking through him. We finished the meal with a discussion about a ritual to resolve some outstanding trauma and to re-write the contract. Morloki came back to the meal with only partial knowledge of what had happened. He walked me to my car and then bent me back over the hood as he kissed me, causing me to lose my breath and stopping traffic.

I went back to the hotel, overwhelmed. I talked to Tom about all that happened, and he wanted to meet Morloki. Morloki joined us at my tattoo appointment the following day. Lantz was doing the beginnings of the dragon that day. Having the two of them there, putting their energy into the mix while Lantz cut into me raised the intensity and the energy tenfold during the session. Lantz and I had only just started working together then. Eleven years later, we know each other much better, and he knows my body almost as well as my lovers do. His art covers many parts of my skin, and includes tributes to my Patrons, my actual collar, and marks for significant transitions.

Presence is fundamental to connection. So rarely are people fully present that most of us notice someone who is present. We talk about them having presence, gravitas or charisma, and many believe that this is some inborn talent. In actuality, presence is a skill that we can learn. It goes beyond what most people employ as mindfulness. To be fully present, a person must be wholly embodied and grounded in the moment. The elements involved in presence are embodiment, grounding in time, a high level of awareness of what is going on around them (grounding in space), and full focus/attention on what is going on moment to moment.

What does it mean to be embodied? An embodied person sits comfortably within their skin. They are integrated physically, psychologically, spiritually, intellectually, emotionally. They often seem larger than life, as many people are never fully embodied. Some choose to stand next to their bodies or not fully inhabit their bodies because their bodies are places filled with physical pain. Others because their bodies contain too many triggers for psychological pain, trauma, and shame. To embody an idea is to give it tangible, physical form. Many of us only embody ideas but never genuinely inhabit our bodies for more than moments at a time.

Congruence is when all parts of us are in sync, all aspects of life are in sync. Carl Rogers, an eminent psychologist, used this term to mean when our ideal selves and our experience are consistent or very similar. This goes side by side with authenticity (living life following the needs of your inner being rather than following the demands of society or your early life conditioning). Presence is more natural when you are living authentically and when you are congruent.

When you are not aware that these are skills, you are more likely to think of the person with presence as magical. They are often exciting to be around. They usually have captivating energy that has a physicality to it that can be hard to describe. Part of this is the intensity of focus they have on whatever they are doing, and on the people they are interacting with.

Having all of someone's attention focused on you is delicious. It can also be frightening. It creates vulnerability. Often we feel as though someone can see into us or see through us. If you have a trauma history, this can feel even more frightening. Being vulnerable has often come to mean being at high risk and even at risk of death. But being vulnerable is necessary for any intimacy. This is one area that we have to work to resolve. If we learn presence and congruence, it is easier to learn how to make ourselves vulnerable and noticed when it is safe to do so

XIII

SURRENDER

I wrote this piece later in my relationship with Morloki, and yet it
feels apt here because of the part of my story that follows.

Cooking at the Aga
Sweat beads between my breasts as I add
A pinch of this
A dash of that
You bury your face in my neck
Pressing into me as I sway my hips
Singing that baritone so creamy
The rhythm of our bodies enters the pot
Our home cooking
Simmering on the stove
Our kisses soul food
My body your platter

Ravenous you feed until all that is left is thick gravy
Juice dripping from your lips, I kiss you, lick you clean
'Never leave the table hungry.'

I wrote this second piece later as part of the blush report, a daily check-in required by another of the dominant people that I served. I have always blushed quickly and so profoundly that for ages, my nickname was Red. People who were not in the know thought it was because of my red hair. This piece is also appropriate for the next part of my story.

Today's colour is rust inspired by chains, irons, the dried blood that stains the iron blade .... the one with the bone handle....used to create the sacrament mixed with the other precious fluids.... creating, amongst other things, red tears.

Bent before the Altar, I worship God and Goddess. My marks of service clear in the torchlight. Tattoos, cuts, bruises, grazes. The brand burning on the brazier. Sweat and smoke stinging my eyes. Drums throb louder softer louder softer louder louder closer closer. Whip lands between shoulder blades. 9 tails graze ass cheeks. Staccato beat of the whip shoulders to feet and back to shoulders. Hoarse cries in syncopation. Drums pound faster skin burning. Cries become moans as they make the cutting. Smith's arms wound in muscle, wrapped round me, holding me still. Smouldering ash from the sacrificial flame rubbed into the cutting. Shriek pain/pleasure cuts the night as the last drum beat fades. I collapse into the arms that hold me, tears covering His chest, mingling with His sweat, dripping into the cup that holds the rum. Vessel open, purified, marked as Theirs. Contract signed again.

Morloki and Tom talked. I was haunted anew by memories of Damien and started having nightmares for the first time in years. It felt as though I were stalked through my dreams. It was time for me to do another piece of personal work, to unravel another strand left from Damien and all that came after. It was time also to revisit the ritual I did that initially brought Damien into my life. As Loki spoke to me through Morloki (No, the name is not a coincidence. He chose it deliberately.), I asked about the contract and we all decided that it would be a good idea to create a ritual that would further banish Damien's shade from stalking me and take the time to re-work and renew the contract between myself and Loki. This was a complicated piece of ritual. Morloki had plenty of experience and since Loki was in-residence part of the time, negotiating what needs to be included was easier than it otherwise might have been. Tom was narcissistic and believed that he had plenty of experience in this realm; however, he did not. Thankfully, he stepped back and allowed Morloki and I to craft the ritual. Tom's principal motivation was to make sure he was foremost in my thoughts, and he knew he was not because of Damien. He said, 'I cannot compete with a ghost.' This is a telling comment as Tom and I had a consensual relationship, and the intrusive thoughts of Damien were non-consensual, traumatic. Yet to Tom, they were the same. Even at that stage in my life, I was involved with someone who didn't understand the meaning of consent and who would punish me for my past. In talking about my experience with Tom, it became clear that he saw me as having been a temptress and believed I invited Damien's treatment of me. I should have taken heed as soon as I realised this. I did not. I still wasn't able to step away from the internal voice that said, 'Don't be silly. You are exaggerating' to whatever I was feeling.

If you have done no ritual work, ritual magick, please know that there are rules that create a modicum of safety when doing this work. The type of work we undertook was risky. It felt somewhat like when Sam and I initially did the sex magick, and I shouted 'Bring me a Master'. Loki found the parallels amusing. When dealing with Gods and particularly trickster Gods, it is essential to be exact with your words and to make sure you have left no details out or left any loopholes.

The whistling was loud in my ears as I worked out the parts to this ritual. Loki's whistling told me I was missing something, yet I was damned if I could figure out what the fuck it is. He chuckled in my ears. 'You will figure it out, and it will be too late' he said as I felt hands around my throat ever so lightly, feathers brushing and then gently squeezing until I gasped. Finally, we worked the details out. Loki asked for a price. He wanted to fuck my ass. Morloki could not be the conduit for this one. Nor could Tom. I asked my playmate who practiced magick and knew Loki well, or so I thought, if he would be the conduit. He agreed without thinking it through. To be a conduit means being God ridden - Loki would take possession of his body and use it to his ends. My playmate was too excited about the opportunity to fuck me in the ass to pay attention to what that might feel like and what it would mean.

We set up time and space. We gathered the supplies to create an unbroken circle (safe space), to call Loki and others in, tributes for the Gods who help, food for after, plenty of water. I prepared myself with a ritual purification bath. Morloki wrote the draft contract, and the draft of the ritual, and Tom approved it.

The day of the rite arrived, and everything went smoothly. We raised the energy high. Loki quenched his thirst through pounding into my ass until my playmate exploded. The contract was signed and witnessed. My playmate was traumatised, and I spent an hour helping him to come back into himself, to ground and to deal with some of his feelings. He has mostly avoided me since this ritual. I found out last year that he was so traumatised, he was still talking about it 10 years later. He told a mutual friend about the experience.

After the rite, I was more settled. Tom was thrilled with the results. He invited Morloki over and told him he wanted to reward him for his help. He knew that Morloki desired me. That was obvious. Tom sat down with Morloki and magnanimously said to him, 'Listen, man, please enjoy her. And don't leave the table hungry.' Morloki paused and replied, 'You don't want to say that to me. Tell me what you are happy with - how much time, what I can do.' Tom shook his head and like the king of the castle rewarding a loyal subject spread his arms and said 'No man. Really. Don't leave the table hungry'. Morloki looked at Tom intently and once again said 'Are you sure?' Tom got annoyed and said 'Yes' in clipped tones. Morloki's wide grin spread across his face as he said, 'Why thank you.' I shivered. I saw the predator's teeth rather than a smile. I wondered why Tom didn't see this. In the 14 ½ years I have known Morloki, I have only ever seen a smile with teeth showing in two situations: 1) Because I have asked him to smile properly 2) Because the predators are peeking out and it is decidedly not a smile. Years later, Morloki mused that Fenris is always ravenous, so telling him not to leave the table hungry meant that he would never leave.

I spent more time with Morloki during the rest of the trip. We had not yet fucked. Despite permission, he waited because of his situation. I returned in the summer at the beginning and the end. Whenever I got permission, I saw Morloki. Things with Tom were not going well. Eve still didn't want to spend time with me. We had two threesomes, and during one I ended up outside in the car park talking with my playmate because Eve had a meltdown. Tom tried so hard to make her feel ok; he ended up being awful to me. I left that date early and went back to LA to my hotel.

Back in the UK, I spoke to Morloki often. I felt him with me, and when I masturbated, I felt him inside me. It amused him when I asked if he was aware of me when I was self-pleasuring. 'Of course. Can't you feel me?' he asked. I was amazed at the depth and intensity of our connection. This was not the first time I experienced a connection like this. When I hadn't spoken to Sereth in months, if I was thinking about him or talking about him, he would be in touch - often within hours but at the most a couple of days. I feel him with me all the time. The same is true for Frost. All I need do is focus on either of them. And Morloki remains with me no matter what I am doing, who I am with, or where I am. Distance means nothing.

During the next trip, Tom didn't make time for me even though I flew over from the UK. I was bored hanging around the hotel and got permission to drive up to the Antelope Valley where there was a pagan gathering happening and Morloki was attending and working the crowd. Grudgingly, Tom allowed me to go but told me I couldn't stay overnight, and he would call me and let me know when he would be free so I could head back to him. I didn't pack clothes for the next day. I left everything at Hotel Erwin and just brought my laptop, phone, basic toiletries in case I wanted to freshen up. I reserved a hotel room, so I had somewhere for privacy. It became clear by 5 pm that Tom would not make time for me and I had to buy something to wear that evening and the next day. While I was there, Morloki and I finally fucked. By the time we physically came together, I was already crawling out of my skin. It was a great first experience. Morloki seemed surprised at how much I was enjoying him and told me he believed that there was something wrong with him because his wife had not wanted to have any sex with him in years. 'There is nothing at all wrong with you. Your wife doesn't fancy men that's why she won't fuck you' I said. I figured this out by watching her for a few hours.

Back in LA, Morloki visited me at Hotel Erwin. The sex was ferocious. When Tom finally made time for me, we didn't fit well together. He beat me past where I was comfortable because he was angry. I was silent around him. I was trying hard not to make him angry and wondered if I could tolerate this anymore. I left a suitcase with Tom, so I didn't have to keep carrying dress-up clothes and toys back and forth. I lost everything in that suitcase when we split up. I left for home with rug burns on my wrists, knees, feet. Bite marks everywhere. Some bruising was so deep that I couldn't sit comfortably. Tom refused to speak with me. I didn't understand what angered him. Perhaps I was showing too much interest in Morloki. More likely it was because his vision of having Eve and me and then adding others was not coming to fruition. He pontificated about 'true slaves' as though we lacked in discipline or training. He neglected to consider that by not telling Eve of his plan or even telling Eve he intended to place me above her, he caused this upset.

In mid-September, I headed down to Glastonbury for the weekend with Neil to clear my head. We spent lots of time talking and finally, I removed Tom's collar. He had been alternately ignoring me and making unreasonable demands, including financial ones. Morloki told me he wished to collar me. I climbed to the top of Glastonbury Tor, taking the steeper direct route as I have always done in life. I was on the phone with Morloki the whole way. I entered the tower, and the wind was rushing through. A man walked through in a black hat with a black dog. He smiled at me and tipped his hat and then, when I turned around, disappeared. Papa Legba had made his presence known.

I knelt at the edge of the top of the Tor - looking out at the vista before me. I removed the collar and set it on the ground next to me. I stated clearly that I no longer belonged to Tom. It was 11 September 2009. Morloki stated his desire to own me and asked if I would accept his collar. I said yes, and it was done. I headed down the Tor and went with Neil to have a meal. My phone ran off the hook after I took the collar off. Tom knew. I didn't want to talk to him. He sent a message to Morloki, saying he wanted to talk. He told Morloki that he knew I had taken my collar off. He asked what was going on and Morloki told him that above all he was my friend and he wouldn't tell Tom anything that I had said I didn't want him to share. Tom was furious. He was threatening and shouting at Morloki, who hung up on him. Tom called back twice and finally said, 'You have taken her, haven't you? She is yours now.' Morloki quietly said, 'I warned you. You told me not to leave the table hungry, and I warned you. I am always ravenous.' Tom tried to be adult about this and wished Morloki well but 30 minutes later phoned him back and was threatening and shouting. He wanted to meet with Morloki. Morloki agreed. Morloki was happy with the resolution, and Tom stopped bothering me.

Morloki and I began our journey together from that day. He moved out of his house at the beginning of October and formally separated, though he has been separated for ages. I informed my son's father that I was in a serious relationship. My son told me he couldn't wait to see Morloki. Before Morloki and I were anything other than friends, my son said to me that when we went to LA, we would visit Morloki. At the time, I was with Tom, and so I told my son we were visiting Tom, but we would see Morloki. My son was six and very insistent that we would visit Morloki, not Tom. By the time I took my son to LA, we were visiting Morloki. But before this, Morloki visited us at home. My son was getting out of his father's car, having just returned from school as I pulled up with Morloki. We got out of my car. My son ran and hurled himself into Morloki's arms and gave him a huge hug. He told Morloki he was waiting for him. The relationship between them remains this close to this day.

Many people scoff at spiritual connection and energy. I am a scientist, and so I am meant to scoff at this as well. My experience does not allow me to deny the spirit's existence. I have always been intuitive. I have ever had a relationship with the Gods who claim me. I studied Wicca, ceremonial magick, eastern mystical traditions, native American shamanistic traditions. I let my intuition tell me where to go. I opened myself, and I listened. I made myself a vessel.

This has never been easy for me. Opening myself requires trust and faith. Making myself a vessel requires surrender. I am and remain a control freak. I must practice surrender every day. I gain peace, wisdom, and joy as well as challenges through my relationships with the Divine. There are symbols on my body from many cultures. I have offended some and they talked about appropriation. The logos on me are of those who claim me. It is a strange mix of cultures. On my back is the Kabbalistic tree of life, Fenris the Wolf, the Dragon wraps around from my right breast to my lower back (whose name is only known to pack members), and Oshun. On my right thigh, Papa Legba's sign. On my left thigh, Thor and Loki. On my right shoulder,

Erzulie. On my right shoulder, Ogun's cauldron and my logo - the yin yang inside an 8 pointed star for integrating sacred sexuality. On my left calf, the Owl. On my bum, the hummingbird (transformed from the original dove). Our family crest on my right calf. My collar circles my right ankle. On my left ankle is the Hamsa. On my right shin is the Phoenix. And on my left forearm, the eye of Ra, the scarab, the ankh and the wings of Isis. Each time I am marked, the ritual opens me further. My Gods demand much of me.

I can no longer have sexual relationships with people who don't understand the spiritual, sexual energy and connection. I don't do pick up play or hook-ups. Sharing my energy with someone is too intimate and taking in their energy impacts me at such a deep level that I must take care. The more I surrender to this energy connection, the more fulfilling my relationships are, the better the physicality. I am surrounded by people who I am connected to emotionally, physically, energetically, intellectually and spiritually.

I teach energy play, which starts with being able to perceive the energy as separate from emotion and physical sensation. Learning to move energy and to understand that all energy is the same - no matter how you have generated it, no matter what the source - gives people more control, more agency. These are skills that can be taught. If you will learn and practice, you can become quite adept. There is no quick route to adepthood that doesn't involve intense trials and lots of pain on all levels. If you want the fast way, the challenges are steeper. Consider carefully as you may wish to take the slower winding route. Both paths end up at the same place.

XIV

THE REAL JEZEBEL

I wrote this piece after a man with whom I had a consensual liaison lied and told people that I pursued and seduced him. He had told my Master and I that he was single, but he was in a relationship. When the woman found out about his liaison with me, he blamed me. He called me all manner of slut, whore, and finally, he called me a Jezebel and a temptress.

Jezebel was not a fallen woman. In the original text, Jezebel was a Phoenician princess who became the Queen by marrying King Ahab. She convinced the King to convert to her pagan religion and then had several Jewish prophets murdered. She entered battle with the prophet Elijah. Once Ahab had died, their sons acceded to the throne. Elijah anointed Jehu as a champion to overthrow the regime. Jehu incited her court officials to kill Jezebel by throwing her from a window. Because of her association with Ba'al, who is deemed a false prophet when Elijah battles many Ba'al religion prophets and proves the God powerless, Jezebel becomes associated with false prophets and fallen women. It is from this derivation that we see her seducing men away from the true God to a life of depravity.

In Judaism, the emphasis is on the fact that she was a false prophetess or a sorceress. Men are at risk from this evil woman. The statement is, 'One cannot suffer a prophetess to live.' In this biblical text, I understand the emphasis on her evil. The Bible is patriarchal.

The emphasis is on her ability to tempt but no focus on his response. He is tempted away – the lesser sin – and she as the temptress, is targeted as evil and killed. They admonish him.

How do we continue to buy into this mythos? A man does nothing to advertise that he is in a relationship and a woman approaches him. She is the pursuer initially. And why not? He is free, and she is free to make that contact. They dance, and it comes down to negotiation. He still maintains that he is free and single. They get together a couple of times over months.

It is after the last time they get together that she discovers he is in a committed monogamous relationship. She learns this not from him, but another. How then can she be the temptress? What did she do to target this so-called committed man? And why is it that women are all too ready to continue to treat him with respect but to treat the woman he had a sexual interlude with like a whore, an evil temptress? They treat her as though she has transgressed against the sisterhood. He is still addressed as Sir and excused for his transgression. After all, he is male, and she seduced him. The woman should have known better.

Hmmm, I suppose we all should be psychic. We should never trust a man to be honest about his status – not even those who are pillars in the community. Why do we do this to each other? We do sometimes target men who belong to other women. We act like there is some extreme shortage of men and continue to raise their already over-inflated opinions of themselves.

Please don't misunderstand. I love men. I've worked hard to move away from the dishonesty in relationships that makes it impossible to have respect and trust. Trust is a necessity, particularly in a power exchange relationship. I am flirtatious, and I am seductive. I will pursue a man that takes my fancy. This behaviour is all with the permission of my Master.

I have discovered repeatedly when you scratch the surface on many people; you reveal their rigid upbringing.

What gives you the right to blame me? What gives you the right to the details of my experience? I felt defiled when you questioned me. I'm still not sure I made the right decision. You were not a part of that transaction. What your partner did was wrong, but I did not know you were his partner at the time of the encounter.

I did nothing not negotiated in advance with my Master. My Master spoke to both of us that evening; I had no reason to hide. I had no knowledge that your partner had a reason to hide.

That he held me in contempt, I do not doubt. Because I aroused his passions and 'made' him stray. Because he needs to hold a woman in contempt to have a sexual relationship with her – not just to do things he finds disgusting or debasing – but those things he wants to do. It was hurtful enough to discover that he held me in contempt, to learn that they cast me as the worst kind of whore was worse. I did not need that judgement from you.

You should direct your anger at him. Not at me. The worst thing I did was to keep this from you when I found out you were

191

his partner. Maybe not my best decision, but I felt that it would be best if he came clean. Both my Master and I worked to get him to do so. We failed. Neither of us could figure out when it would be appropriate to say anything to you, so we did not. We also did not lie when you asked directly.

This was not the first time your partner behaved this way, so I suspect you have known for some time. Why put me in that position? It was horrific and humiliating. I felt awful for you because he betrayed you. You do not deserve to be treated the way he treated you. I did not treat you that way.

I did not deserve to be treated the way he treated me. It was out of respect for you that my Master didn't confront him and tear him a new asshole because he treated me with such disrespect. I begged him not to say anything because I did not want you humiliated. Now you are treating me as poorly as he did. How dare you contact my Master and not me. You want me to be comfortable with you talking to him while I am described as some sort of whore? Sorry, no. You call your partner Sir and treat me as though I have tempted him into evil. I read your writing, but your behaviour belies your words.

I cannot even gain support from any in the community. Out of respect for you, I keep quiet while you post many things to work this through. I am left to sit here quietly enraged – I can't call him out. I can't post in ways that will bring his deception to light, even if I don't call him out directly. I feel constrained expressing my feelings as I don't wish to cause you any more pain.

If I had the moment to think again when you asked me – I would tell you that the details of my encounter with a man I believed to be single are none of your business. I would have said that, but he will lie to you. You said you needed the truth. I needed the experience to retain its form, not be reduced to something sordid. Both of us could not have what we needed.

It is not the first time I have been vilified for my sexuality and my enjoyment of sex. It is not the first time that my path has caused me this type of pain. It is the last time. I will not be quiet through this anymore.

I have had to be quiet at home to protect my son, though his father was the one who broke our vows and though he did so with someone who targeted him and pursued him. She has spoken to the entire world. Everyone hears her side of things, and she is the one who has had support. I have remained dignified and quiet and kept most of my anger for him – as he is the one who violated our vows.

I am tired of keeping quiet. I am tired of behaving with 'dignity' or out of concern for others and allowing people to believe what they wish of me.

I am reminded of when I was raped and held prisoner. Damien destroyed my apartment during the time he held me prisoner there. Then the CSIs made even more of a mess. I couldn't stay there after they captured him and took him off to jail. My best friends, DeeDee and Sam offered for me to stay at their house. I was finally finished showering and wrapped in a robe when in walked a woman I had never met. I remember her long painted pointy nails in my face as she tried to scratch me. She screamed that she would have taken anything willingly from Damien, she would have eaten his shit and thanked him. She would have died for him. How dare I think I was better and put him in jail? DeeDee, in her typical ambivalent style, had invited Damien's live-in girlfriend Debbie to come to stay as she was afraid to go home. I had not even known she existed.

I am reminded of Eve telling me she could never accept me. Tom had not told her I existed until after he visited the UK in March. We had been together since July. He told me she was aware of me. It didn't matter that she had always known he was poly – that she was the third in a relationship of his at first. I remember Eve shouting at me because I was willing to do all the things she was not willing to do and saying I would 'steal' him.

It took me years of therapy and personal growth to come to terms with my sexuality. To learn to feel good about me as a sexual being. To stop feeling disgusting or guilty or ugly for my desires. I deplore experiences that make me go back there – the experiences where I can hear my mother calling me a whore for kissing a boy on the couch when I was 12.

I will not accept this anymore. I refuse.

The man who called me out and blamed me for his infidelity was a well-known figure in the leather community. He took the role of so many men I had known in my life who took no responsibility for when they acted on their impulses and their desires and blamed women for causing them to stray. He and the woman he was in a relationship with made my life miserable within our POC leather community for quite a time. I did not call anyone out in public. I didn't have the confidence to do so. I didn't want to air even more dirty laundry in front of our large social group. This was the repeat of a pattern I experienced many times from the time I was 14 until my late 40s. As a practising sex-positive slut, I was the target for all the shame that these men and women carried around with them.

Targeting me meant that they did not have to take responsibility for their trespasses, their conflicting feelings, and their lack of skills.

I was ashamed of my sexual desires & the intensity of my appetites for many years. I grew up with the message that good girls don't. Good girls don't desire sex. Good girls don't have sex outside of marriage. Good girls don't have sex other than for reproduction. Good girls definitely don't want to have sex with more than one person at a time. I love sex. I want sex a lot, and when I connect with someone, I want to have sex with them. I don't always act on these desires, but the urges are there. For many years, I carried the shame like a millstone around my neck.

Recently I realised that sometime in the last 20 years, I dropped the millstone from my neck and it shattered into pebbles that disappeared as I walked forward in life. I am happy being a slut, enjoying my desires and impulses whether or not I act upon them. In the last 15 years, I have surrounded myself with people who don't judge me for being a slut, and many say that my sluttiness is one of their favourite qualities. I am surrounded by a group of people who are happy to enjoy my sluttiness, partake of my sluttiness and help me get my needs met regularly.

I know that some of my readers will find this hard to understand. Many are still under the spell of the culture that says that women who have strong sexual drives are sluts and sluts are bad. Some find it hard to understand because they don't have strong sexual drives or their drives are confined to one person only. Others are afraid to look at their drives and desires. If I begin to feel judgmental towards these people, I remind myself that for a long time I had lots of shame that I carried too.

As women, they often teach us that other women will compete with us, will try to 'steal' our lovers from us. They teach us that there is a shortage of 'good' mates - be they men or women or non-binary or transgender people. They bring us up to compete in ways that are destructive rather than encouraging. As a result, when a partner is unfaithful, we don't tend to blame the partner. Instead, we blame the other person for the infidelity. The other person had no contract with us. Frequently, they are unaware that their relationship is considered cheating. It is the partner who is to blame for the dishonesty, unfaithfulness, breaking of the rules. So many women still look at the 'other woman' as a Jezebel - a sorceress who sets out to seduce their partner away. They don't look to their partners to take responsibility. Instead, they shore up faulty beliefs that say that their partner has no responsibility for the infidelity and that if the seductress hadn't set her sights on him, he would have remained faithful. They ostracise and attack the other woman without even seeking an explanation from their partners.

The man who labelled me Jezebel has often been at events that my Master and I have been at over the last ten years. Occasionally he would try to speak to me, but my Master would intervene. While I was writing this memoir, out of the blue, I received a written apology from him. It was most unexpected and surprisingly real. It seems that experiencing loss in his life has caused him to examine his way of interacting, the things he has done in the past, and he chose to take responsibility for his harmful acts. Even though all of this happened a decade ago, my reaction to this apology was strong. I experienced relief at his acknowledgement he was at fault and that nothing I did deserved how he treated me. Even though I have long since learned to reality test and to trust my internal experience, there remains a part of me that is that little girl and the young woman who was always gaslit, who was told that reality was defined by others. The relief was the confirmation that I was correct in how I felt, that my experience of his behaviour as abusive was not the result of my imaginings; it was reality-based.

XV

CONTRACTS & AGREEMENTS

Two pieces from the time of this part of my journey.

The Contract...

'Master, what happened to the hard limits thing?'. He chuckles, 'slaves don't have limits...I agreed not to damage you permanently. Did I not?'. 'Yes Master but Grey had a detailed contract and a non-disclosure agreement....' His laughter is deep and raucous. 'So he did. Grey has 50 shades. I only have a few. No need for absolutes.' He ends the conversation by taking me by the throat and plunging balls deep into my cunt.

He's beating my feet with a set of acrylic rods. He drums them to the Prince set that is playing. I am screaming, my face drenched with tears. Oh, Gods, I hate this. His complete and utter enjoyment rolls off him in waves. He will not stop soon. Not until he finally tires or until he can feel something give way in me. When I move from fighting him to accepting what he chooses to give. When I yield entirely, he will make me come while doing this thing that I genuinely hate, enjoying my distress at the mind fuck. After 15 minutes or so I wail, 'Where was this in the contract Master?! I don't remember signing it!' His laughter is sinister. I lose track of time. I yield despite myself, and I feel his joy as I do. The energy explodes through my body - I can feel the blows rise up my spine and out the top of my head. His teeth are at my throat. He growls as he chews. He tells me to cum, giving me the release I so badly crave. The last thing I hear before sleep takes me is 'Don't you remember the magic ink Jewels' and the wolf howling.

We are talking about bastinado and the beating that Sir gave me - viciously using a dragon's tail amongst other implements. 'I don't remember signing a contract' I say to Master who cannot stop laughing. 'I don't remember this being in the contract if I signed one. Where was the clause that says whoever you choose gets to beat my feet with various awful things until I cry?' Amidst your laughter, you ask, 'Is this slave humour? You remember you consented, right?' 'Yes, Master' I say. 'But where was the contract that said I agree to no limits except you and whoever you choose will do your best not to cause me harm as defined by permanent damage?" "You remember when you agreed. You swore a blood oath, " you remind me. I am quiet, remembering the various rituals that cemented my overall contract. 'Hmm.' I grunt, and you bite at my nipples. I moan as you move lower, tonguing and chewing my stomach and then biting my pubic mound. You dip your tongue into my thick sweet juice and bite at my clit, causing me to throw my legs around your neck and squeeze. You nibble and suck and lick until you hear me panting, begging to cum, pressing my pussy up into your mouth, grabbing you by the ears and pulling you further into me. I am so close.

Suddenly you stop, raise your head - looking at me with a smirk on your face 'Did you want me to tell Jack that he needs to stop beating your feet because it is not in the contract? Did you want to give him a list of limits? Shall I let you decide what happens to you - at my hands or his?' The laughter in your voice has an edge to it. "God, no Master. No limits. No bossy slave." I reply. " Good, I'm glad that is settled," you say as you bend to lick me again and this time you don't stop until I'm screaming in orgasm bathing your face in my sticky sweet nectar.

As my pulse calms, you slide up my body and plunge your dick into me in one clean stroke. You fuck me fast and hard, fingers digging into my hips, my thighs, my ass. You groan as you cum and that sets me off again. My pulse is out of control. You bite into my shoulder, deeper, until you draw just a drop of blood. My world explodes... I crack wide open - energy rushing like fireworks in the summer sky. 'You are sure you don't want to see that contract again?' you snicker. 'No, Master' I rumble. 'I remember signing it - the contract that says this slave has no limits... I remember consenting to all of you' "Good. I was just checking, " you chuckle.

Later in the wee hours of the morning, lying together wrapped up in your arms... a mischievous grin crosses my face.. 'Master... are you sure I signed that contract... the one that says you can beat me with any implement at any time? The one that says I will take what you choose to give me?' I can't help but giggle. 'Yes jewel' you reply, smacking me on the ass, pulling me into you 'be still and go to sleep' you say. So I do.

And the second piece which illustrates the intensity of the struggle at times. This is mind fuck at its best. If I do what he wants me to do, he will punish me. If I don't, he will punish me.

No, I Won't.

"Yes, you will" I hear you growl in my ear. "No. I. Won't" I reply, my mouth filling with liquid. I shake my head and hope that the urge diminishes. I feel your hands on my waist; your teeth graze my neck. "No" I maintain as you bite deep. My knees buckle. Your arms hold me up as you feed on my neck. There is a direct connection between your teeth in my throat and my pussy. I feel scalding juice come from both points and smell the metallic musky tang of my blood. I pull myself up and begin to struggle again. I growl. 'No. I. Won't' as I try to turn in your arms and feel my mouth about to overflow.

"Yes, you will" you laugh into my ear, your hands wrapping in my hair and turning me around. I dig my nails into your chest, lower my head to resist the urge, now almost overwhelming. Your body shakes with laughter, even as I draw blood. Your dick is hard and pushes into me.

I struggle to stay close as I know if I push back, I will. I cannot resist much longer. The air crackles with the energy surrounding us. You grip my breasts, digging into that scar, the one Loki helped to place there when I was 19. I scream with rage, lean back and spit full in your face. I wail as I realise I lost control, surrounded by your laughter; look at the glee on your face as my spit drips from your chin. Your eyes sparkle with anticipation as you strike out.

The first strike hard across my face draws more rage from me. "I told you you would, bitch" you exclaim "And I told you what would happen". You flip me over and push me down onto the carpet, hitting me the whole while. I cannot keep still for this beating. I cannot stop myself from struggling, though I know that the more I struggle, the worse it will be. You claw my back and ass raw, beating me in between the clawing, using your full strength with each strike, holding me down with your body.

My struggling brings me up onto my knees as you shove them apart. Tears course down my face as I curse you as I have never done before. All it does is make you laugh as you beat me harder. Despite my struggling and my professed resistance when you thrust you slide into me with ease. My pussy is hot and dripping natural lube. I am bent back like a bow, gripped by the hair as you pound into me. I collapse onto my stomach as I feel your teeth close on the back of my neck again. I freeze, relaxing into your bite, cry my submission as your claws bite into my tits, blood flowing from the wounds. I cannot form words. My jaws and teeth are not the right shape. I want to beg to come, and I cannot say anything. My moans turn to whimpers and grunts, deep growls in my ears.

"Come" you growl in my ear. I feel your tongue lap the blood from my neck. I bellow my release as energy tears through my body, sharp peaks, one after the other until I collapse into tremors. You lick the blood from the rug burn, the welts, the bites, coaxing me to come again, squirting until I am completely spent. The last thing I say to you when I finally regain the strength. 'No. I. Won't'.

Morloki and I enjoy playing on our own, but wanted to spend more time playing in public. There is an extra energy that enters when you play in public. All the people watching and aroused by your play add their energy to yours. It isn't easy. You have to be able to stay focused on your scene and also to harness the power from the watchers. Sometimes people interfere in negative ways. Other times their energy is not favourable, not pleasant. It takes skill to manage public play effectively and get the most out of it. We played at a local club and had a superb time.

We talked about the structure of our relationship. We agreed on a polyamorous relationship at the beginning. We agreed that as we were entering a 24/7 authority transfer based relationship, he had control over my other relationships. Much later, we talked about this in detail, and I wrote about our 'time-share' method of polyamory. This has evolved to his model of our system: the lake. I have reproduced some of that below. Part of the joy of polyamory is that you can get needs met elsewhere, that your partner doesn't fancy meeting or can't meet. I wanted a D/s relationship with a woman and also wanted one that would be very structured. Everyone I play with is a serious player. We play hard and often for keeps. Morloki agreed to keep an eye out for possible partners for me.

In April, we attended Kinkfest in Portland, Oregon. Portland has the most exceptional atmosphere. It makes freaks feel at home. Even TSA agents work to make the experience a positive one. While waiting in the queue, they joke and do what they can to help us pass the time while we wait and stay in good spirits. The event was OK. There weren't many classes we wanted to attend, and the energy in the dungeon/playroom was odd at times so although we played, we didn't play for long. We ended up spending a lot of time in the vendor room. I noticed them first. As I now know how they identify, I am using their chosen pronouns, but when I met them, I saw them as women - one very butch and the other in between. They were working one of the vendor stalls. Martin noticed me looking and smirked. He looked me up and down, and I blushed from my toes to the roots of my hair. His partner, Jeff, smiled. They said hello to Morloki. 'Say hello girl' Morloki prompted. My mouth was dry. I stumbled 'Hello'. They made leather small talk. (Leather small talk is about events, people you know, kinks, etc.). I added when I could. I regained my tongue and my usual bouncy energy.

We headed over to the corset seller. At that time, my event uniform was a corset and tutu. I love corsets and look great in them. I love to tight lace. I miss how they held me, restrained me, paced my breathing. I can no longer wear them because I have an active hernia. But then, I wore them to my best advantage. I tried on a red leather corset with a matching corset skirt. Morloki had me walk around the whole room. I got some applause, which made me want to hide. I struggled to walk pleasingly, to avoid clumsy. I hoped for grace but was convinced I wouldn't ever get there. Both Martin and Jeff complimented me.

In the summer, we attended Black Beat. This conference was much more our style. It was a POC event. The atmosphere was energetic, and we connected with others quickly. We headed into the Crucible to play as part of the event. I bought Morloki a pair of light up acrylic drumsticks. There was a conversation area with some tables and some couches next to the area. Prince came on and Morloki bent me over a table and drummed on my ass. For the next 45 minutes (the whole of the Prince set), Morloki beat me with his hands, wood sticks, acrylic sticks. When he finally stopped, I was limp. It was an intense beating and a very erotic one, a very satisfying one. When I opened my eyes and looked up, there was a crowd of people sitting around us who were watching. They clapped, and I blushed a deep crimson.

We attended the O'Kink family BBQ hosted by Mistress Max Rulz, for the first time. She held this event in her home and garden. The food was outrageous and the play even more so. People performed. Mistress Max is a fantastic photographer. At one point that day, Morloki was playing with me with steel claws. I opened my eyes and looked down, and Mistress Max was between my legs with her camera taking photos. We had a great time that day and agreed that we would return.

We agreed that we would attend Black Beat the following year and also decided to attend LLC in Los Angeles. Before LLC, Morloki and Martin were in touch. We all agreed to meet at LLC and a play date was arranged for Martin and I. Martin negotiated parameters with Morloki and interviewed me to find out my kinks, limits, desires, and any limitations. When we met over a drink and bar snacks, Martin and Jeff enjoyed making me blush. It tickled Morloki to see how flustered I was. The playdate went exceptionally well, and I asked Martin if he would consider a D/s relationship, if Morloki agreed to it. More negotiation happened, and I began my service to Martin. Martin and Jeff are leather dykes, and there are other family members. I was excited to take my place in a larger family again as when I was running with El, V and C.

Martin provided more structure. I journal and I was expected to learn household rules and rituals. My first trip out there coincided with the coaching course I took (which was based in Portland). The first trip went well. I got along well with Jeff, who is also sadistic and occasionally bit me or pinched me. My interaction with Martin was excellent. I was in chains for the weekend and I loved it. At the beginning of the relationship, I discussed with Martin that I like my sex with my D/s and BDsM. I was clear that I wasn't willing to engage in a D/s and BDsM relationship with someone who would not have sex with me. This was (and is) important to me because this is what turns me on. I didn't want a relationship in which I had to either gain satisfaction during the pain alone, by masturbation or waiting until I was back with Morloki. Martin said that this was no problem. He was into me and was looking forward to fucking me again. One thing about being fucked by a woman is that interchangeable dicks are a thing. It is entertaining to have the option to pick the size and shape you want. Martin had a fucking colossal dick he called Mandingo. He also liked to engage in temperature play so a dick might be warm or ice cold.

For the next 18 months, my relationships grew in tandem. Morloki and I spent as much time together as possible. We attended Black Beat once more, and then it closed and Weekend Reunion took its place. We developed a solid leather family. Time spent relaxing with people who share our views, and our relationship styles was (and is) a blessed relief. There was just one issue with my relationship with Martin: the sex disappeared after the first weekend. The longer the relationship went on, the clearer it was to me that this relationship would not work.

The first Weekend Reunion was a blast. Master and I enjoyed ourselves from beginning to end. One evening we were hungry and ended up eating sushi off our neighbour. This evening finished up with the four of us having a seriously hot time. We hosted the after party in honour of my 50th, and the cake was so fucking delicious that people snuck into the room where it was kept in the middle of the night to get extra pieces to take back to their rooms. We spent time getting to know the Blues and I enjoyed time with Frost and Kimi, remembering how much fun it is to just spend time with other women. After weekend reunion, we went to the O'Kink BBQ again and made new memories.

And then in October, my father was diagnosed with lung cancer. I was devastated. I was due to spend time over Valentine's Day with Martin and Morloki, and I agreed that this was still what I should do. I got to Portland and things were awkward, and I did not understand why. Martin was impatient with me and always angry. Jeff was apologetic and tried to help me succeed. After 24 hours, Martin told me that Jade was coming to visit as well and that I would have to give up the guest room I had been staying in. I was shocked that I didn't know, and I realized Martin had forgotten I was coming and so said yes to Jade but didn't have the guts to tell me. I resolved to make the best of this, but things got worse. Jade cannot stand me because she is jealous of me, and I didn't understand why. Both of them were being cruel, and I wished I could fly down to LA to Morloki. I was furious because it would have been no big deal to do that if Martin had come clean and spending Valentine's Day with my beloved would have been excellent.

I was part of their show for the leather events that weekend. I had fun on stage, but the rest of the time, I was told I was not doing well enough. I was expected to know things without having served Martin like this before. It was clear I was annoying him. By the time I left, I was a mess. I met T at San Francisco airport for coffee and burst into tears. I decided to confront Martin. When I got home, I wrote a respectful letter and requested a conversation. It did not go well. Three weeks went by and then Martin asked to talk. We came to a truce. The family was getting together for IMsL, and they have invited even Morloki. The weekend should be full of family events. I was told there would be playtime. There was some family time, but there was always something going on, that meant playtime didn't happen. I spent more time with Morloki than the rest of the family. This wasn't a problem; it just wasn't what I expected.

Martin presented a class on knife play and cuttings. He needed a second demo bottom. Master agreed that I could be the demo bottom, but no detailed negotiation happened. The scene was hot, and I knew that I was in front of a class full of eager people. Amidst the scene, Martin carved 'toy' into my ass. Martin called me toy as a nickname. I was stunned that he made a permanent mark on my body without discussing it with Master and only with a cursory request for consent from me during the class. There was no way I could say no. It would have significantly embarrassed Martin in front of the class, and I just couldn't do that. I felt coerced, but I couldn't say anything. Master was seething. I begged him not to make an issue of this during the event.

Event over, I headed back home to the UK, and Master headed back home to Los Angeles. As the cutting scarred, I found myself more and more upset. My relationship with Martin deteriorated. It was late May, and I decided to end the relationship. The ending video call was awful. I asked for permission to speak freely and say, 'This isn't working for me. I don't feel you are attracted to me. That's OK. You cannot help your attractions. But I can't serve at this level without mutual attraction, the energy that brings and the sex that comes from that.' I don't know why I expected Martin to be a grown-up and admit that he had no attraction for me and that though he loves me, he agrees that this wasn't working. I knew that was the truth. He would not admit it. Instead, he was furious. He said 'Are you begging for release?'. I did not respond. He asked again and added 'No one leaves me' I formally requested release.

A month later, my father asked me to come home. I knew that I was flying home to say goodbye. He was lucid and told me that Morloki is a good man and that he was pleased I was finally settled. He told me that my son was my greatest achievement. He spoke on the phone with my son. We talked the day away. The next day he was delirious most of the day. I sat with him and my brother, singing to him to try to settle him on the Sunday night as he didn't know where he was, and he was combative. At 2 am, I headed home because I had an early flight. I took off at 8 am. My father died at 8:30 am. When I landed, I opened my iPad and there was a message from my son's father telling me. I got home from the airport and started planning to go back to the US with my son for the funeral.

My son's father was a pain in the ass. He was angry because I told him I didn't want him at the funeral and my mother didn't want him in her home. He insisted that our son needs him, and I told him that my son could gain support from me and that by coming to the funeral he would cause more harm than good. He had a tantrum, but I held firm. I wasn't putting my mother through having to deal with his pretend caring and obsequious behaviour while he spouted lies. My son and I left for NJ. When I returned with my son after the funeral, he took my son away to join friends on holiday. He didn't consider that being in an empty house while grieving my father might be hard for me or that my son and I might need to support each other. He left me on my own. My son called me from the trip crying that he wanted to come home but his father refused telling me he believed it was good for our son to spend time with friends. I was on my own with the dogs, trying desperately to stay grounded as I grieved.

While I was in the US, Martin called to see how I was and gave me his condolences. It was awkward, but I appreciated the contact and the sentiment. T and I had started a relationship, so she checked in on me. I wanted Morloki with me, but my mother didn't know him well yet and didn't approve, so we decided that it would be inappropriate. We spent lots of time on the phone while I went through all the grieving rituals and supported my mother, my grandmother and my brothers. I had little space for my grief. I was home only a few weeks when I went to Portland for my course intensive. It was hard to be there and not see anyone, especially when I was grieving. I returned home again and a couple of weeks later headed to Weekend Reunion. T and M negotiated a double topping scene with me. We were aiming for catharsis, and they whipped me and flogged me. It was hard and fast, and I broke more quickly than usual into a complete catharsis. The whole event brought more cleansing. I was surrounded by debauchery and also by love and connection. The barbecue was fun.

I returned home to the UK. Morloki and I were now together for four years. We finally agreed on a wedding date a year and a bit away and began to prepare. I would bring Morloki to the UK on a spousal visa. We married in the US and then started the process.

XVI

FAMILY

If He makes of me a cup, I am a cup;
I am a dagger if He makes me a dagger.
He is the Writer; I am the pen in His fingers.
Who am I to obey or disobey?
- Jalal-ud-Din Rumi

These pieces illustrate different aspects of my relationship with Morloki, my Master and my husband.

> *This is the blush report for 22 September 2013 at 18:27*
> *BST. Today's colour is Dorothy's Slippers Red inspired*
> *by*
> *Waking in sweat alone in this emperor sized bed*
> *Aching for your caress*
> *Burying my nose in your robe*
> *Petting my pussy in time to the beat I hear in your head*
> *A drummer's syncopated rhythm*
> *Then the soft stroke of the brush*
> *The one that makes that softly rising tinkling sound*
> *Breathing deeper faster*

Tone rising
Colour changing as it moves over my body from pink to
almost dark as an eggplant
Rubbing my hard slippery clitoris as the beat moves to
9/8 time
Increase in tempo, + increase in volume until
Crescendo = splash
As my breathing settles, I click my heels three times
hoping to bring you home.

Second piece

The ice and fire games
Teeth at my neck kicking the temperature higher
The alpha bitch that rises in me when you tease me
That wanting, that desire that drives the flames ever
higher
Until the bitch is growling and spitting, unable to speak
words
Only able to make the sounds - the yelping, the howling
When I eventually surrender to that primal force, you
can see the blood pulsing at my throat
Across my breasts, my neck, my forearms and wrists, the
veins rise
Adrenalin courses through
Gods help anyone who crosses me or threatens you at
that time.
Gods help the unmannered and disrespectful who
approach then, assuming that a slave could not be your
twin soul

Assuming that this usually friendly, open girl suffers
fools even for a nanosecond or has patience and
restraint when pushed to rage
The fire must burn through me before it soothes the
beast
Or the ice push through me
And you will not allow that until you have taken all
you wish from me.
I don't think they know what a predator looks like.
Don't they realise that often your smile does not reach
your eyes?

The Rumi piece at the beginning of the chapter describes well what I strive for in my surrender to Morloki and in my relationship with my Gods. I have always loved this poem, and much that Rumi wrote reflects flavours of surrender.

Morloki and I married in the gay Catholic church in North Hollywood. They were happy for us to have our reception there as well. As a wedding gift, one of Morloki's best mates DJ'd for us (and he is an excellent DJ at that). T was my maid of honour and her partner Brian was Morloki's best man. Morloki's friends, set decorators extraordinaire, decorated the space for us with flowers and props from Omega Cinema Props (where he worked). The space was so romantic, somewhat noir and perfect for us. Initially, we planned to have three weddings: one on the west coast, one on the east coast and one in the UK. In the end, the west coast is the only one that happened. We did this on a budget, so we made the reception a potluck. I found a great house on AirBnB with a decent kitchen. I spent a couple of days cooking a ton of food for the reception dinner.

I love to cook for the people I love. Some of it is cultural. Though my mother was never much of a cook, my grandmother was always cooking something delicious. Jewish people use food to show love, for comfort, to share with friends and family. A guest never comes to a Jewish home without being offered something to eat, no matter what the occasion or situation.

My son and I arrived in LA a week early, and the three of us ran errands, picked up the marriage license, and spent some time having fun before the other people got into town. My son and my husband had matching outfits for the wedding and they looked fantastic. My love for Morloki grew exponentially while watching him with my son. He is the role model I wanted for my son: A good man who works hard and takes care of the people in his life. He has stayed that excellent role model and taught my son most of what he needs to know about being a man at each new stage of life. He loves my child unconditionally, and for that, I will forever love him in a way that I cannot explain. It feels like my heart is so full it will burst.

Our wonderful friends from the Green Man on Lankershim conducted the pagan ceremony. Jill sang 'At Last' as I walked in on the arm of my son who gave me away because my father had died. My mother and both my brothers came to see me get married for this third time. All of them took part in the ceremony. Most of the other guests are friends of Morloki's except for a half dozen of our leather family and a few friends we have in common. The photographer was a kink friend of ours who knew us well and our wedding pictures reflect his knowledge of us. The videographer was a friend of Morloki's.

The wedding was brilliant. Morloki added an extraordinary part to the ceremony where he pledged his love and care for my son. It was so beautiful it moved my son to tears. The magick was completely present during this ceremony. Positive energy surrounded us and so much love. I finally married someone who loves all facets of me and does what he can do to encourage me to live present, congruent, authentically and all of me. This is no small accomplishment. We danced – to the Time Warp, to Soul Train. We danced the hora, and I fell on my ass. I laughed, got up and kept dancing. My son and I did a special dance to 'Putting on the Ritz'. Morloki and I did our first dance to 'Fly Me to the Moon'. The food was delicious. One leather friend flew down from northern California and brought cooked wings with her on the plane. Everyone ate well and took some food home with them. The cake was incredible. I have an intense sweet tooth, and this cake was perfect. Our families sent us home to begin our wedding night since we only had two nights together before I had to leave Morloki behind and they all stayed and cleaned up the church.

We arrived back at the house and there was a trail of rose petals to our bedroom and on the bed. T and my son decorated for us! Our wedding night was scrumptious. T took my son out the next day so we could have the day alone. It was a beautiful day, but also a difficult one. I never liked to say goodbye to Morloki, but leaving my husband behind was somehow worse.

We started the immigration process with the help of a lawyer in the UK. She predicted that his visa would come through in March, so we planned for Morloki to emigrate in April. He organised with his brother to make the cross-country trip from Los Angeles to Atlanta so he could put some stuff in storage near his brother and then he flew out of Atlanta. Organising his retirement and sorting out his pension getting started became more difficult than expected.

Money was tight, and so things were stressful. In March, Morloki's father died. I flew out to be with him and his family for the funeral and then returned home.

My son's father and I had agreed that we were all going to share the house, the parenting and the bills. I knew I would pay for more than anyone, but he was supposed to get a job. He had not bothered to get a job at all from the time I gave birth. We agreed he would go back to work when our son was in full-time school, but he always found a reason not to work. Even when we divorced, he felt entitled to do nothing and expected me to support him. One week before Morloki was to arrive, my son's father told me he was moving out because he 'can't do this.' I was enraged. Morloki could not drive immediately, and I was working as many hours as I could, so my son's father still needed to get our son to and from school. We had a huge row, but eventually, he agreed to be in the house three days a week to transport my son to school. As soon as summer break began, my son's father moved out and moved in with a girlfriend. He had little contact with our son over the summer.

Morloki arrived, and though I was so happy to be living with him, finally, the financial stress was high. I decided to downsize and was looking for a buyer for my home and also looking for a home for Morloki, my son and I. My son's father did nothing to help to get the house ready for the move. He spent no time getting rid of a large amount of junk he collected over the years, let alone helping with getting the house in order. He bitched at me because I didn't agree to store his stuff until he had a place. He wanted me to pay for storage for him.

During the years he lived in the annexe of our home and I supported him, he got along well with Morloki. We even took two

218

family holidays. Now he was rude and entitled. He behaved as though I were the one who had an affair, and somehow it was my fault that the marriage was over. He took no responsibility for his behaviour in any area of life. It was a difficult period, but Morloki, my son and I got through it together. By the end of the summer of 2015, my son's father moved in with friends and my son visited him every other weekend. This went reasonably well until the end of November 2017.

Adjusting the part-time Master/slave relationship to full-time Master/slave relationship and husband/wife relationship is often a difficult time. Keeping a dynamic at the forefront can be difficult when life intervenes. When the dominant is earning less than the submissive and/or the submissive has the most substantial financial responsibility for the family, and there is financial stress, this can play havoc with the M/s dynamic. Rituals can help to stabilise the situation; however, it is often difficult to commit to consistent routines. It is particularly hard when the dominant partner feels as though they are not doing enough. The submissive partner can become resentful as it thrusts them into a dominant role and they see few ways to redress the balance. It is at times like these that having external support from either knowledgeable professional or mentoring from peers can mean the difference between the M/s dynamic surviving and it disappearing entirely.

People often have trouble understanding the transition to surrender, that point where a slave becomes a slave – handing over authority to the Master. Raven Kaldera speaks about limits (which is a frequent topic when talking about M/s and D/s relationship) and says that the slave does not have limits, but rather it is the Master who has the limits.

The discussion of limits happens in the negotiation, but it is not that the Master agrees to the slave's limits. It is that the Master understands these and that if they have honour and integrity, they will uphold those limits they believe are healthy for the slave. The Master is limited by their integrity, by their honour, by their desire to protect their property and help their property become the best they can be so they can be of most use to the Master.

The struggle is around surrender. In my experience, the difference between a submissive and a slave is where the limits and the control lie. With the submissive, the limits are theirs and as a result some control is theirs. With a slave, the limits belong to their Owner and the control rests with their Owner(s).

It seems simple in writing, but the actual doing can be complex and/or difficult.

Excellent communication skills are always needed if an M/s dynamic is to be successful. At times like these, excellent communication becomes even more critical. At times of stress, people are often quick to interpret reactions, facial expressions, silence in negative ways. They sometimes jump to conclusions. Taking the time to journal, talk with a peer mentor and/or professional before talking with your partner makes it far more likely that conversations will resolve difficulties and help to re-boot the M/s dynamic. Exaggerating some daily rituals can further contribute to shore up the dynamic when most of the day requires either a reversal of roles or is merely mundane.

Often when marriages break up, there are concerns about court involvement. Angry ex or soon to be ex-partners frequently threaten to bring in social services, the police or the courts to 'protect' their children. Most times, these people are well aware that their former partner's behaviour has no negative impacts on their children. They act out of jealousy, anger and spite. In doing so, they raise the stress for their children and all the adults involved.

CHAPTER XVII

PLAYMATES

I wrote this piece for a woman I was involved with for a short period. She met someone and became monogamous.

Though I left plenty of time, I did not count on leaves on the train line slowing things down. The last thing I needed was to be late. I hate being late and she likes it even less. I arrive at the theatre with 4 minutes to spare, hair escaping from my upswept 'do', the one that Annie put together. At least my makeup wasn't mussed or running. My sleeveless black Bettie Page swing dress, red heels and red Balenciaga bag held up well. I am all too aware of my lack of undergarments. I take a deep breath and go to look for her at the entrance to our box. Tonight the show is a jazz concert with a well-known bassist.

I can feel her looking at me and know that I am turning scarlet. Her eyes take in my clothing, hair, makeup, the slight tremor of fear and excitement. I stammer a greeting. She dressed in a black suit with a dark burgundy silk shirt. She is wearing a hat and carrying a leather topcoat. I release an audible sigh of appreciation. She looks smooth and so tasty. She takes my arm, leads me into the box.

The theatre is old, beautifully decorated with sumptuous velvet curtains. The seats are not nearly as comfortable as they are pretty. The box has room for six, but there is only the pair of us. She hands me a glass of crisp champagne and raises her glass in a silent toast. "You look great" she says, and I whisper "thank you, Sir.". "I am not sure about the hair. You don't expect it to stay up, do you?" "No, Sir" I sigh. "good". "Sir, you look fantastic," I say, and she chuckles in response. I am chewing on my lower lip, which she knows signals my desire and my anxiety. Her fingers trace patterns on my neck, causing me to shiver.

The lights dim and the concerts begin. He arm is around me, stroking the side of my breast, my waist. She grunts in approval, feeling no bra strap or panty line. She lets me know she wants me to lift my skirt, so my bare ass is in contact with the seat. I sit down again, feeling her fingers slide into my centre. I gasp and try not to squirm. Her thumb grazes over my clit, already full and pulsing. I bite my lip to stifle a moan and close my legs to trap her hand. She laughs "open girl" she directs, and I comply allowing her deeper access. Within moments, I am ready to cum. She reads my predicament in the line of my body, the tautness of muscles, laboured breathing, pulsing clit, copious juice. 'Cum' she whispers in my ear and bites down hard. I cum hard, biting my hand to stifle my moans. She remove her hand from my cunt and wipes it across my lips, encouraging me to suck her fingers clean. As I do so, I reach over to gently squeeze her hard dick, surprising her with my brazenness. "You usually ask permission" she says through a groan as she pulls my head towards her crotch. You unzips and shove my head down onto her. It takes my breath as I suck her dick, inhaling her scent, moaning with pleasure at her response. The song ends, and there is a discreet knock at the box door. She throws her coat over my head, holding my head down. 'Enter' she says, and I hear the stammering of a man asking if we would like some refreshment. She orders ice cream and coffee. As he leaves, she presses down on my neck, shoving her dick further down my throat. She is controlling my breathing with her thrusts, pushing towards orgasm. She cums just as the knock comes on the door. Her shout of 'enter' is more ragged than before. Before the young man leaves, she notes the bulge in his trousers and grin. She tips him, and he stammers 'thank you, Sir'

She pulls my head from her lap. My carefully constructed hair is now unravelling, my lipstick smeared over part of my face. My lips look swollen. She pulls the pins from my hair, causing my curls to cascade down my back. She wipes the excess lipstick from my face with her handkerchief. My lips feel swollen and raw. She reaches out, twisting my nipple until I gasp. She pinches and turns until tears pool in my eyes. 'Ice cream?' she asks as she continue to spin. 'Yes please, Sir' I squeak. 'Good girl' she says as she lets go and I almost scream. I am shuddering with pain and desire. The music begins again as you feed me. I sigh in pleasure at the cold sweetness sliding down my slightly raw throat. The heat of the coffee contrasts with the freezing cream to create tactile confusion... Delicious moving between the extremes.

I want to sink to the floor at her feet. I must be sliding in my seat as it takes her very little to pull me to the ground at her feet. I am content and secure, even in semi-public, even in my finery, at her feet. We watch the rest of the concert this way. Sometimes her hands are on me. At other times they are not. My cheek is against her boots. My eyes close while I enjoy the different sensations: the smell of the leather, the scent of her body and my heat, the sound of the bass, her breathing and my heart beating. The feel of the leather under my cheek and lips, the feeling of her hands in my hair make me sigh. The concert ends. She helps me up from the floor. 'Sir, I need to visit the ladies before we leave' I say. 'Hold it' she replies an evil edge to her voice. I am shifting from foot to foot as I mumble 'Yes, Sir'. We head off into the night. She takes pity on me, and we catch a cab to my hotel instead of the tube. She can see that I am struggling each time we ride over a bump. After 20 minutes, we finally reach my suite. The luxurious bathroom boasts a sunken tub and a two-person dual head shower. 'Please Sir' I cry.... bouncing from foot to foot. She walks with me into the bathroom, strips my dress from me, and puts me in the shower cubicle. 'Go ahead then' she says as she stands leaning against the doorframe, watching me intently with the faintest slightly cruel smile on her face. I am dying. I hate peeing in front of anyone - worse even to know she is observing me. My body tries to freeze up, but I am so full, I cannot stop myself. The piss gushes from me, drenching my legs, collecting in a puddle at my feet. My whole body is beet red, the blush rising from my toes to the roots of my hair. I'm trembling with need. I can feel her eyes on me, triumph registering when I look at her face. 'No' she hisses. I lower my eyes to the floor. 'Clean up' she says and turns the shower on. I wash quickly but thoroughly, enjoying the strong spray of the water.

I enter the room; the lights are low and temperature comfortable. She is still fully dressed and lounging on the sofa.

She has mixed a drink, and the TV is on. British television amuses her.

I approach her and sink to my knees in front of her. I remove her boots, socks and continue to undress her until she is down to her jock. I do so efficiently but with enthusiasm, enjoying the task. When I finish, I get up and get a refill for her drink, bringing it back to he and presenting it to her from my knees. My need is palpable. I have to work hard not to squeeze my thighs together to gain some relief. This amuses her. She begins to tease me further, pinching my thighs, breasts, that sweet spot on my ass. Watching as I squirm - running a finger up into my pussy, tweaking my clit - listening to me moan. I am so close to orgasm, and I don't dare cum without permission. I cannot distract myself without displeasing. I would have to take myself mentally away from the situation. This would surely be noticeable. 'Please, Sir... please oh please,' I wail as she gnaws on my breasts. 'Not yet' she says. She is biting harder now - I am sure she will draw blood and know that when she does, I won't be able to stop the waves from crashing over me.

It feels like time is standing still. I focus on staying perched on the edge of orgasm. I focus on her teeth. She stops biting abruptly and begins to smack me - my tits, my stomach, my thighs, my pussy - hard spanks that bring me close to tears. She grabs me by the throat, choking me as she rain blows down on pussy and thighs. She eases back off my throat for moments, taking me to the edge without pushing me to lose consciousness. She watches my face with interest, holding my gaze while she scratches at my thighs, digging her nails in deep. Moving back to my throat, her nails marking me. She whispers in my ear, 'You need an ass fucking'.

I am on my stomach on the bed and cannot figure out how I got there. She pulls me up to elbows and knees, grab my hips and shove her dick deep into my ass. I scream from the surprise as much as the pain. She fucks me fast and hard, and I moan desperately, pleading in screamed jumbled syllables.... not so she could make out the words... 'Please please please Sir please I need to cum so badly need to cum want deeper harder more, but it hurts Gods it feels so fucking good please' I wail and 'Now' she groans. Waves crash over me; my orgasm almost drowning me. She pounds into me, and I can feel her move closer to orgasm. I cannot meet her thrusts. She holds me in place, giving her more purchase so she can fuck my ass harder. She moans as she cums, then collapses on top of me. We are covered in sweat, both panting still. When she regains her breath, she slowly withdraws from my ass, causing me to wince. 'Sore?' she asks. 'Yes, Sir' I reply.

I wrote this piece for someone I met at an event and became friends with, though we never had a sexual relationship of any type. Debbie is a butch dyke. Her energy struck me when we were attending a leather event. That led to eye contact and then a conversation. Timing wasn't on our side and never has been. She inspired this by her carriage, her energy and a conversation we had about military bearing and ritual.

The Whistle

'Damn' I swear under my breath as I throw my stuff in the car. 'Running late. I hate hate hate being late. And today is not the day to be late. Damn'. Anyone watching might have been amused. I stop short of blaming Fen for my lateness. His morning 'wake up' ate up the 90 minutes I set aside for spare time - just to make sure time - the time I only need when I am so anxious I cannot think straight. 'And damned if He doesn't know it' I grumble under my breath. I can hear his laughter in my ears.

Dressing appropriately is a challenge, as it always is when dressing for someone I don't know terribly well. As it is, one of the main reasons I am being sent for this training is a perceived lack of 'formal' service skills. It is a fair comment. I have never done restaurant service. I preferred sales jobs as I worked in high school and university. By the time I hit graduate school, I had other skills. I can type and take dictation of a sort - it is my own shorthand rather than a standard shorthand, but I keep up. It helps to have a sharp memory for language - so I can repeat back what has just been said to me. My memory goes out the window when I'm anxious, and in a setting like this, I am guaranteed to be anxious.

I am told I will learn formal service to include valet, meals and anything else that the Captain thinks might interest my Owners. I am told to expect to be away a fortnight and to pack 'suitable' clothing. I will be allotted a certain amount of time per day for email and contact with family and owners, time to take care of work-related business. So, along with me come my computer, iPad, phones and assorted paperwork. I pack dresses with boots, bring a couple of pairs of low heels, praying that I will not need to wear these to serve as my ability to be graceful in heels is only fair at the best of times. I pack leather corset and skirt, a pair of jeans and a couple of t-shirts and some walking boots - just in case - and a new leather journal in which to take notes along with my favourite pens - one rollerball and one fountain.

I wear my collar, my tags, my watch and no other jewellery though I pack a pendant for my collar, some earrings and a bracelet in case I am required to dress and one nice bag. I have packed far too much, but anxiety makes it impossible for me to think more clearly. I choose a black and white Bettie Page dress, sleeveless with a neckline that has a triangle cut out to expose some cleavage, v in the back. The bodice is tight, moving into a lovely swing skirt. Underneath, I wear black lace bra and matching panties. I decide on bare legs and black sandals with no heels. Why risk breaking an ankle before I even get started? 'Play to your strengths, girl' I think as I work to tie back my unruly curls.

The drive to the airport is quicker than expected thankfully so I make up some lateness. I am in plenty of time for my flight. Security goes smoothly. The new full body scanners make the need to remove my collar obsolete. This eliminates uncomfortable discussions with TSA personnel and makes my travel much smoother than it was in the past. I spend the short flight time thinking about how I came to this place. I had been observing the many ways people navigate a personal leather journey. Progress along my path highlighted a desire for more ritual in relation to service. The only problem was that I lacked the skills. I studied Japanese tea service when I was an adolescent and loved the order and rituals involved. I always wished to study it again in more depth as an adult but had never found the time - nor had any of my Owners expressed an interest in being served in this manner. However, there is definitely a use for me to perform a valet's tasks creditably and serve a formal meal well. My cooking skills are good when I am not anxious and are continuously improving since I love to cook and to learn new methods and recipes. But presentation has never been my forte. I hope that this work will change that. Master expressed an interest in my learning some formal skills, and this is step one. He agreed that training in tea service (eastern and western) and presentation (including flower arranging) can follow. Master chose my instructor with great care. It has to be someone who values precision, who is strict but fair, and with whom there was at least some spark as when my sexual energy is not involved, I don't learn nearly as much. When my energy is engaged, I strive to please, which is exactly what is necessary to get the best out of me.

I have always thought of myself as clumsy and I tend to be clumsier when anxious. The more I am criticised, the clumsier I get. It is a longstanding issue for me, one that has never been adequately addressed by any of my owners. Perhaps I just did not spend enough time in situ to get past the obstacles. I just seem to consistently get in the way of myself. One of my Owners maintains that this is because I think too much. He may well be right, though I am not conscious of thinking at the times I am being clumsy. I am conscious of blind panic at those times. I hope that this fortnight of training will break through some of my blocks.

The flight passes quickly and before I know it I am at baggage claim picking up my suitcase. I walk rapidly towards the exit doors, looking for the person bearing the sign with my name on it. The man with the sign is dressed in traditional chauffeur's livery, including cap and gloves. He addresses me as 'Miss' as he greets me and slowly looks me over. I haven't been called 'Miss' in many years and this makes me smile. He nods once when he finishes looking me over, as though he approves of my choice of outfits. I am relieved I chose a dress instead of travelling relaxed in jeans or worse in a sweat suit as I sometimes do. The ride to the house is pleasant and not overly long. There is cold mineral water and classical music playing. I spend the time looking out the window, making myself pay conscious attention to what I see so that my anxiety quiets. I focus on the sights, the sounds of the music and the car, the smells of the leather in the car, the driver's cologne, the taste of the cold water and the feel in my mouth as I sip. I don't drink too much. The last thing I need is to find myself desperate for a loo before I am invited to freshen up.

We arrive at the house. The chauffeur opens my door and takes my arm as I get out of the car. 'I'll bring your luggage along, Miss. Just go up to the door and ring the bell.' I press the bell and then stand with my arms behind my back, a posture that I often take when I am not sure what to do with my hands. The door opens and a housekeeper in old-fashioned dress invites me in. 'Wait here Miss' she says and leaves me standing in the hall. There is a mirror on one side and I try to tie my hair back again as it is wild around my face after the trip. As a result, I am facing away when the Captain enters the hall. The whistle catches me off guard and makes me jump. I hear her chuckle and I try hard to turn gracefully. I was told that she prefers to be referred to as Captain or Sir when we first met.

'I find the whistle useful' she says, and I am reminded of Maria's response. Before I can stop myself, I say, 'Oh no Sir, I'm sorry Sir. I could never answer to a whistle. Whistles are for dogs and cats and other animals, but not for children and definitely not for me. It would be too humiliating'. My voice catches on the word humiliating. I feel my face flush red and my nipples tighten. 'Precisely' she replies. The flush rises through me from toes to the top of my head. Now I am crimson. Soon I will be scarlet.

The Captain strolls around me, examining me as though she were taking inventory. I struggle to remain still and keep my eyes on the ground. 'Strip' she says. I move to obey quickly, again thankful that I didn't wear stockings, or any complicated clothing - getting out of the dress gracefully is hard enough.

My clothing falls in a pile at my feet. I hear the whistle of the cane too late to brace myself. The strike lands precisely in the middle of my ass, causing me to stumble forward with a gasp. 'Clothing will be folded neatly when removed' she says quietly. 'Eyes will be lowered unless told otherwise' and I realise too late I have been staring at her face. The whistle precedes the strike by only a second. This strike lands precisely above the last. I yelp but hold my balance. 'Better' she says. 'You will not speak unless spoken to. You will acknowledge with Yes Sir or Yes Capitan.' 'Yes Captain' I reply. My voice is shaky.

She kicks the pile of clothing to the side and presses on my shoulders. I sink to my knees and bend my head towards her highly polished boots. The smell of the leather and the polish makes me dizzy. As I kiss her boots, I melt. My blush turns to scarlet as I feel juice ooze onto my thighs. My smell becomes the top note to this perfume. The smell of her boots, her cologne and just a hint of sweat underneath create the bottom and mid-notes. I bite back a moan as I continue to inhale, my lips remaining on her boots. I hold my breath as I feel her hand in my hair, pulling out the hair tie and spreading the curls onto my back. I sigh with pleasure at her touch on my scalp and the back of my neck and cannot help but moan as she pulls my head back by my hair until I am looking up at her. My colour darkens to brick red as she looks at me. Her hand moves under my chin, pressing over my jaw. My breathing is shallow. I struggle to relax into her touch. She lets go and steps back. I lower my eyes. 'Good girl' she says. I moan softly.

The Captain walks over to the bureau and picks up a leather portfolio. She opens this and begins reading. 'Your Master says you cannot be on your knees for too long, is this correct girl?' 'Yes, Sir' I reply. 'When you need to shift position, you may do so. Just be sure to sit well, with your back as straight as possible'. 'Yes, Sir'. I adjust my position. The transition is awkward. 'We will work on grace.' she says. My heart sinks. I have 'worked' on grace before. I remember hours of practice walking and walking in heels when I served the General, the feel of the crop on my back, thighs and belly when I failed to please. My fear is clear on my face. She chuckles 'Not to worry. We will find a way that works. I will not fail so you will not fail.' I hesitate for a moment and too late again hear the whistle of the cane just before the strike falls across my breasts. 'Yes, Sir' I squeal. 'Keep still' she warns. The cane falls again, landing just above the first strike. And again landing just below the first strike and right across my nipples. I howl but I keep still. 'Good girl' she says. The strikes resume. They come in quick march rhythm, peppering my breasts from top to bottom, extra attention being paid to my nipples. I can feel the bruising begin. I am howling and soon I cannot be still, dancing from foot to foot in place as she continues to methodically cane my swollen nipples until the tears course down my cheeks. It has only taken a few minutes but feels like it has taken hours. She wipes the tears from my face with her hand, bringing it to her mouth and tasting them. I sob quietly. 'Sandra' she calls. The maid arrives quickly, 'Yes Captain?' she inquires. 'Take her to her room to freshen up'. 'Yes Captain' she says and helps me rise. She turns her back and leaves the hall. The maid escorts me into the house. She walks quietly in front of me. My face burns now beet red. The marks on my breasts are rising. The breeze on my nipples is sharp and painful. My pussy is soaked.

We reach the room. My case has been unpacked and my things put away. There is a platter of fruit, biscuits and cheese on the table with a bottle of still and sparkling mineral water and a full ice bucket on the dresser. 'Freshen up and then rest. I will come get you for a tour of the house when it is time. Dinner won't be until later so you best have a snack now whether or not you are hungry. My best advice: Drink, eat and rest whenever you have the opportunity'. 'Yes, Ma'am' I reply. I enter the bathroom and sigh in pleasure when I see the claw-foot bathtub and the thick, plentiful bath sheets. I turn on the taps and begin filling the tub. I add a bit of arnica oil, some musk, vetiver and ylang ylang and a few drops of neroli. I eat and drink as the tub is filling. I sink gratefully into the deep tub, wincing a bit as the water engulfs the fresh cane marks. After soaking some soreness from my muscles and cleaning the travel sweat off my body, I slowly leave the tub. Towelling off causes me to wince anew. I slide between crisp sheets and comforter and drift off to sleep almost immediately.

I startle awake at the sound of the whistle. I quickly get up, make the bed neat and run my hands through my hair to neaten it. It is still damp from the bath and the curls are thick and tight. Sleeping on my hair when wet is never a good idea, but it takes almost four hours to fully dry so finding a time to wash it that doesn't conflict with seeing people or sleeping is always difficult. I am standing next to the end of the bed when the Captain enters the room, my hands behind my back, my eyes lowered. I quickly fall to my knees and bend to kiss her boots. I keep my head lowered until she lifts my head and resume standing hands behind my back. My face is crimson again. I know I reacted exactly as she wanted to the whistle and I hate that I did so. Part of me wants so much to be defiant. The rest of me wants so much to be a good slave. I have been in situations I felt were humiliating before, but something about this whistle gets under my skin. I cannot put my finger on it but it is not simply that whistles are for dogs and other animals. Or maybe it is? There is also the desire to run. The whistle is the beginning of the hunt and the prey in me recognises that. It announces that the predators are coming, giving prey a sporting chance - or giving everyone the change to race - or telling the dogs to lead away. The dogs have all been trained to the whistle. I shudder at these thoughts. 'You learn despite yourself' she says, the amusement clear in her voice. I want so badly to stick out my tongue, but I know better. I bite it instead. 'Yes Captain' I reply -the words forcing out between my teeth sound clipped. 'It is time for dinner. Tonight you will dine with me. Tomorrow you will begin your lessons. Come along' she says and leaves the room. I fall into step quickly behind her, working hard to keep up and maintain a consistent distance between us. Her stride is quicker than mine and slightly larger. I try to adjust my rhythm failing miserably when the Captain stops short. I run into her at speed, almost knocking her over. 'I'm so sorry Sir' I say as I fall to my knees, my lips to her boot. 'Stand up' she says and I do so quickly. 'Now bend over and put your hands on your thighs.' I make sure my ass is a clear target and that my hands are out of the way. The whistle of the cane makes me shudder and the first strike makes me howl. She places 5 more strikes evenly spaced. Six of the best, as they would in an English public school. My face is covered with tears. 'You will thank me when I correct you' she says. 'Thank you Sir' I reply, trying not to sob.

We enter the dining room. She pulls out a chair for me and smiles as I gingerly sit. My ass is swollen and stinging. Soon that sting will turn to burn. It will not be easy to sit still during this meal. The meal begins with smoked fish of a variety of kinds. The Captain is served and once her plate is full, she allots me my portion. I wait patiently, eyes lowered. They pour wine. They pour water. My hands are in my lap. I am biting my lip as I listen to her begin to eat. After a short while she asks, 'Are you hungry?' 'Yes Sir' I reply quietly. 'You may eat'. 'Thank you, Sir'.

I take small bites, eating slowly, savouring each bite. The fish is delicious. It melts on my tongue. I savour the smoke salt flavour. 'You may drink at will' she says. 'Thank you, Sir'. The white wine is crisp, sweet and light.

'Have you questions for me?' The Captain says. My mind goes blank, as it often does when I am put on the spot in this way. I can think of nothing productive to ask and yet, not even 5 minutes later I might think of a ½ dozen questions or when writing a journal I will ask a dozen. I know this is something that drives Sir crazy. He wants a direct answer. He believes I am being difficult. I am not. My mind goes blank. I have yet to learn a way to get past this block. I have never been good at speaking my mind in these situations. Writing has always been easier for me. 'I am sorry, Sir. My mind has gone blank.' I reply. 'That is a problem we will help you overcome. But for now, you can write them in your journal when you retire this evening. In the meantime, let us enjoy the rest of this meal.' 'Thank you Sir' I reply as my shoulders relax for the first time since we entered the room. The main course is roast chicken with all the trimmings - stuffing, roast potatoes, and sugar snap peas. The gravy is thick and delicious. I salivate at the smells and turn carmine with embarrassment. She chuckles and puts a portion on my plate. 'Eat' she says and I work hard to cut small pieces and eat slowly when I feel like eating like a farmer who has just come in from the fields.

Dessert is black Muscat grapes, and cafe reale. The sweetness and the spice are perfect. The food is cleared away, swiftly and silently. I marvel at how efficient staff are, wondering if I will be half as graceful by the end of these lessons. 'What are you thinking?' she asks. 'I was wondering if I would be even half as graceful by the time we are through' I reply quietly. 'You will' she replies. She stands and I follow. She comes around the table and runs her hand over the welts on my ass, slides her hand in between *my legs to discover how wet I am. I blush blood red. 'Good' she says and then snaps her fingers for me to follow. My blush has covered my body. I follow without hesitation despite the visceral humiliation at her finger snapping. She leads me to my room. 'You now have an hour free to catch up on business, communicate with friends and family, read for pleasure, or listen to music. Following that, you will write in your journal and you will go to bed. Sandra will send you up a nightcap for you to have before bed.' 'Yes Captain'. 'I will see you in the morning. Sleep well.' 'Thank you Captain and you as well'.*

I settle down on the bed and open my iPad first. I check all the mail, discarding junk, replying to what business mail I can without the computer. I check in on Facebook briefly and Fetlife. I don't try to catch up with what friends have been doing as I realise the whole hour will disappear. I text both Master and Sir and by then the hour is over. I turn on some music while I write in my journal. As I write about the day, I reflect on my naked state. Though I have been doing this for many years, I have never become accustomed to being naked when others are clothed. It still has a profound effect on me - highlighting my position and causing extreme awareness of my body and my reactions. Naked with collar, collar and bracelets or chains all have the same effect - though chains add the element of physical restriction, which deepens my state further. I wonder if they will allow me to wear any clothing and so I ask in my journal. I realise I have not asked about masturbation and orgasm. I know that the Captain has control for the time I am here, but I did not ask about the rules. I ask this in my journal as well, all the while acutely aware of the wetness seeping onto my thighs, my tight nipples, and the throbbing of my welts. Sandra enters with rum hot toddy 'To help you sleep' and smiles as she sets it down on the nightstand. I thank her, eyes lowered, and wish her good night. I drink the toddy as I read a couple of chapters in my book. By the time I am finished, they turn the lights off. I slide under the duvet and fall quickly asleep.

My dreams are erotic and intensely charged. I am running through a forest with predators in close pursuit. My hair is flying round my head as I run. I am panting with the effort but determined to elude the chase. As I run, my nipples tighten, my clit throbs, my body is covered in a sheen of sweat. I am perilously close to orgasm when I am knocked to the ground by the beast who has landed on my back. His arms snake round me to feel his prize. His panting is loud in my ears, breath searing. His claws scratch round my breasts, over the welts, digging and scratching until blood flows. I feel his tail winding round me, pressing legs apart. I wake with a start as my body convulses and hear the chuckle in my ears. I am mortified and wonder if coming in one's dreams will be judged orgasm without permission and what kind of punishment I might suffer. I drift quickly back to sleep.

Sandra wakes me from a deep, mercifully dreamless sleep. 'Time to rise. See to your grooming and be ready for inspection when you hear the whistle' She says. 'What shall I wear?' I ask. 'Anything you need will be laid out for you Miss'. She replies. 'Thank you'. I slide out of bed and pad off to the bathroom. I quickly shower including a hair wash, brush my teeth and use the toilet. I apply face and body cream; squeeze more excess water from my hair and pad back into the bedroom. There is a gossamer

240

thin large length of emerald green silk, and six large gold clips on the bed. There are no shoes. I move the silk and clips to the dresser and quickly make the bed. I tidy my business materials back into their case and turn to dressing. I have never been very good at these sorts of things, preferring clothing to have a clear structure. However, I create a short dress, clipped together high on my left hip and over my left shoulder. I use one of the largest clips to clip my hair back.

I am adjusting the dress as I hear the whistle. It startles me though I am expecting it and I jump. I hear a chuckle behind me and flush deep red as I turn around. I walk to the Captain, kneel and kiss her boots. I rise slowly, trying to maintain my grace. 'Good morning Sir' I whisper, eyes still lowered, breathing shallow, cheeks bright shades of pink. 'Good morning, girl. Did you sleep well?' I turn vermillion as I remember the orgasm in my sleep. 'I did Sir, though I woke from a very intense erotic dream and...' I stutter. She taps her quirt against her hand, 'Go on, girl'. My blush gets even brighter as I whisper 'I woke from an orgasm Sir'. I am shaking, nipples hard, pussy hot and slick, face and body burning. 'Did you have permission?' She asks as she reaches out and twists my right nipple. 'No, Sir' I gasp. I briefly think about explaining but decide it is better to take responsibility. 'Bend over' she scolds and turns me to face the bed. She unclips the silk at my hip and pushes it up to expose my ass. She kicks my legs apart and lifts me from underneath so my stomach is not resting on the bed, and my ass is pushed out. She begins by tapping the quirt back and forth between my thighs. It stings, but just serves to inflame. The quirt comes down in the sweet spot, on the bottom of my ass cheeks. She beats me quickly and efficiently. Not too hard and not too lightly. Hard enough for me to gasp, squeal and eventually to get some tears but not to make me scream. She halts and presses into my ass. I can feel her heat as she pulls me against her and I moan softly. I push myself harder against her, silently pleading, and she pushes me down onto the bed. 'Don't move' she says. She spreads my legs wider and then pushes into me in one stroke. I groan as I feel her hit my cervix. I am working ever so hard to stay still. She lifts my hips into the position she wants and begins pounding into me. I can feel my orgasm so close. The combination of the deep fucking, the feel of the pounding on my welts, and being asked to be still is driving me spare. 'Please please please' I wail. 'No' she says. She keeps fucking me until she comes, pressing me flat onto the bed. I am barely holding on. I know if I come without permission I will be beaten again - and likely it will be much worse than the first beating. I struggle to maintain control, breathing slowly and deeply, thinking of things that annoy me. Finally, I have some control. She gets up and asks me to stand, turn around and look at her. I look into her eyes, struggling again for control. 'You will come the next time you hear that whistle' she says. 'Yes Captain' I reply, my face turning the colour of cooked pickled beets. 'You may look down' she says. I am relieved to look away. 'You will start this morning's lessons with formal table service.' she says and walks out of the room. I hurry to follow her. This time, I do better at keeping pace and do not run into her, even when she stops rather suddenly. 'Good girl' she says. I smile quietly, 'Thank you Sir'.

'This is Grant' the Captain says as she introduces me to a tall bald ebony man dressed in an impeccable pearl grey suit.

He has paired the suit with lilac shirt, pocket square and socks. His tie is a slightly deeper shade of grey and shoes match the suit perfectly. He is wearing a fine watch and a steel eternity bracelet. 'Good morning Sir' I say and Grant chuckles. 'Grant is fine. Good morning, jewel.' His voice is lovely and deep and that is all it takes for me to blush, ruby this time. 'I will leave you in Grant's hands. I will see you at luncheon' the Captain says as she turns to leave. 'Yes, Captain' I reply.

There are a few different table settings laid out at places on the table. Grant talks me through the different services. The first is for a formal dinner. The second is for an informal dinner. The third for an informal breakfast or lunch. The fourth for a formal breakfast or lunch. To the side there are some additional service pieces, glasses and silverware. I have my notebook with me and am taking rapid notes. 'Breathe jewel. I will give you the opportunity to study these more fully. This is just an overview.' I can hear the humour in his voice but do not feel any malice. I smile and breathe deeply. We spend about 30 minutes on the overview and then put away all the table settings and linens. While we are doing this, I get an idea of the kitchen, pantry and the rest of the dining room. Following the overview, Grant spends some time talking with me about various ways of presenting a dish. I try out a few until I find a stance that is comfortable for me. I'm feeling a little more relaxed. Before I am aware, two hours have gone by and it is time for a coffee break. We enter the kitchen and I am shown the various machines, coffees and teas. Grant prepares café au lait for me and espresso for himself, grabs a bowl of assorted fruit and a cheese plate and I bring in the plate of biscuits, crackers and biscotti. I lay out informal table linens,

243

plates, cheese knives, forks, teaspoons and butter knives. I wait until Grant is seated and then take my place. I wait as Grant starts eating. He beams. 'You need not wait for permission to eat with me'. He says. I realise that I have become used to doing so, and that this is now my norm. I am pleased as the more that this becomes habit; the easier I will find my service. We eat as we talk about our backgrounds and current situations. I discover that he has served the Captain for the past 5 years and is a bisexual switch. We discover as we talk that we both view our attractions similarly in that we are both primarily drawn by energy and after that a variety of physical characteristics. This makes us unpredictable as to what genders the people with whom we are in a relationship will be. He tells me that at one time he served a homosexual trans-man and owned a heterosexual cis-female slave and at another time he served a butch cis-female and owned a bisexual trans-woman. We both note that there are times it is difficult to explain our way of relating to others and talk about how often we have felt that there was not a community in which we truly fit. We both experienced prejudice from heterosexual and homosexual communities and did not fit within the trans-gender community either. Sometimes the 'B' in LGBT really disappears 'Back to work' Grant announces and I quickly clear the table and sort things into the dishwasher.

I spend the next two hours on an overview of the wine cellar and liquor cabinet along. Grant tells me I will be able to use cheat sheets for drink making and helping to pair wines but that often I won't have lots of time so it is good to become familiar with everything so I need only glance at the cheat sheet quickly in most cases. I take copious notes - working hard to make sure that I will later be able to read my own handwriting. As we are finishing, I hear the whistle. I shudder as I turn crimson and Grant laughs. 'That has an intense effect on you' he notes. 'Yes Grant. It does. Both humiliating and sublimely erotic' I admit. 'Yes, that is obvious' Grant replies 'I can smell you from here'. I am mortified, turning blood red. 'I'm sorry' I whisper and he chuckles 'Nothing to be sorry for. You smell delicious'. 'Thank you' I stammer as I hurry off to find the Captain.

She waits for me out in the hall. I rush into the hall, hairs flying wildly, face flushed, but avoid running into her. I drop to my knees and kiss her boots. She keeps me head down for some time. My breathing slows a bit. She raises me up and escorts me in to lunch. This time, there is one place set. She sits and points to the floor to the side of her chair. 'I will have a guest for lunch. Get comfortable here. Today you will listen as we eat and converse. Soon you will serve the meal.' She says. 'Yes, Captain' I reply.

The Captain stands as Sandra enters the room with a beautiful woman. She is red-haired and curvy with cinnamon eyes that carry a mischievous glint. I quickly look down and I hear her giggle. She gives the Captain a long hug and then sits in the chair to the right of her. I am now on the floor in between them. She reaches down and puts her hand in my curls, grabbing a handful and lifting my head so I am looking at her. She greets me and tells me her name is A. I say hello quietly. As she examines my face, my blush deepens until I am again the colour of pickled beets. 'Why she is lovely!' She exclaims. 'Yes, she is and seems not to be aware of it often' the Captain replies. I do not thank her, as I am not being spoken to. The appetiser is served - shrimp cocktail with a choice of sauces - spicy cocktail or Marie rose. 'Wine?' The

Captain asks, and A accepts a glass. The Captain opens a bottle of semi-dry white and pours each of them a glass.

They toast to good friends and good food and each sip the wine. They start to eat. After they have taken a few bites, the Captain picks up a spare linen napkin and ties it around my neck. She feeds me a shrimp dipped in Marie rose sauce. The shrimp is extremely fresh, the texture delightfully firm. The sauce is delicate. I chew slowly and clean the sauce from her fingers. I go to thank her and she says 'After the meal'. I nod my head, remaining quiet, as it is clear she wishes me to be. She gives me a sip of wine and turns her attention back to A who has been nibbling on a shrimp while watching me. I work hard to remain still, but it is difficult not to squirm under her gaze. The two chat about people they have in common and various upcoming events. They both feed me titbits as they finish the first course and work on the main course. Eventually, I settle a bit and enjoy the experience while letting go of my anxiety. Sandra clears the table and Grant enters with a cheese plate, fruit, petit fours and coffee. He offers dessert wine but both decline to drink any more with lunch. They linger over coffee. Jewel is delightful. When she has completed the next few days training, I might like to borrow her if that is OK?' A says. 'Of course you may.' The Captain replies. Grant enters the room and the Captain snaps her fingers to gain my attention. This has almost as disturbing an effect as the whistle. I look up at her and reply 'Yes Sir?' 'Say good bye to our guest and then go with Grant. You will have one more lesson before your siesta.' 'Yes Sir. It was a pleasure to meet you, Ma'am. I hope that I will see you again' I say. A grins 'No doubt you will jewel' She replies and Grant leads me from the room.

We arrive in the library. Grant has me sit in one of the overstuffed chairs. I always feel so young sitting in these chairs, as my feet never reach the ground. Grant brings out a large humidor and a liquor trolley. On the trolley are a decanter each of port, brandy and single malt scotch. The glasses are heavy and crystal. 'Now we will cover an overview of cigars, port, brandy and whiskey' He begins. We spend the next hour learning about the parts of the cigar, how cigars are made, characteristics of different regions, the basics of humidors, and cutting and lighting cigars. The hour after that we spend going over vintage port, brandy (including regions and houses) and types of whiskeys. Grant tells me we will have in depth lessons on all these topics over the next week and not to worry too much about remembering as this is just the overview. Again, I am taking copious notes. Finally, Grant tells me it is time to stop and leads me to my room. He ruffles my hair and tells me he will see me later. I head into the bathroom and have a shower. Dried and wrapped in a large fluffy bath sheet, I crawl into bed and close my eyes. I am asleep in an instant.

I startle awake at the sound of the whistle and work hard not to swear under my breath. I knuckle the sleep from my eyes and pad into the bathroom to wash my face and go to the bathroom. The whistle sounds again and I hurry out into the hall. I have only gone three paces before I hear another shrill blast. I run down the hall and quickly to the door of the Captain's study. I take a second to calm my breathing before I knock on the door. 'Enter' she says. I walk into the room and quickly drop to my knees and kiss her boots. 'When you hear the whistle, you need to quick march. One blast should be enough. Two if you are in the midst of something you cannot leave off immediately. If you have not responded by three, I will discipline you. Am I understood?' she asks. 'Yes, Sir' I reply, my voice heavy with tears. More than anything, I don't like to disappoint.

I am still on my knees, with my lips to her boot. The smell of the leather makes me high. The desire to lick and kiss her boots, to worship, is overwhelming. I begin with another kiss and then am subsumed in the worship. My tears overflow and run down my cheeks. A tear runs off the end of my nose. My breath comes in gasps. The Captain reaches into my hair and grabs a handful. I moan, a low rumble rising from my toes. She grips and releases and grips again, pulling my head up just a little and then bending it back. She grips harder, bending my head back further until she can see the tears on my face. Her hand traces my jaw, finger on the pulse in my throat. She watches my reaction carefully, noting my shallow breathing, my dilated pupils, the saliva gathered at the corners of my lips. Her hand slides up to my throat and she slowly squeezes. I work to avoid the panic as it becomes harder to breathe. I breathe at her pleasure. I am within moments of passing out when she lets go. I somehow keep my position and kiss her hand. She sits up and runs a hand through her hair. Her colour is deeper, flushed, and her pupils dilated. 'Dinner will be informal. Afterwards, you will have a lesson in moving with grace. Then you will have an hour free and then you will go to bed. Understood?' she says. 'Yes, Sir'. I whisper.

The Captain takes my hand and helps me rise. She leads the way to the dining room. She sits and sends me into the kitchen to help serve. Grant hands me a full plate and I bring it carefully into the dining room, placing it down in front of the Captain from her left. There is grilled asparagus, polenta and roast duck. 'What would you like to drink Sir?' I ask. 'Water please' she replies. I fill her glass carefully. I return to the kitchen to get my plate and wait until the Captain gestures at a seat at the table. I place the plate down and stand quietly behind the chair. 'Sit' she says. I sit and wait patiently as she eats a few bites and makes appreciative noises. 'Eat' she says. I begin to eat. As before, I find my appetite as soon as I start eating and have to work to slow myself down. Grant brings me some water and pats me on the head. I can feel the smile in his touch. We have little discussion tonight and I am happy for the respite. I am very tired even with the naps. Dessert is a Pavlova with strawberries and I have mint tea with it.

When the Captain stands, I follow and we go into the living room. 'This will be a short lesson as I can tell you are already tired. We will start walking in bare feet.' she says. She stands behind me, adjusts my posture, pushing my shoulders back, reminding me to think as I learned to do when I briefly studied Alexander technique - as though there is a wire running from the top of my head straight down through my feet into the floor. She adjusts my head position and first has me put my hands at my side. This feels awkward, but I know it will get easier with practice. 'I will use my whistle to set the tempo' she says and I groan before I can stop myself. She chuckles. 'There will be a penalty for that' she says. She blows the whistle so I have a cadence and I walk the room in tempo. Or at least I attempt to walk the room in tempo. I am too self-conscious to keep the rhythm. My critical self-talk takes over and all I can hear is 'You have no grace. You are clumsy. You lack rhythm'. The more I listen to this, the worse I get. I am pulled out of this line of thought by the quirt on my breasts. I yelp and I jump. 'Start again' she says.

The whistle blows the tempo again and this time I can cross the room repeatedly without stumbling. 'Much better' the Captain says and I can hear the approval in her voice. 'Now, let's work on some position changes' she says and has me kneel, move to sitting on the floor, change to standing position and then get back down again. After some trial and error, I make these changes with some grace. 'Good, very good' the Captain says. I am beaming with the praise and also exhausted. 'Off to bed with you then.' she says. I get to my knees and kiss her boots. Her hand tangles in my hair. I rumble with pleasure at her fingers on the back of my neck. There is a special way that she has that is difficult to explain. She grabs the hair on the base of my skull and presses into the spot just at the base. My mouth waters with pleasure. She chuckles. 'Hungry girl?' 'Yes Captain' I reply. 'You need sleep' she says. 'Yes, Captain' I reply. She pulls my head against her thigh and continues to rub my scalp. I groan in pleasure. 'Bed. Now.' she says and I rise with as much grace as I can muster and run off to my room. I sit down with my journal and write only a few words about her smell, her touch and my need before I yawn. I close the journal and slide under the sheet and am asleep before I can think another thought.

I wake to hands spreading my thighs wide. 'Lift up' I hear and I comply quickly. I am impaled on a dick before I am fully *awake. I scream in pleasure. Hands turn my head to the side to taste the dick at my lips. I am pulled forward by my hair so I swallow deeply. I am being double fucked in perfect rhythm. All I can do is receive their thrusts. My pussy is overflowing. I am so close to coming and I cannot ask for permission with a mouth and throat full of dick. 'Come now' the Captain says. The release is like a tsunami, contractions intense enough to trigger orgasm for the Captain and Grant. The waves take minutes to leave my body. It is only when they withdraw that I realise it is still the middle of the night. 'Help her back to sleep' the Captain says and leaves the room. Grant strokes my face and runs his hands through my hair. 'Girl you best get some rest. You will need all your strength tomorrow.' He kisses my forehead and pulls the sheet up over me. 'Thank you Grant' I mumble as I drift off again. I don't have the energy to ask what tomorrow will bring.*

The whistle wakes me. I have begun to lubricate at the sound of it. Just like one of Pavlov's dogs. I slide out of bed and pad into the bathroom for a wash. I am drip drying my hair when the whistle sounds again. I sprint from the room and head to the Captain's study. She is in the hall waiting for me with a tall dark woman at her side. Her energy is intoxicating. She has delicious smooth chocolate curves, a piercing gaze and an enigmatic smile. I realise that I am staring and drop my gaze. I quickly kneel and kiss the Captain's boot. She leaves me there, hand in my hair. 'She is lovely' the woman remarks and I all but purr at the sound of her voice. My body turns a deeper pink and I tremble. 'This is Mistress.... you can call her Mistress or Ma'am' The Captain says. 'Yes, Captain' I reply. 'Where are your manners jewel? Don't you have a greeting for Mistress ....?' I can hear the smirk in the Captain's voice. I move to Mistress' feet and bow my head low, kissing her boots. 'Very nice to meet you Ma'am' I say, my voice trembling and my body now vibrating like an aspen leaf in spring winds. 'Lift your head, girl and look at me' She says. I look up into her deep umber eyes and get lost there. She laughs again. 'Delightful. She is so sweet and though I know from you she is not innocent, there is a shyness to her that is engaging'. 'Yes this is so. She was sent here at the behest of her owners. But since her training began, her situation has changed and she now belongs only to One', the Captain goes on 'So it is possible that she will be available for more than just some practice or play'. I work hard to keep my emotions under control. I am still raw from the end of my contract and have been focusing on this training to recover. I drift into my own thoughts and do not catch Mistress' reply, but they are both chuckling. 'You will see Mistress later' the Captain says as she calls for Grant to take me. I rise carefully and drop my eyes, square my shoulders and wait patiently until Grant attaches the lead to my collar and takes me from the room.

Grant sets a quick pace and I struggle to keep up. We arrive in the library, sweat beading on my back and forehead, my breath somewhat shallow. Grant hands me some water and I try not to gulp. 'This morning, we will go into more depth about drinks and cigars. We will cover wines including champagne and other sparkling wines, sherries and ports, beers and ales, whiskies, other spirits, brandies, mixed drinks, cigars and other tobacco products.' 'Yes Grant' I reply. 'Let's start with Scotch. Here you have a choice of blended and single malt. There are some rare blends that are made at some of the best distilleries, but in a fine house, we use blends in mixed drinks and a choice of single malt is available for drinking alone or with water. Many whisky snobs believe that water and ice should not be added as they pollute the flavour, however there are still many folk who will add one or both. We have whisky stones that will keep the drink cool without melting.' Grant described malts with lots of peat versus those without, the different barrels that whiskey is distilled in (sherry barrels or simple oak, for example) and how this adds to the flavour. Different vintages and different distilleries. I take detailed notes.

After the overviews, Grant has me taste a variety of whiskies and I note the nose and the flavours in my book as well. 'It is a good idea for you to have tasted everything that you are offering to guests so you can well describe what you are offering them. If you have wide knowledge, it also allows you to advise your Master on what to purchase and keep in his cellar. This applies to all drinks. In fact, the same should be true for food. Though there are cooks and in some houses sommeliers, if you are first girl, your job is to know about the running of the whole house. You take advice from the specialists and inform the Master of what is important. You should be able to answer detailed questions about his household - all of it - even if you are not personally responsible for an area. If the household is small, you may not need as much detailed information in your head, but you best know where to get it for the times that your Master entertains or when you are loaned out to another household, or even for when you are visiting folks so you can advise Master if need be.' Grant says. 'Now let's move on to other spirits'. We spend the next hour going over a variety of other spirits and the time leading to lunch break discussing cocktails and other mixed drinks. 'After lunch we will practice pouring spirits, making cocktails and serving in various glasses' Grant says. 'Yes Grant' I reply. The whistle sounds and I run from the room. The sound of Grant's laughter rings in my ears as I go.

I arrive at the dining room and am greeted by the Captain and the cook. 'You will serve lunch.' The Captain says. 'When you finish serving us, come sit at my feet and I will feed you.' 'Yes, Sir' I reply quietly and follow the cook into the kitchen. Cook ties a pretty apron around my waist and ties my curls back into a thick ponytail. This takes some effort, but she gets my hair tied in a way that keeps it off my face and looks pleasing. She cannot do anything with the few curls that escape to fall into my eyes. 'That will have tae do' She says, her gentle Scottish accent making me smile. 'Thank you, Cook' I say. She hands me the appetiser tray of Insalata Caprese and motions for me to serve. I enter the dining room and start when I see Master and Mistress.... at the table with the Captain. I place the first plate of caprese in front of Master, the next in front of Mistress.. and then finally a plate in front of the Captain. 'Greet your Master girl' the Captain says. I kiss Master's boots passionately. He lifts me to him, crushing me in a hug. He kisses me until I am breathless. When he lets me go, I slide to the floor at his feet. 'I will feed her Captain, if you don't mind' Master says. 'Be my guest, Morloki' the Captain replies. 'Jewel, sit comfortably' Master says and I adjust my position with some grace. Grant enters and offers black pepper for the salads. Sandra brings in water and wine. All eat. There is little conversation at first as they enjoy the flavours. Master feeds me my first bite and has me suck the extra oil off his fingers. My face turns flame red as my nipples tighten. The second bite has me moaning around his fingers. Conversation stops as the Captain and Mistress... watch my responses. The energy rises up my spine, burns through me as Master pushes with each touch. It looks as though he is simply stroking me, or pinching me, or scratching me but each touch contains a push that sends the sensation throughout my body, multiplies it until I cannot catch my breath. If I could look at my Master, I know the expression on his face - unmitigated joy. As it is, I cannot keep my eyes from rolling back into my head each time the energy peaks. 'Look at me' my Master says. I drag my eyes to his face as he feeds me the next piece of mozzarella. I savour the flavours as I take the food from his hands. I revel in the texture of the soft cold cheese, the dry heat from his somewhat rough hands. 'Now come' he says. The orgasm builds from my centre, intense heat rippling outwards, hot juice covering my thighs. 'Nicely done' says Mistress ..... 'Thank you.' Master replies.

I am still shaking when the Captain says 'Jewel, we are ready for the next course'. 'Yes, Captain' I reply, rising slowly and attempting to clear the table gracefully. My body is glistening, awash with pinks and reds. I enter the kitchen to the sound of Cook singing. She runs a hand through my hair and gives a gentle tug. 'I love your hair'. 'Thank you, Ma'am' I reply. She pulls my hair harder, observing my trembling. 'I mustn't make you late' she says, almost to herself, letting go of my hair and turning to the plates. I gather up the tray of roast duck with polenta and sautéed spinach and walk slowly into the dining room. I place plates starting with Master again as no one has told me I should do differently. I remember Grant's instructions 'Guests first, always. If your Owner is a guest, your Owner first.

If not, women first and then men'. I return to the kitchen and get the wine caddy and place a towel over my arm. 'Mistress... would you like more wine?' I ask . 'No, thank you' she replies. I move to the Captain. 'Sir would you like more wine' I ask, making sure that I lower my eyes. 'No, thank you jewel' he replies. I bring the wine back to the serving table and return to refill the water glasses. When I finish, I return to my place at my Master's feet. The conversation flows over me. Each bite I am offered, I savour. I take the opportunity to focus on all that is in front of me: the sights, sounds, tastes, and smells. When I hear the cutlery still, I get up and clear the table. I re-enter the room and brush the crumbs from each place. Then I put out the settings for dessert. As I walk by Mistress.... she stops me with a hand on my thigh. 'May I?' she asks Master. 'Please' he replies. She slides her hand between my legs, initially stroking lightly and then pinching. I yelp but keep still. She goes back to stroking, pulling a moan from me. 'Responsive' she says. Her tone of voice suggests she is thinking 'slut'. Master replies 'Thank you'. After a few moments, she lets me go so I can continue serving dessert. I head off to the kitchen, now shades of sex red to blood red.

'Come here, girl' Cook shouts as I enter the kitchen. I move quickly to her side. 'Bend over' she says. I comply, feeling the cool of the marble countertop on my thighs. The smack of the wooden spoon makes me squirm. 'Keep still' she says. 'Thwap thwap thwap' the spoon sounds against my flesh. She hits me a dozen times. 'Up girl. Take the dessert in' 'Yes Ma'am' I reply, my face as red as my ass cheeks. I bring the tray of strawberry shortcake into the dining room.

I have always loved to have intimate relationships with people I like without having to define these relationships. I love to drop the need to say 'We are dating.' Or 'We are in a relationship' and to say 'This is my playmate'. When I connect with someone, I often feel attracted to them. It goes with the flow of energy. I love to express myself physically. So while this isn't always the case, it happens quite a bit, and in the past I have suppressed these desires and kept good boundaries and prioritised the friendship over all else. It is beautiful to belong to a man, to be married to a man who understands how my desire works and how I express myself and supports me in this type of expression. He knows that my other attractions don't take away from our relationship and most of the time, they add energy to our relationship. He knows that I will not leave with the next shiny thing that comes along, and I am not comparing him to anyone.

I love it when we can share playmates. Morloki and I have a couple of people we enjoy playing with together and sometimes separately. It is so much fun to watch my beloved create pleasure and joy in another and receive them from another. I know that there will be many more shared experiences in the future and personal ones as well.

Sometimes people have difficulty with the term 'playmate'. I love this term because it is accurate. Sexual intimacy (with or without kink and BDsM) is adult play. For me, there is light-hearted energy to this play even when the activity is an intense one - even when there is pain involved. The flirtation, the negotiation, the anticipation are all reminiscent of play for me as a child. I have always loved imaginative play. I liked to dress up, to role play, to create scenes and develop relationships between the characters. I love to use the characters and scenes to explore different stories, sensations and experiences.

Please don't misunderstand. I am not talking about casual relationships, though some relationships of this type are casual and I apply no judgement. Most of my relationships are at depth. The energy exchange involved in my physically and emotionally intimate relationships takes stamina and vulnerability, so I do not enter them casually.

Compersion is when you get joy out of the joy of another. My favourite example of this: Have you ever watched a toddler - 18 - 30 months old? When they discover something new or that feels good, they break out in glee, often toddling at full speed with joy clear on their faces, and chortling. People who see this cannot help taking part in the joy and often laugh out loud or find themselves grinning long after the child is out of their purview. This is how it feels to be compersive.

Most people who have grown up in modern western cultures have grown up believing there is a scarcity of everything in the world and that to get your needs met you need to make sure you don't lose out to someone else. People are taught to compete for resources, for partners, and to do so ruthlessly even against family and friends. They are trained to hold tight and not to share. They are taught not to trust because it is hard to get your needs met and that most people are looking out for themselves. It is a sad state of affairs. Instead of multiplying happiness and joy, they multiply mistrust and fear. We become worried that we are not good enough, will not get enough, will find ourselves alone. They teach us to expect the negatives; the glass is half empty. Instead, we could look at the glass being half full, and we could expect the positives.

We are also taught that to be open and vulnerable is to put yourself at risk. Even after all of Brene Brown's research on vulnerability highlighting that it is powerful to be vulnerable, it builds trust and intimacy; it increases self-worth, promotes compassion, aids in creativity and motivation and reduces loneliness, we still fear that vulnerability means weakness and risk and alienation.

To be vulnerable takes courage. We have to combat our shame. We have to learn to be comfortable with negative assessment by some people. We have to have the courage of our convictions. The gains from being able to be vulnerable and authentic are huge. With partners (lovers, play partners, serious relationships), the benefits from being willing to be vulnerable are an exponential increase in emotional intimacy, physical intimacy and pleasure. Living out loud requires being vulnerable and authentic in a variety of parts of life, not only when it is easy.

If you want to encourage vulnerability and compersion, practice being non-judgemental and learning to speak in a way that communicates that lack of judgement. Practice your vulnerability and compersion. Seek feedback and support from people you admire who are living out loud.

Sometimes people think living out loud means you are always very vocal about and in people's faces with your opinions, your life, your needs and desires. That is not always the case. Many people live out loud quietly. They go about their lives without compromising on their message and their integrity. They tell their story and live their story daily. They are confident and unconcerned about being accepted or rejected by others. What would it be like if you lived out loud? What are the gains, and what are the potential pitfalls?

'You are not only responsible for what you say but also for what you do not say.' Martin Luther.

Lies beget lies. Dishonesty begets dishonesty. Disrespect breeds disrespect. It is much easier to come clean, apologise to those you have wronged, and move forward.

People choose to have relationships behind the back of their significant others for many reasons. Sometimes things happen quickly. Sometimes these are relationships forged in anger. Even in poly relationships, where the permission is there to form sexual, emotional and deeply spiritual relationships with others, people can choose not to follow the agreed-upon rules. Sometimes this is because of anger, other times this is because the person does not believe permission will be given and still other times it is merely because the person finds the communication and negotiation necessary too hard to confront. In some ways, it is much easier to have an affair. But it is not respectful – to self, to significant other, to the new partner – to the dynamic.

I am polyamorous by choice and work hard at being open and honest with all potential partners and playmates. I am Owned, and when my Owner chooses to share me, he expects his gift to be acknowledged. We don't play with people who are in committed relationships unless all parties are in on the negotiation. This feels respectful to us. It makes for less drama. This community is not all that large. There are a wide variety of views how to 'do poly'. There are many folks with lots of experience who are happy to share their experiences – good and bad – so that others may learn from them and make new and creative mistakes.

In my relationships, I work hard to respect others, to treat them with acceptance and approach with a lack of judgment. It is much more challenging to do this consistently in my personal life - when people are close to me I want their approval, and I want to know they value me. Sometimes, I avoid conflict instead of confronting a situation head-on. I work hard at personal responsibility, at being as honest as I can be with myself and others.

Because of my chosen profession and my 'non-mainstream' lifestyle, I have been exposed to many people's definitions of respect. I have seen the consequences of treating people with disrespect, the results of spending a lifetime feeling disrespected - either by family, friends, community or society at large. In my work, I find it easy to afford respect for others, regardless of their life circumstances and choices. I can sit with people without judgment, respecting their humanity, accepting them and offering them the opportunity to change knowing that they are acceptable whether or not they change. That they are worthy whether or not they change.

I remember as an adolescent challenging my father's beliefs about respect. My father has always had strong opinions. I remember accusing him of not respecting my beliefs when they differed from his ideas. It was hard for me to understand how he felt disrespected when I behaved in ways he felt challenged his world view. When I reached my 30s, I finally understood how difficult my father found it when he saw that my lifestyle differed from his own. I learned to express my respect for him and his beliefs, even though I was choosing a different life path.

I was taught to respect others and to work especially hard to respect the opinions of others. I have clear memories of my father explaining to me it was important to treat others with respect unless or until they proved themselves unworthy of it. I remember asking how someone could prove himself unworthy of my respect and his reply 'through dishonesty, deceit, a lack of respect for you, your family, your values or a lack of respect for humanity'.

Buber speaks of the I - Thou relationship. Authenticity psychotherapy - congruence - those moments of real connection. As I age, love of this type - genuine connection on as many levels as possible, becomes

261

more important to me. Those individual encounters I have with others have meaning because of connection. There is deep emotion, real contact and intense healing possible in these relationships - whether they last for decades, years, months, weeks or even only for one night. It is not the amount of time that is key (though certainly, intimacy in long-term relationships has many more flavours), but rather the ability to make actual contact - openly, honestly - accepting the other as they are whole human being and agreeing to explore together without trying to mould each other into some pre-conceived pattern or role.

The deepest wounds in my life have been betrayals of trust. I remember the first time I looked at my first husband and didn't recognise him - when I realised that he had been lying to me and that I had no inkling he had been lying. The feeling of unreality - as though I were Alice and had fallen through the looking glass - suddenly familiar things changed. Nothing looked right, smelled right, sounded right. Felt right. My reality had been torn, and now I did not know what was real. Had I imagined my reality? Was I deluded originally, or had what I experienced as reality been true?

The worst thing that growing up with a parent who gaslights produces is a child/adolescent/adult who no longer trusts their sense of reality. Learning again how to trust one's view of the world - one's perceptions - is a slow and painful process. It is the most significant emotional harm perpetrated by abusive parents of all types. It is most evident in sexual abuse where when a child feels uncomfortable with a parent's touch or intrusion; the parent tells the child that this isn't uncomfortable, and nothing is wrong. Children learn to trust their perceptions from their parents - or they learn to distrust their perceptions. Those who do not learn to trust their perceptions are more susceptible to gaslighting and predators than others.

Reality testing is a skill, and like any other skill can be learned. If you haven't learned it growing up, it can be learned in therapy via the I - Thou relationship Buber speaks of. This type of treatment is not one where the therapist is silent or reflects back. In this type of work, the therapist is authentic in the session. They help the client to look carefully at their reality, to learn to trust that deeper inner voice, to change it if necessary so it reflects their reality and moves them towards their most authentic congruent selves.

Authenticity and presence bring connection. If you have never experienced what this type of connection feels like (and many people have not as they live their lives disembodied, working hard to fit into society's or parental expectations), you may not see the value in it. I, for one, could not live without it. I wither when cut off from those deeply connected interactions. Being wholly present, fully my self and vulnerable to another (by sharing my thoughts, feelings, dreams, spirit and sometimes my body) brings me more joy, more healing and allows me to provide healing in a way that is far more tangible than you might think. Being seen for who you are and not rejected, being granted all your feelings, even the negative ones, being given safe space to experience all aspects of you are all transformative. Most humans find this kind of contact, not only important but necessary. This is love without conditions. This is what we feel the first time we gaze deeply into the eyes of someone we love who loves us wholeheartedly. I see you. All of you in all of your glory. All of those hidden recesses, the parts you have tried to bury. All of your gifts that you don't acknowledge. I see you. I hear you - your laughter, giggling. Your sounds of passion. When you are sobbing with grief. When you are shouting in rage. I hear your song. I hear your pregnant silence. I hear you.

XVIII

POLYAMORY

I wrote this next piece for the double dominant couple I was in a relationship with.

Fire and Steel

I arrive at the suite first. I stow my clothing in the closet, make sure my toiletries and medications are where they can be easily found, put my suitcase away. When you arrive, I am in a modified kneeling position, dressed in my black and red leather harness and cuffs and black silk panties.

'Empress' I cry as I you enter the suite, my joy at seeing you again shown in my voice and in my grin. I don't rise as I am unsure if that will be acceptable and I don't wish to mar our time together by impulsiveness. You come and run your hands through my hair, gripping and pulling my head back, so our eyes meet. Your greeting is full of warmth and excitement. The sexual tension between us is high and gets higher as Pharaoh enters the room. My grin lights up my face, and I struggle for a respectful greeting that contains my joy at seeing him again.

I bow my head towards the floor. 'jewel' he says, and I can hear that he is pleased as well.

After a few minutes of bringing cases and kit into the room, you ask me to unpack for you both. I rise and open cases, closets and drawers, finding places for clothing and toys so that every-thing is neatly stored away from prying eyes and yet comfortable for you to access.

Once there is order, I return to you and ask if I can make you both drinks, tea or coffee. You request tea, and I get the teapot, the kettle and my selection of loose tea that I brought from the UK. This travel set makes creating a tea ritual much more comfortable when I am away from home. The items are all lovely and unique, which is necessary. An essential part of tea ritual is the guest gets a treat for their senses – from the tea ware to the water, to the ritual itself to the sweets, to the taste of the tea. I have brushed up on my Japanese tea ritual (formal), a Chinese ceremony (less formal), an English ritual (semi-formal) and two rituals that are my creation to honour the people I am serving.

I make sure that you both have comfortable seats and are dressed comfortably. I have loosened your travelling clothing, taken all that is superfluous and put it away, and brought you both comfortable choices from the clothing that I put away for you when I unpacked. I also offer you both yukata I have brought for you. They make these relaxed kimono from light cotton and the colours are those of your house, purple and black.

I gather my tea supplies and set up the table so I can perform the ceremony. I present the teas to each of you and wait for you to choose. You choose a spring sencha green tea – bright and full of flavour. Pharaoh chooses the lapsang souchong – the smoky flavour complex and rich.

As I begin, Pharaoh stops me with a hand on my head. 'Come here, girl' he says. His tone of voice tells me not to question, to obey. I kneel in front of you both, within his reach. He threads a length of chain through one ring on my harness and then through a ring on each cuff. The chain is strong but not overly heavy. The sound it makes is musical rather than brash. It is an extended length of chain, more than needed to restrain me. Pharaoh creates a harness out of the chain, just as one might do out of rope. The chain is cold, and its weight reassuring. There is something about it that creates a feeling of being held firmly, and yet it could be menacing. I moan as he tightens bits and pieces between my legs. You comment on how good it looks. There is a length of thick chain between my legs, tight up in my wet pussy and rubbing against my clitoris when I move. The chain separates my breasts and yet does not impede the nipple jewellery. I moan when I move as the chains rub, press and push on my breasts, nipples, ass, cunt and clitoris.

Pharaoh has me rise and turn so you can both get a good look at me thus adorned. I do so slowly, fighting my embarrassment, knowing that I am blushing a deep red as I turn. 'Come here, jewel' he says with intention, creating a command voice so quickly so I am moving towards him without volition. My gaze is on my feet, head bowed. He lifts my chin with one finger so I cannot avoid his gaze. I bite my lip. He watches me as he moves the energy between us with one finger until a blaze ignites. Your attention on me stokes the flames higher until I feel hot juice collect between my legs. You reach out and grab a nipple, stroking then pinching, then scratching, then pinching until I am whimpering. I am still standing still and not trying to get away – even though the pain is rising, even with the impulse to pull back. I keep my place. 'Good girl' you say and I sigh.

My chains rustle as I prepare the tea and serve you both. When I have finished, you have me sit comfortably at your feet as you are drinking, eating and talking about the plans for the weekend. Every so often, one or the other of you feed me a titbit or give me a sip of tea. You run hands through my hair or pull stroke or pinch nipples, or any part of me you can easily reach. Once you have finished most of the tea, you explain the schedule for the weekend, ask if there are any goals I have, if I understand what I am to be doing. You have me with you for one day, and with Pharaoh for the other and during the evening events, I am with the both of you unless plans change.

You both feel that a siesta would be a good idea as the formal events have not begun yet, and all of us would benefit from the additional rest. I am too restless to take a siesta. You ask if I think some fire play would help me relax. I have only had two experiences of fire play. The first was at Desire when I was lit on fire and thrown into the pool. I remember being really excited and so zoned out that they had to push me into the pool so I wouldn't burn myself. The other experience was with Martin, and he used fire cups. I remember this was part of a larger scene where he was pushing me towards things I found extraordinarily frightening. The fire cups were not as scary as I expected. I didn't have a good understanding of using them. I worried about losing my hair and had trouble focusing. The scene was very intense, and our relationship wasn't in a good place, so it was a hard scene.

Given my previous experiences, you choose to put the fire play off until the evening events. 'Orgasm will often help you sleep' you muse, and I agree. 'Show us how you masturbate' you say and offer me any toys I might want to make things easier. I have always found masturbating in front of others to be extremely difficult but also extremely hot. I shake as I request the chains be given more slack, so I find it easier to use my hands and the vibrator to put on a show for you.

I start slowly, just running my hands over my body. I have never found this easy to do and doing it gradually is even harder. Sweat has appeared between my breasts, and my breathing is more shallow. You are both watching intently, making this hotter and yet harder to do. I close my eyes as I push two fingers between my outer lips and stroke my clitoris for the first time. My breath catches in my throat. ''Open your eyes, jewel and look at me' Pharaoh says. I moan as I do as I am told. I find it almost impossible to look at him, or either of you and yet it is equally impossible to disobey directly. I open my eyes as I reach for the small burgundy Pom vibrator. I love the feel of the soft silicone on my clitoris. The shape has it fit perfectly in my hand, making it easy to stroke myself and gain the pressure I need to cum. My juices quickly coat my fingers and the vibrator as I meet his gaze. My breath catches in my throat. I am stroking more rapidly. 'Breathe jewel' I hear you say and take a ragged breath in as I realise I have been holding my breath. 'Slower jewel' Your voice is like molten gold – beautiful, hot, silken. I slow my strokes, my moan more like a cry as I do. I am so close.

'jewel look at me' Pharaoh says again. My gaze has drifted, and then my eyes closed. They snap open as I realise I have

disobeyed. My expression shows my awareness. His deep chuckle causes me to shudder, and I understand this is one I cannot win. The more aroused I get, the harder it is to keep my eyes open. He knows this, and he will press this button repeatedly. My desire to obey is as intense as my desire to close my eyes. Allowing anyone to see into my soul when I cum is terrifying and also compelling. My heat rises, steam coming off my skin. My fingers moving faster. I drop the vibrator and press my clitoris in the rhythm that I use for self-pleasure since I stopped rubbing my teddy bear between my legs when I was 20 years old. The chains clank together, catching some of my flesh in between, and the pinch causes me to moan louder.

I am no longer aware of anything but my building orgasm and the energy flowing through our triangle. You are behind me, and he is in front of me. Both pushing the energy and circulating it. I feel like I will explode. My moan is steady, musical, rhythmic in time with the energy flow. I am desperate to be touched physically and yet no simple touch alone could feel like this.

The fire first appears between my breast – small flames, yellow to orange, glowing bright. The burn is no more painful than that of a seriously hot shower. The line of fire descends to my pussy – becoming more intense – turning to white blue with yellow, orange-red tips. Mesmerising. The fire burns, bites, and spurs me on. The chains are hot now, burning as they move against me.

'Faster jewel' he intones, and my hand moves more quickly – the flames intensifying. 'Faster' and I can feel the fire burst from me, the energy burning ever so bright. 'Please' I moan 'please,

please please'. 'not yet jewel' he says. My fingers move faster, covered in super-heated ambrosia. I feel your lips and then your teeth on the back of my neck. 'Not yet' he says. 'Please,' I wail as I feel his hand cover mine and continue to feel your lips, your teeth as you taste the energy flow and add to it. He is pushing me further and closer. The flow of the energy, the flames, the rhythm increases. Our pyramid glows white, searing white. 'Now jewel' he commands and pushes me over the edge.

My release tumbles from me and washes all over us. Sharp eddies of pleasure on waves of bliss. He catches me as I fall forward and wraps me up tightly. You both kiss me, sharing the after-burn. We all head for a short sleep before the evening's activities commence.

We met Pharaoh and Empress at a POC event at the beginning of us going to public events. The connection between the four of us was great from the start. I love when we have connections with other couples. It makes for far more fruitful relationships. The friendship blossomed quickly, and I quietly nursed my desire. There was lots of flirtation over the years.

After a few years of doing a lot of travelling to events to volunteer or speak on my own and not playing because I don't pick up play, Master talked to Pharaoh and Empress and arranged for me to be in service to them when I was local. To say it excited me is an extreme understatement. The first opportunity to be with them was at a leather event. It was an event full of obligations and expectations. I love serving at this type of event because there are always a lot of ways to make things easier on the people I am serving. It allows me to show value is so many ways, and that feeds my soul. They taught a workshop on service to more than one dominant, which is often a controversial issue. Many people believe you can only serve one at a time, so that means only one authority transfer based relationship at a time. Pharaoh and Empress are a dominant couple, and anyone in service to one is also under the care of the other. I sat at their feet during this workshop. I turned out to be the perfect example of what they were talking about. I was in two authority transfer based relationships at the time: One with my husband/Master and the other with them.

I engaged with them both most days. I checked in with them the same way I check in with Master. I got to see them 4 times per year on average. The relationship differed greatly from my relationship with Master, and that is part of why it is so much fun. I love serving a couple. It is fantastic to have that connection with both people. . I enjoyed all of my time with them whether sitting, chatting, packing Empress' suitcase, getting morning drinks, energy play, or being thoroughly beaten until I scream in pain then pleasure. The pandemic changed the rhythm of this relationship and it has now moved back into a leather family friendship connection. Life often deals us challenges that require relationships to morph.

Sam and I resumed our relationship after many, many years break a few years ago. He was living in an M/s relationship with the Tina. My relationship with Sam is not authority transfer based, and it never was. When we were first together, we enjoyed lots of rough sex, but there was never a clear authority transfer. When we resumed our relationship, it stunned me that his kiss was still the same. He still smells the same. It brought back everything from our past in a rush. I was able to introduce Sam to Morloki when we all attended Master slave Conference in 2018. Sam and Morloki connected quickly. Both share some same esoteric interests. It was such a joy for me to watch them, listen to them in conversation. I saw Sam about three times a year prior to the pandemic. Travel has been more restricted since.

Kevin and I started talking again in 2008 briefly and then again in 2010. We continued our connection until 2020. In 2019, 30 years after we said goodbye, we met for lunch in Encinitas, California. The intensity of my feelings again blindsided me. It was as though no time had passed. He smells the same, and his kisses are the same, and I still feel the love for him I felt 30 years ago. Our relationship remains complicated. As a result, all we have done is kiss. I went to see him on two trips and after talking regularly for another few months, he told me that he couldn't do polyamory with me. He said he wanted to be the one I came home to so he knew this would not work. I was gutted but I respect his decision. I miss talking with him, flirting with him but I understand that he is doing what he needs to do.

We met The Blues at Black Beat. For a few years, we would chat at events. We spent a bit more time as time went on and before the pandemic we joined LHOCC and got to know them even better. We began spending more time together at events and would talk in between as well.

Shortly after the first lockdown, I called Frost for some advice about a mutual I was having difficulty with. In that conversation, we ended up talking about being long-term in collar and being married to your master as well and some of the unique challenges and unique joys that come with this type of relationship. We agreed to talk weekly and started spending between 2 and 8 hours per week on Zoom and that has continued to this day. Our relationship deepened further over that time. I had to shelter in place for most of two ½ years and I would not have made it through this period without our relationship.

I have always been oblivious to women being attracted to me. I had always been attracted to Frost but had no idea it was reciprocal until the first edition of this memoir came out and I was doing a reading at the online book launch. In our community, it is not unusual for leather houses that are close to each other to play together. The lines between leather family, friend and playmate can be somewhat blurry. When my Master and I put together a few online play parties, all the LHOCC houses got involved in doing demonstrations. The sexual energy between Frost and myself by that time had increased. We began to spend a bit more time together on zoom as two couples interacting which was a lot of fun.

Sometime in 2021, Frost and I began to engage in play despite being separated by an ocean. I became and remain her toy. I love being a toy. Toys bring enjoyment and fun. Toys are entertaining and I find being entertaining extremely satisfying.

In early 2022, I was able to make my first trip back to spend time with family. Frost and I have often tried to find a word that describes all the facets of our relationship. She has called me Sister for a number of years now. When we don't use Sister, we use partners. It encompasses the emotional intimacy of our friendship, the energy we share with each other alongside the physical/sexual connection. The Blues are leather family. We support each other in all that we do, are there for each other when things are difficult and celebrate each other's triumphs. Our values are in alignment. And we have an abundance of fun.

My partners make life so rich. They stimulate my mind. I am continually learning, and I partake of their energy and their passion. I know that I am deeply loved for who I am and that there is always someone there to have my back. This is what I have been striving to create again since Damien. A group of friends/lovers with whom I have deep intimacy - physical, emotional, spiritual, and where loyalty, authenticity, integrity and just straight forward realness are the values embraced. When people ask how I balance all this, I reply 'carefully' and laugh. It isn't easy to balance all of these intimate relationships. It takes time and attention and energy and a willingness to be present for the event when I am finding it hard to be present for myself. As difficult as it can be, for example, when everyone is in a real crisis, I wouldn't trade this for anything in the world.

In 2019, Master and I discussed that some of my needs were not being met in my then current relationships. He decided I should find a playmate or two closer to home. As a rule, I meet people in person first - at events, through friends, through colleagues. I have done little online dating, and the only person I ever met online was Tom in 2008. But in 2019 people meet on dating apps and sex apps. So I had to bite the bullet and create a profile. I agreed to do this but still hoped to meet people in my usual way. I was not looking for hook-ups. What I want and need is very specific. Most of the people who've approached me have been awkward, rude, arrogant or all three. I met a couple of exceptional and exciting people. None of them worked out. My body and my energy are sacred, and I don't share impulsively. I have three people who will vet potential suitors before I am permitted to play, and I love it that way.

I learned long ago that for me, love begets more love. I have no shortage of love. I have a lack of time. When I am satisfied sexually, I give more love to everyone. Every partner benefits from each other in my world. People who don't have multiple relationships don't realise how much work it takes to maintain these relationships. Communication is essential and regular communication necessary to manage many relationships, so they all thrive. Older relationships need to get regular attention, especially when there is a new relationship around.

New Relationship Energy (NRE) is delicious. Our bodies release lovely chemicals that make us high. Learning someone new is exciting. It is essential to pace yourself and do a reality check with someone objective so you don't dismiss red flags and find yourself in a relationship that is not a good fit for you or worse one that is negative for you. Remember when you thought his forgetfulness was cute? Or when you thought her inability to ever put down her phone was something you could live with? Or when you didn't mind that she always told her whole workplace your private conversations? Once the NRE has worn off, these traits are still there, but you are much more likely to mind them. Existing Relationship Energy (ERE) is also delicious. It is beautiful to have a relationship where they always know the right spot to touch, lick or kiss, and the correct pressure to apply. Or when they know exactly what to do when you are sobbing, wanting to curl up in a ball with grief.

Balance is the key to introducing new relationships into your life and to your existing loves. Maintaining balance can feel like a full-time job, but it gets easier with time. Bring some of your NRE excitement back into your existing relationships and feel the fireworks explode as that relationship is revitalised.

In the 21st century, all varieties of consensual non-monogamy have become trendy.. Over and over, I read about the best ways and even the right way to do non-monogamy and I am regularly interviewed on these topics.

As an accredited advanced GSRD therapist, sex & intimacy coach and psychologist, I have spent the past 30+ years helping people to find, construct, create and maintain many relationship combinations and structures. As a person who has practiced ethical non-monogamy in one

276

form or another since I was 17 and occasionally unethical non-monogamy, I have an insider's view. I can tell you unequivocally: There is no one right way to be non-monogamous. Each relationship is as individual as a lip print because each individual is unique.

On Open House: The Great Sex Experiment, I help couples open up their relationships in a space where they have access to support before trying something and after trying something. In the two seasons of the TV show, I have highlighted a few things that everyone who is considering non-monogamy needs to do:

Become excellent at communication.

Have good self-esteem. Non-monogamy is easiest when people are secure in themselves.

Have excellent emotional skills, especially self-soothing skills (emotional regulation skills) and boundary setting skills.

Be committed to working on yourself and all your relationships.

When I was 17, I had no language to talk about non-monogamy. My first polycule was made up of 3 permanent members and a fourth rotating member, depending upon who I was dating at the time. We didn't know we were creating a polycule. We didn't even know we were practicing consensual non-monogamy. Initially, we reluctantly formed a triad because both women did not wish to give up their relationships with the solo man. The relationship between the women grew strong, though rarely sexual. We formed a polyfidelitous triad at first and then, I was encouraged to bring in a second male to the polycule. The other woman in the relationship was more comfortable when I had another man to relate to besides her live-in partner. I was the person allowed to be involved sexually with others and encouraged to bring dates/partners home.

If DeeDee had been asked to describe our relationship, she would have said she was Sam's primary partner, and I was his secondary partner. Chances are, Sam and I would have agreed. To her, it needed to be clear she was the person to whom Sam gave priority. Her needs and wants came before mine. We all accepted that this was necessary for the triad to function well. At that time, I would have described my relationship with them as my primary relationship and any other relationships as secondary. I prioritised time with them over dating others.

Later in life, I took the role of the secondary several times and found this difficult at times and wholly fulfilling at others. For me, having a hierarchy highlighted how time and responsibilities were prioritised. It had nothing to do with how much love and commitment existed in my relationships. And it still does not. I love my partners and am as committed to the ones I don't live with as I am to my husband.

The other factor in how my relationships were structured, was and remains my involvement in power exchange/ authority transfer relationships. These are, by nature, hierarchical. In all power exchange dynamics, someone is leading, and someone is following. Someone commands and the other obeys. Someone holds the authority and/or power, and the other surrenders authority and/or power.

You cannot take the hierarchy out of power exchange dynamics. When people are in power exchange dynamics and also polyamorous, there will always be a hierarchy. The amount and strength of the hierarchy may vary, but it will always be there. For some people, this is not a problem at all. For others, hierarchy is seen as inherently either problematic or even wrong.

It is popular in polyamorous circles to criticise anyone who sees their relationships as hierarchical or who organises their relationships hierarchically. People frequently say things like 'Love has no hierarchy' and 'All relationships should be equal.' Many polyamorous people become vexed at the mention of prioritising one relationship over another. Using the terms 'primary' and 'secondary' can get a person excluded from some polyamorous groups.

Yet almost all relationships are organised in hierarchies. We may not openly admit it, but we all prioritise our relationships and our time. We cannot help but do this. I may love equally, but I cannot honestly say that I would give equal weight to the needs of the partner I see four times a year and the husband who shares my bills, my home and looks after me when I am ill even if both relationships involve a lifetime commitment. The responsibilities in each relationship are different. If my husband and my lover both express a need for me to be with them on a particular day, I would likely prioritise my husband if the needs were equivalent.

This is called sweat equity. Sweat equity is a term coined in 1937 to refer to the equity built up in a project when someone did not take a salary. The term started being used in relation to non-monogamy around 2020. The term refers to the fact that relationships are prioritised depending upon how much time and energy has already been invested in them.

Let's consider an example:

My husband is having surgery on 4th December. My lover is moving house on 4th December and would like my help. My priority would be my husband. If it were my husband who was moving house and my lover who was having surgery, I would negotiate to be with my lover if possible as having surgery is a weightier need.

But what if we are looking at merely choosing who to spend holidays with:

279

Both my husband and my lover want to spend my birthday with me. If they don't agree to all of us together, my husband has priority – even if we were not in a power exchange dynamic – because there is more sweat equity in this relationship. This gets even more complicated when we have more than one or two relationships.

Part of the reason that it has become de rigueur to insist that all relationships should be equal is jealousy can be a serious issue when there is perceived inequality. Quite a few of my clients have come with problems managing the holidays, time, activities, social media posting because one partner is unhappy unless everything is 'completely equal'. In reality, it is often not only impossible to divide things completely equally but not desirable either. Partners who do not live with each other rarely want an equal share of the dull stuff. They don't want to split household chores, or other monotonous tasks like budgeting, car maintenance, errands for work. They want an equal share of the fun stuff – holidays, nights out, attending work 'do's, date nights and weekends, birthdays, Thanksgiving/Christmas/New Year's/Easters, summer, winter breaks, etc.

How does the person who is doing the errands, caretaking and the other mundane stuff feel about equally splitting the fun time but not the responsibilities and the other things that often form the day-to-day pattern of a committed long-term relationship? Usually not so happy in my experience. I frequently hear, 'Why should I give up half of my holiday time with my partner to their other lover when that lover isn't paying the bills, sharing medical care, or looking after the dog?'

When a dominant/submissive or power exchange dynamic is added into the mix, this becomes even more complex. By its nature, a power exchange dynamic is hierarchal. The person is in the dominant position is the one who controls all the relationships the person in the submissive position forms if the power exchange/ authority transfer relationship is a full time (24/7) relationship. In this case, the only person with agency is the one in the dominant position.

I have written about this model of non-monogamy before and called it the loaner model or in my case, the time-share model of non-monogamy. I am in a 24/7 power exchange /authority transfer relationship with my husband, who is my owner. As my owner, he is the one who has the agency, authority to control any other sexual, BDSM, or romantic relationship that I have because I have surrendered authority for all aspects of my life to him. My husband used to say I was a time share because each of my other partners have several weeks per year with me. They are granted a percentage of my time based on their desires and my husband's agreement to grant these desires. If my husband no longer wants me to have a relationship with someone or wants me to spend less time with someone, he may change or end any agreement.

Some people who practice polyamory have been horrified by my description of the non-monogamy that we practice because the hierarchy is clear. There is very definitely inequality between my relationships. There is no inequality in how I feel about my other partners. I love all of them. There is inequality in how much time I spend, whose needs get priority, and where my responsibilities lie. All parties consent to this arrangement and on that basis, why should anyone be judgemental?

When I break down how they divide their time, decide who gets what priority in any given situation, it illuminates hierarchies even in the relationships of the people I have met who are most adamant that there should be no hierarchies in polyamory. Though this surprises them, it doesn't surprise me in the least. It is nigh on impossible to divide time equally between several people, even with the best will in the world. Life doesn't present us with equal challenges. We have a wide variety of blessings and challenges, and though our love is infinite, our time and energy are finite. Ultimately, we have to make choices. If we are hell-bent on creating total equality, we will end up spending an excessive amount of time working to do this. And we spend an excessive amount of energy judging people for having hierarchies in their non-monogamous relationships.

In my experience, a better way to spend the energy is looking at where needs intersect and how we can balance our relationships in ways that responsibilities, needs and wants are in balance in each relationship. The less time we spend comparing within our relationships, the better. Increasing our communication skills, including our negotiation skills, is a better use of our time. Learning how to identify our own needs and differentiate them from wants is paramount as well as creating balanced.

Why is it fashionable to trash hierarchies wherever they are found? Perhaps looking to broader mainstream culture and politics may give us answers. We often see hierarchies as binary: Rich/poor, good/bad, though they run primary, secondary, tertiary. There are many levels, not just two. If we can keep this in mind and also recognise that there are multiple hierarchies in any set of relationships, then maybe the reality of the hierarchies in our lives will no longer be seen as unpalatable. Instead, we can look at them as structures that enable us to order our lives and relationships so it is easier to find and maintain balance.

The model of polyamory we use has evolved since the first edition of this book. My husband/Master created a new model in 2023 when two of my other relationships became deeper and he wanted a way to describe how he sees these relationships, how they are prioritised and how any new people who wanted to be involved with me or us would be prioritised. He is the owner of a lake with property surrounding it. I am the lake. There are houses on the lake. Sereth has one house. The Blues have another house. There is an undeveloped lot that belongs to one of our people. There is a guest house where extended leather family and few select others can come and stay for varying periods of time. And occasionally, there are pleasure boats that can be taken out on the lake. He says that there is no more property available on the lake because to add more would damage the natural resource. The people who have property here and those who visit have full use of the lake and take care of the property along with the access to the lake. He has overall responsibility. For us, this model encompasses the multiple authority transfer based relationships and the depth of the existing relationships, all of which are committed long-term relationships and gives a guide for how a new person might approach if they wanted to have a sexual relationship and a deeper interaction with me.

XIX

ONWARD JOURNEY

This piece comes back again and again as I write, speak, teach, listen to people and work with people. Authenticity and congruence are the keys to progression, to joy, to the evolution of each of us. Will is necessary but will without congruence and authenticity damages. With authenticity and congruence comes presence, and with presence, the message is always heard.

"You stand before me". His voice resonates, a thick bass. I am unaware of the splendour of the room.

"It is my privilege, my honour to do so" I reply softly. "It has been a long time. Let us go somewhere quiet to talk'. I incline my head. I don't trust my voice. "How is the business?" he asks. "Well, "I reply. "Do you bring my word into the world?" he demands. "I hope so" I reply. "Good, that is what I hear". I relax at his approval.

"What is it you want from me?" I ask. "As always child, everything" he replies. "Now that we are alone come here and greet me properly". He commands.

I stumble forward, am quickly caught in the circle of his arms – the velvet-covered solid oak – I'm enveloped. I inhale deeply his scent burnt vanilla with a hint of spice. I have never felt as protected as I do in his arms. His lips find my neck, then my mouth, and he drinks deeply of me. His hands wander over my curves. I am more fleshy than the last time we met, softer, rounder. I worry that he will not find me pleasing, but he does not seem to mind, stroking and pinching my body, bringing the heat with his fingers.

He allows me breath, pulls back and looks down at me, still holding me in the circle of his arms. "It is good to look on you once again", he says. I look up into those deep brown eyes and mine fill with tears. "Why do you cry, little one?" he asks as he tastes the salt from my eyes. "Too long. When I am away, I only remember a shade of you. I cannot keep your full presence in my mind. Now that I am here, I never want to leave again, and I know that all too quickly, it will be time for me to return home." I reply. "Why not greet the time with laughter instead of tears?" He chides me. "Come, we will eat. Then we will talk. Later we will make love. Then it will be time for you to return home. Speak to me of what ails you?" he says. "It is unclear to me what you wish me to say. What is the Word that I must bring to the world? I find words so difficult to come by – to explain the fullness of your love – your care. How am I, a mere mortal, to describe magnificence?" I reply.

"You will find the words. It is not magnificence that you must describe, but congruence, authenticity. If a soul stays in my embrace, she is congruent. Then all actions that flow from her will be just and true. It is when you leave my embrace that doubt enters in and actions become merely will." He replies. "But is not true Will the way?" I ask.

"True Will must come with compassion. Truth, honour, loyalty to powers higher than yourselves. To your further development – the spiral rises ever higher. You have chosen a body for a reason. It is as you always suspected it was – there are lessons to be learned whilst enfleshed that cannot be learned from without. There are lessons to be learned in time and space that cannot be learned when you are part of the limitless void. Duality has its purpose, but it is only one state of being. The original state of being is oneness. As you are now, you can only touch that concept in the briefest of fashions – at moments that feel as though they stretch to eternity. Once you have fully mastered the lessons inherent in duality, then it will be time for you to return home to the unity. Until that time, it is at moments you are truly congruent, authentic, that you reclaim the feeling of unity. It is at moments that you truly connect with your fellows you reclaim the feeling of unity within community." *"And my mission?"* I ask.

"To communicate this – to make this understandable to your fellows. Your life serves as a backdrop – a set of lessons to translate. It is not because you are above your fellows – all of you are special and unique. It is because you agreed to take on this task – to take this mission – that you have the gifts this time around. It is like you tell the others – it is not easy for no path of growth is ever easy – to appreciate great joy you must appreciate great sorrow. To feel truly safe, you must have felt terrified. To know deep in your soul, you must have been at one time lost and confused, even deluded. It is the nature of a dualistic universe – the one you at present inhabit. Congruence is when you can integrate the dualities, keep cognizant of them, and act as one

whole being, in keeping with your mind, body, emotions, and spirit. It is then that you act with authenticity, strength and humility and unity of purpose." He says.

"I am frightened, and when I am frightened, I freeze, wanting to hide under the covers, in a fantasy, until the danger has passed or I feel strong enough to cope," I say.

"Have you not wondered about those fantasies you seek out. They are not escapes as they continuously remind you of your mission, your responsibility. You do not have the benefit of all the gifts that others have in those fantasies. Your world is more restricted at present. Acknowledge your fear and then do as you have always done – act. You do that now, sitting here, using technology to speak to me though a large part of you wishes to run and hide." He says. "That is true. I am tired. I need to rest." I reply.

"You have rested! It is time. You will find respite periodically in my service. Too much respite and you become bored. When you become bored, you create dangerous challenges for yourself. There is no longer time to waste. You will be much more tired before this is finished – but more exhilarated too." He says "What do I call this message – how do I frame it?" I ask.

"You call it congruence, authenticity – you name it unity – you call it walking the tightrope – spanning the abyss – bridging the gap. Look to the bridge across forever – re-read the words of Bach – study Haydn, Handel – visit the places you used to call home. Think long on Silistra and how you can take from her philosophy – frame it so they can hear it in this modern age. That is not merely a saga but rather allegory – my message is there – it has spoken to you – take refuge and solace from it."

"We do not wish to make this too strenuous a journey – we want to you to experience joy as our teachings can only be understood in the light of love and joy. All is not serious – you must retain that child-like sense of awe and hold fast to your passion. Passion speaks to you – that is why we use it so often to reach you – it touches you on the most basic human level – in the most basic of places. You are woman – indeed – clothed in spirit – having bathed in star's breath – having experienced the bowels of the earth. Hold fast to your knowledge – to the secrets of the eightfold spirit – for sevenfold is not truly enough. Use your sign, your site, your vision – your hearing – use all your senses and then more."

"Go to work now. All will be clear as you write." He commands. (And now, I obey).

This next piece was written with a man I was newly dating in mind.

'What a spectacular view of the river' I think as I enter the room. The view is unexpected, given the price. 'The upgrade' I think. 'Red hair magic strikes again' I giggle.

Too many long days and nights in London over two weeks before the holidays means a need to spend at least a couple of nights in a hotel. Too many commutes always equal exhaustion. And when I am exhausted, my service suffers, and Master becomes cross.

The king-size bed is covered in crisp white sheets with four good-sized pillows. The wall-mounted flat-screen TV is large and at the perfect height. In the corner are a floor lamp and a comfortable leather club chair. The lights of the city reflecting off the river, shining in the window, the chair is shrouded in shadow.

I startle when I see him sitting there in his immaculate windowpane suit, quietly, comfortably in the mood-lit room. 'Good evening jewel' he says, soft, smooth voice penetrating my shock. 'Good evening, Sir' I murmur as I quickly unpack and stow my belongings in the wardrobe and drawers. There is a robe laid out on the bed and slippers next to it. 'Shower and change and then return here'. He says. 'Yes, Sir'. I reply as I strip off my dress, tights, bra, panties and head for the shower. I spend a few extra minutes under the hot spray working to calm my nerves.

Negotiations are always complicated for me as in some way they always include my Owner. This is not a complaint; it is a simple statement of fact. I don't have the agency to negotiate on my own. This negotiation didn't include me at all. I had been told where I was staying, what time to check-in, and what to pack.

I exit the shower, towel dry quickly, and put on the robe and slippers. I walk to the chair and kneel at P's feet. He places his hand on my face, thumb under my chin and lifts my face until I make eye contact. 'You will strip, get on the bed and display yourself for me. Then you will make yourself come as I watch. I may give you instructions, or I may not. If I ask a question, answer fully and quickly.' 'Yes, Sir' I reply as my stomach turns flip flops. I find displaying myself so difficult, even after all these years and all my experience. There is something about that level of objectification that makes my blood boil with desire and yet paralyses me with embarrassment. I could never work out if it is because I feel humiliated or because I feel like a sex toy or both.

I strip and climb onto the bed – first on hands and knees so he can see my ass and then lying on my back and spreading my legs wide for him to see my moistening pussy. I start by stroking myself from breasts to booty. Quick strokes all over until my skin is pink. I pull on my nipples until they are brick red and taut. My pussy lips darken to the same hue.

As I begin to stroke my pussy lips, I glance up and see that P has unzipped his trousers. His cock is in his hand, and he is slowly stroking himself. I moan as I watch him, rubbing my clitoris and pressing a finger into my juicy core. I bring my soaked finger to my lips and suck off my savoury, sweet, sticky nectar.

'You can use the vibrator if you wish' he says. I reach for my favourite vibe and turn up the speed to high. I press it on my clitoris. My hips rise to meet the vibrations, and I moan louder. I will not be able to wait. I will come quickly.

P strips and sits back down in the leather chair. He is pulling on his cock, harder, faster as my pleasure rises. 'You may come when you wish' he says, voice choked with desire. I come a minute later. As the waves of my orgasm roll over my body, I feel him standing next to me. His hot come hits my chest as my first orgasm dies down. The second spurt of semen lands on my lips and my tongue darts out to taste the thickly sweet treat. He wipes his cock on my cheek and goes into the bathroom. I can hear the shower running. My second orgasm overtakes me as his come dries on my body as I think 'I am his come slut. I have no other purpose than to provide him with the pleasure he desires.'

He returns from the shower with a damp towel and cleans the dried come off my body. He wraps me in the robe and points to his feet. 'You will sleep at my feet. If you do not settle on the bed, you will be sleeping on the floor at the foot of the bed.' I work hard to quickly settle my body so I will not be on the floor.

I have never been the best sleeper, and over the last 19 years, my sleep has become more erratic. Getting comfortable is often a challenge. A few times a week, I wake in the middle of the night to strip off any clothing as a hot flash takes me, though I am through the menopause already. If my pain levels are high, I wake when I become stiff and need to turn over. I lie at the foot of the bed, trying ever so hard not to toss and turn, but it is no use. When things are this bad, I often masturbate to tire myself out. I know that I cannot get away with this while sleeping at his feet.

After an hour or so, I feel his hand in my hair. He tugs my head up, so I am looking at him. 'Girl what is the problem?' he growls. 'I cannot get comfortable, Sir'. I reply. 'Come up here'. He says, and I move, so I am lying facing him. He grips my face, his thumb under my jaw. He moves to squeeze my throat slowly, taking my breath, watching me carefully as he does. I struggle to control the panic as I cannot breathe. Just as I am about to truly panic, he lets go of my throat. My moan mixes with a deep, hoarse growl. It amuses him. 'Growling? Perhaps not the best idea.' He chuckles. He pulls me towards him, bites my lower lip until I am humming with pain pleasure.

His dick is hard and pressing against me. I want him to fuck me so badly, and he knows it. 'No, I will not tonight'. He says as he pinches my arm tightly. He is stroking his dick again. 'Turn on your back' he instructs. He presses hard cock into my cheek but doesn't allow me to suck him or even to taste him. He wraps my hair around his dick and pulls and strokes his cock with my hair. He moves above my face and presses his balls into my mouth. 'You can suck on these, lick these. Do it now' he says, voice jagged with his rising desire. I love the smell of him and inhale deeply.

He tastes of his sweat - salty and a bit sour, and I shudder with pleasure as I bury my nose and tongue in his balls. He moans as I suck them into my mouth. His stroking picks up speed.

I know he is close to orgasm. So am I. 'Rub your clitoris' he says, and I am so grateful. In seconds I am on the edge of orgasm. He stops my hand suddenly and moves off my face. He is flushed, holding himself at that edge of orgasm as he straddles my chest, pinning me to the bed. He pulls twice on his swollen cock and shoots hot sticky jizz all over my neck, face and hair. 'I bet you would love to be at the centre of a circle jerk' he says 'with a bunch of men covering you in come.' I wail as I reach another peak, the orgasm so intense that I collapse after.

'Go shower' he says, and I pad off to the shower in my bare feet. I wash my hair to get his dried come out of it. I towel my hair until it isn't too wet and pad back into the bedroom. 'Now go to sleep' he says as he points to a pallet he has made up on the floor at the foot of the bed. I whisper 'yes Sir' and curl up on the pallet under a thick down duvet and fall asleep within moments.

I wake to the sound of the maid entering the room in the morning with a bunch of clean towels. I am naked on the pallet on the floor. I blush crimson with embarrassment as she notices me. 'Thank you.' P says as he takes the towels. 'Don't worry about her. She is fine' he goes on. The girl asks if she can look at me more closely. 'Yes, and you can touch her if you like' he says. She squats down beside me and runs a finger over my now hard nipples. She pinches them lightly and then harder and grins when I moan. 'Thank you, Sir' she says as she leaves the room.

Within a few minutes, the room service waiter arrives. P opens the door and lets him in the room where he sets up breakfast.

I haven't moved as I have not been told to dress. The young man blushes when he sees me and his erection is quickly visible. 'You can touch her tits - and you can wank off over her if you like' he says. The young man immediately takes his hard dick out of his trousers and strokes over my tits. It takes only a few seconds for him to shoot a copious load all over my chest and neck. I moan as he does and come hard as he wipes his dick off in my hair. 'Thanks' the young man says to P and hurries to leave the room, almost forgetting to have P sign the bill. P lets me lie there in this stranger's come as he eats breakfast. 'Eat' he says as he moves me between his legs and puts his half-hard cock in my mouth. I suck him until he comes in my throat, savouring the taste of him and the feeling of him in my belly. After cleaning me up, it is time for P to go and for me to head for work.

I made a commitment to write a first draft of this manuscript during Nanowrimo 2019. I had been working on it and found in early June 2019 that I was having trouble putting all the disparate pieces into a structure that made sense. I realised that I had not returned to Boston, MA, since I graduated from university. This seemed to be more than coincidence and as I thought more about it I realised that I was avoiding going back. I planned a trip for October, hoping retracing my steps would help me break through the block and the writing would flow. It worked. I had not counted on how much emotion would rise by retracing my steps, nor had I counted on the cravings and desires that stepped to the fore. When I left Boston, I was craving so many things. And despite having one play mate and three partners, no one was available to play with me, to help me relieve the cravings. It was very difficult to manage my impulses, but I did so. When I returned to the UK after the epic journey, I remained emotionally raw. 'I need structure.' I told Master. 'I need structure so that I can feel my core self, stay seated in my core self. I need the structure to make it easier to surrender, to help me come away from being 'Dr' and dominant independent woman and wife or I will stay in that space all the time and the longer I stay in that space, the more likely I am to get myself into trouble.' 'You have structure' he replied but added a bit more structure daily.

My core desires were up front throughout the trip and have remained up front since my return. Master has never been interested in water sports. Initially, he apologised several times. I responded by saying that I am well aware these aren't his desires and I am not asking him to make them his desires. I asked to be allowed to find one or two people who can meet those desires because they are into them. He agreed to let me do this. I already had one person in mind. For the other, I tried a dating site. That did not work.

I was determined to make my dating experience more authentic and to be positive about the experience. I took the advice I give my clients: Go out and do things you enjoy and meet people in the old-fashioned way - face to face while engaged in some type of pursuit.

My advice shifted during the Coronavirus – 19 pandemic. I still recommend meeting people through activities you enjoy but for that moment, most of these were online. Watch parties, classes, workshops, theatre and concerts have all taken to the internet.

Re-entering the world after the main part of Covid-19, was not easy. Both my husband and I remain extremely vulnerable so we stay up to date with boosters and both of us mask when in public a good portion of the time. We also think before we go to places that are crowded so I go out and about less than I did. As a result of these changes, I thought I would not likely meet anyone local and focused on finding ways to maximise the contact with my existing partners, even though we are long-distance.

Earlier this year, when I started giving regular talks all over the UK, I began to meet people at events. Dating locally is on the table again with all the excitement and angst that it brings.

XX

EPILOGUE TO THE FIRST EDITION

I chose these three short pieces to illustrate focus. This is where I am going on my journey. Further down the road I have been on since I can remember, further into surrender in as many layers as possible. Fully into presence in as many moments in each day as I can manage.

Heat and pressure, slick juices between my legs, sliding onto my thighs, down between my ass cheeks. I can feel skin, fur, and scales underneath my fingers from where I have scratched and clawed and my screams still ring in my ears. My desire so intense that nothing exists but my need. I smell burnt flesh, and I believe it is mine. My throat is raw from screaming; tears still stream down my cheeks, steam rising as they land on my overheated flesh. I am not speaking coherently, I cannot think. I feel the weight of the creature on my body -the spread of my legs so wide, hear him tell me to open to him. My hips move of their own accord - my body's rhythms overriding any thought or control. I am dancing for his cock - moving faster and harder and with more abandon - the beat in my body is the beat in my blood. I need to feel teeth, heat, liquid, sweat; to taste sweat, blood, tears, piss, cum. To press

297

edges, sharp sharp edges and hardness smooth hardness. To feel cold and ice - all male, all female extremes. I need to fight until made to surrender. I need to submit without a fight, yielding softly and fully.

I need to feel lips and tongue - soft strokes and caresses - flow and also force. I need to contact the steel of my collar. I need to serve in silence. I need to serve with sounds only. I need to serve with words. I need to have space to worship through body service - bathing, grooming, pampering; through domestic service; to worship through sexual service every crevice, every hair, every inch of his body. I need to worship through obedience, through love, through focus on them.

I wrote this piece in 2010.

Surrender
Reminds me of Glow Sticks, that popping sound when
the plastic breaks and the two chemicals mix to produce
Bright, brilliant colourful light
Surrender
Reminds me of wax melting
Dripping at first until the heat rises, then liquefying
My body glows bright
My body warm, honey dripping
The heat rises from the base of my spine
Up my back, spreading slowly until I am completely enveloped
The Dragon uncoils from slumber at the bottom of my spine
Glory in His beauty, His sinuous motion

Surrender
When I can no longer resist
When I can no longer fight
The Wolf's teeth on my throat, the throat I have bared
in submission
The smell of his fur, his musk interweaves with mine,
desire and fear intertwine
His fur surrounds me
My body, my heart, my mind, my soul
All that I am, all that I ever was, all that I ever will be
Offered to you.
Now your body, your heart, your mind, your soul, all
the talents and skills at your disposal - to be turned to
your Will, your Pleasure
Yours
Surrender
Your collar around my throat reflecting the wellspring
of emotion
Reflecting the intensity of heat
Reflecting my joy serving you
Pleasure coalesces

I wrote this final piece in 1983. Despite Damien's concerted attempt to destroy me in 1982, my desire for power exchange is still ever present. My willingness to yield felt in every cell in my body. There was no one on the horizon when I wrote this piece. No one who was the muse.

Full Moon Ritual 1983
Honey bourbon moan pierces hot vigilant mist.

Hail intuition!
He approaches
Drums whisper, silk skin
slaps the coarse sand
His tongue circles her violet
tension
Rope bites hands bound
Leather belt on her tight bound bruised ass.
Fire scream
salt-filled eyes
Trust as a steel collar.
Waves tongue menstrual blood from his half-hard cock.

I have written little about my early life here, nor have I written much about living with autoimmune disease. The flow of the book would have been very different if I had included my entire life to date. I will write about those topics in the future. For now, this is my story. And in the future, who knows? I will see where my intuition takes me, where my Gods decree I should go, and where my Owner and Handlers decide I should take off my boots and rest my head. I greet each day knowing that I am on the path I am meant to be on, and if I apply myself, I will certainly get where I want to go or at least where I am meant to go. I am grateful for my life, all the people who are in my life, all I have including the difficult bits. I reach for joy with both hands, partake of all aspects of life until I am full to overflowing. My people are exacting taskmasters, and I wouldn't have it any other way.

EPILOGUE
TO THE SECOND EDITION

Be careful what you wish for as
you will get exactly that.
Said by every spiritual teacher I have ever had.

Toy

Packing I grab clothing that helps me to look my sexiest and also clothing that I also don't mind losing. You sometimes play roughly with your toy. The feel of a blade as you cut through the fabric, the point grazing my flesh without opening it. The sound of the fabric tearing as you rip it – intoxicating.

I feel your heat, that energy connection all of the time. I can smell your scent as intoxicating as the finest fragrance. I can taste you - -savoury, smoky with a touch of molasses. texture lustrous on my tongue.

You are a feast for all of my senses so I work to make myself a feast for yours. Your laughter, the sounds of your passion, the edge of cruelty in your commands – bring joy in so many ways.

You know all my secrets. Every single quirk and kink – the ones I reserve for the favoured few intimates who understand that edge I dance and who dance it with me. Our pleasure complex from tender to tightrope. All the while I seek to entertain.

The best toys inspire imagination, meet your sensory/sensual/ sexual needs, are sturdy so you can fully engage with them without worrying about breaking them, are good for more than one use and are a bit challenging but not frustrating.

The toys that are too simple, we discard. Those that are too complex, we give up on. I strive to be the toy you will always want to play with – exciting, fun, at times surprising.

I love it when I provide a show for you alone and I love it when you share me with your Sir. Dancing that edge for the two of you is sublime.

And after playtime, after I have been ridden hard and put away wet... After playtime, our emotional intimacy, laughter, deep talks and comfortable silences are priceless.

I love being your toy and I love being your Sister.

I was clear that I wanted balance when I started retracing my steps in Boston, Ma in 2019. I thought I knew what balance would look like but no matter how hard I looked, nothing was working out. When I retraced my steps, I was not in active contact with Sereth. In my eyes, we had moved on to a friendship and that was not going to change.

I varied my profiles on a variety of dating sites hoping someone might approach who not only wanted to engage in the same kinks and sexual activities I enjoyed and who also understood what it meant to interact with someone who was owned. The first inter-action ended through nothing to do with me. The second was cut short by lockdown and we didn't have enough of a connection to survive the long enforced separation. The others didn't even make the screening call. They were too uncomfortable with talking with my Master or even negotiating with me. Some of the approaches were so outrageous that I did an episode of my podcast, The A to Z of Sex®, W is for Wanker, talking about how often myself and some of my colleagues are approached on dating apps and social media. Though the show was great fun to make and telling the stories made all of us laugh, it was discouraging.

Loki reminded me that I needed to have faith. I did an updated version of my wish list and waited. I was approached by someone at the launch party for the first edition and it looked as though that relationship might be the one that could bring balance. I gave it a year but in the end, he had too many commitments to devote time to integrating into my leather world and to meet my needs for balance. The parting was amicable.

I focused on work, my existing relationships including deepening things with my sister, spending more time with leather family and then focused on selling my home with a view to moving to Scotland.

Every so often, I forget what Loki's sense of humour looks like. I asked for structure, for balance and he sent Sereth back into my life. The lesson I have learned is that timing is everything. This time, our relationship is different. It is not easy. He is learning what it means to be in a polyamorous family, Fendragon Pack style. He was never really in a polyamorous relationship before this one. I am learning to breathe before I automatically chafe at the control and structure I have asked for. Both of us communicate far better than we did in years past so this relationship looks very different. He has committed to providing the structure I crave, the structure that my Master does not enjoy providing and I have committed to surrender.

Exploring the past together has allowed Sereth and I to say goodbye to more ghosts and get rid of at least one stubborn shade. He has helped me to illuminate the edge that I dance on daily and to understand the thoroughly erotic sweetness of that precarious dance.

I have a good start to the balance I have been craving. I am complex. The balance comes from my three major relationships with extra joy and spice from the other relationships (including my friendships). My gratitude knows no bounds. My Gods have given me exactly what I begged for, pleaded for, asked for. I am truly blessed.

GLOSSARY

Arousal Non-Concordance

Arousal non-concordance is when your genital response doesn't match your internal experience. For example if you have a vagina, you are feeling really turned on but your vagina is bone dry. Or if you have a penis and you are being sexually assaulted, you get an erection.

Authenticity

The quality of being real, true and genuine
An individual's actions are congruent with their beliefs and desires

Bastinado

A form of torture that involves caning someone's feet.
Can be beating the feet with another instrument besides a cane

BFF Best Friend Forever

https://www.urbandictionary.com/define.php?term=BFF

Boundaries

Personal boundaries are the limits we place on ourself and between ourselves and others that allow us to feel safe. They are the rules, guidelines that allow us to note when someone is behaving appropriately and gives us a roadmap to how we might respond if someone passes those limits. Boundaries are different in differ-ent contexts. They allow us to connect with others and have intimate relationships

305

because they define the space between us and the places where we connect. Good boundaries mean we understand our feelings and our responsibilities to ourselves and to others.

Bugger

Fuck in the ass. British slang. Used to refer to men having anal sex with each other. It now has alternate meanings: A term of affection 'You poor bugger'. Something that is awkward or annoying. Cause harm or act in a stupid way or cause trouble. 'He buggered everything up when he didn't telephone the helpline and insisted on fixing things himself. Used to express anger or annoyance 'Oh bugger! Joe said when he dropped the vase and it shattered.

Catalyst

A person that precipitates an event - often major change.
The substance that induces the chemical reaction with-out permanently changing itself.

Chuntering

Grumbling – slowly - This isn't an exact definition as the word doesn't have a perfect definition.

Congruence

Agreement, harmony, compatibility
Psychologist Carl Rogers said that therapists must have three core attributes in order to create the right envi-ronment for clients to make progress and become able to become their true self:
Congruence (genuineness or realness)

Unconditional positive regard (full acceptance without judgement) Accurate Empathic Understanding (Empathy is when you are able to place yourself in the feelings of the other)

Consensual Non-Monogamy

Relationship styles/structures where people may have sexual and/or intimate (including emotionally inti-mate) relationships with more than one person. There are a wide variety of structures. The key here is that there is consent from all parties that multiple relation-ships are acceptable in whatever form that they are agreed upon.

Consent

Giving one's agreement to do something, to receive something, to a situation or an action. Consent involves having agency, under-standing the detail of what one is consenting to, having the ability to consent and being free from coercion.

Crell

A slave

Crucible

A situation of intense challenges, when various ele-ments may interact with each other and in their inter-action (and reaction) catalyse the creation of something new.

D/s

Dominant/ submissive dynamic. The dominant is in charge and the submissive obeys the dominant.

Dissociation

The act of separating or the state of being separated. In psychology, one set of mental processes separates from another and functions independently.

Existing Relationship Energy

The energy experienced in an existing relationship

Fetish

A form of sexual desire in which gratification is linked to an abnormal degree to a particular object, item of clothing, part of the body. For example, a latex fetish where someone finds latex sexually arousing to the point that they need latex to be present (or in fantasy) in order to reach orgasm.

FOMO

Fear of Missing Out

Gaslighting

To manipulate someone into doubting their own sanity - replace their reality with your own. This is a psy-chological manipulation where the person defines the victim's sense of reality by contra-dicting them and insisting their own views, thoughts and feelings are accurate.

Hypervigilance

State of increased awareness, increased vigilance, awareness of all that is going on around you.

Leather (leather house, leather family)

People who are part of the leather subculture have an affiliation with BDSM practise and wear leather - not just for style but because it is seriously hot. The com-munity has been considered a subculture of the BDSM culture. The subculture started primarily in the gay male community and Guy Baldwin says 'It is very important to remember that the modern leather scene as we now know it first formalized itself out of the group of men who were soldiers returning home after World War II 1939-1945.'

Some people identify as leather and this often includes a set of values and BDSM (Bondage, Discipline, Dom-inance, Submission, Sadism, Masochism). In many cases the emphasis is on Dominance and Submission and equally many focus on Sadism and Masochism. A leather family is a group of people who are part of leather culture and who organise themselves like an extended family. This is chosen family - people whose bonds are by choice rather than by blood.

A leather house (or household) is a group of people who are in relationship to each other, often including authority transfer with a head or heads of the house-hold being in the dominant role and other members having switch roles or submissive roles. Some houses are made up of a group of people who are all involved in BDSM relationships with each others and others have members who are not actively involved in BDSM. This can be likened to a nuclear family as compared with the leather family with is an extended family.

M/s

Master / slave dynamic - A relationship where the dom-inant partner is the master and the submissive partner is the slave.

Magick

Aleister Crowley's Thelema - This term is used to show and differen-tiate the occult from 'stage magic'. 'The Sci-ence and Art of causing Change to occur in conformity with Will' including ''mundane' acts of will as well as ritual magic.

Malkuth

The tenth sephira in the Tree of Life, at the bottom of the tree. It is the earth. Representative of the Garden of Eden and the entire universe.

Masochism

When someone gets sexual pleasure from their own pain or humiliation.
Unrelated to sex: When someone enjoys doing some-thing that is boring or painful.

Monogamy

A relationship between two people where they agree to only a sexual and/or intimate (including emotionally intimate) contact with each other.

Mustard Seed Parable

It is a short parable of Jesus. 'The Kingdom of Heaven is like a grain of mustard seed, which a man took, and sowed in his field; which a man took, and put in his own garden. But when it is grown, it is greater than the herbs, and becomes a tree, so that the birds of the air come and lodge in its branches." Matthew 13:31-32

New Relationship Energy

The excitement experienced at the beginning of a new relationship.

Non-Binary

Not relating to, composed of, or involving just two things.

Non-Consensual Non-Monogamy

Cheating, having an affair. When a person has multiple relationships and has not sought the consent of all par-ties, often lies and hides what they are doing.

O/p

Owner/property. A relationship dynamic where the dominant party is seen as the owner and the submissive is seen as property.

Ordo Templi Orientis

The Order of the Temple of the East or Order of Oriental Templars is an occult organisation that required initia-tion. It was started at the beginning of 20th century. It is most infamous because Aleister Crowley was one of the best-known members.

Pantheon

All the gods of a people or a religion collectively

Petechiae

A small red or purple spot caused by bleeding into the skin
Playdate
An adult get together or date - usually involving sen-sual or sexual activity of some type. Many talk about getting together for BDSM as a playdate.

Polyamory

A relationship style where people have multiple loving relationships (that may or may not include sex). The practice of intimate relation-ships with more than one partner with informed consent from all parties.

Polycule

All of the people linked through their relationships, usually romantic and/or sexual - a romantic and sexual network or a subset of a network

Power Exchange or Authority Transfer Dynamic

A relationship dynamic where one person has the con-trol and the other person willingly consensually gives up control. One person is in charge. This is completely consensual. It can be in the bedroom only or extend to parts of daily life or all of daily life (called 24/7). Authority transfer is used more often now because no one really gives up power, they ceded authority to the other.

Presence

When someone is completely embodied, fully focused on what is happening at that very moment. Showing up in every way in the moment.

Sadism

When someone gets sexual pleasure, pleasure or gratification out of cause someone else pain or humiliation.

Sephira (ot)

In Kabbalah - the word means emanations. These are the 10 emana-tions or attributes that the One reveals himself through to create the physical realm and higher metaphysical realms.

Shag

Have sex with, fuck - British slang

Shekinah

The Shekinah is the Goddess in Judaism - literally means settling or dwelling and it is the dwelling of the divine presence of God(dess)

Slut

Someone who has a lot of sex, sometimes indiscriminately with many different people. A woman who has many casual sexual partners, is promiscuous. Often used to humiliate women who enjoy sex. This term has been reclaimed by women who refused to be shamed because of their sexual desire.

Stockholm Syndrome

A situation in which a hostage develops an alliance or positive feelings with their captors

Submission (sexual)/ Submissive

When a person gains sexual pleasure, pleasure, and/or satisfaction out of giving authority over to another person and allowing them to control the sexual activity, or control all activity.
Submissive is the person who follows the orders, sur-renders to the dominant, cedes control to another.

Trauma Bond

A strong attachment that is developed between the victim and the abuser during prolonged trauma

ABOUT THE AUTHOR

Dr Lori Beth Bisbey is a clinical psychologist, accredited advanced GSRD (gender, sex, relationship diversity) therapist, & a sex & intimacy coach. She has spent over 35 years helping people to create and sustain meaningful and exciting relationships with fantastic sex. She also specialises in helping traumatised people to move from victim to survivor and back into life.

Dr Bisbey hosts a weekly podcast, The A to Z of Sex® She speaks at events, conferences and presents workshops worldwide.

She is currently starring as the resident specialist therapist in Open House: The Great Sex Experiment on Channel 4 in the UK. Seasons 1 & 2 can be streamed on All4.

She has authored 7 books and has chapters in an additional two. She regularly writes for media outlets, is interviewed on podcasts and contributes to all manner of media. She has been writing erotica since she was a teenager. For more information https://drloribeth-bisbey.com.

Milton Keynes UK
Ingram Content Group UK Ltd.
UKHW041826220923
429211UK00002B/6